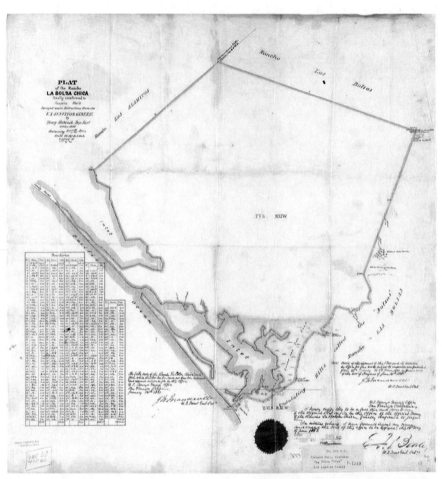

Frontispiece. State surveyor's 1858 map that officially confirmed title of Rancho La Bolsa Chica to Manuel Nieto heir Joaquin Ruiz. (Map courtesy Bancroft Library, University of California, Berkeley)

BOLSA CHICA

Its History From Prehistoric Times To The Present
And What Citizen Involvement And Perseverance Can Achieve

by David M. Carlberg

Published by Amigos de Bolsa Chica
P. O. Box 1563
Huntington Beach, CA 92647

2009

ISBN: 978-1-934379-92-9

Cover photograph by author

Printed in the United States of America

Dedication

To Margaret

And to all those
who contributed
in myriad ways
to the
preservation of Bolsa Chica.

Acknowledgements

An huge debt of gratitude is owed to a group of individuals who agreed to set aside a significant slice of their valuable time to review parts or all of the manuscript of this book. These were not a randomly chosen few, but a select team of people most of whom have intimate connections with Bolsa Chica. Any one of them could have written this book. My thanks go to Shirley Dettloff, Vic Leipzig, Jim Trout, Craig Frampton, Mel Nutter, Marvin Carlberg, and Margaret Carlberg for their enormously helpful comments. But of course any errors that may have slipped by their critical eyes are mine alone and with humble apologies I take full responsibility for them.

I also wish to thank the following for their help in the preparation of this book:

Bancroft Library, University of California, Berkeley

Bowers Museum, Santa Ana

California State Lands Commission

City of Huntington Beach

County of Orange

The First American Corp.

Fort MacArthur Museum

Honnold/Mudd Library, Claremont Colleges

Huntington Beach Co.

Moffatt and Nichol Engineers

University of Southern California Special Collections Library

U.S. Historical Archives

Pacific Coast Archeological Society

Rancho Los Cerritos Museum

Sherman Library, Corona del Mar

University of California, Los Angeles, Special Collections Library

Charlie Boulé

F. Scott Nickerson

Jay Robinson

Publication of this book was made possible through a generous gift from the Griswold Foundation.

All proceeds from sales go to the Amigos de Bolsa Chica

Table of Contents

List of Illustrations

List of Tables

Preface

Bolsa Chica
A Story of Citizen Involvement and Perseverance

The need for a book on the extraordinary history of Bolsa Chica and the Amigos de Bolsa Chica was obvious, but when to write it? When the state acquired the wetland? When restoration was begun? When it was completed? When surveys began to show that the restoration appeared to be successful? As you will learn when reading this book, there is not one of these questions that can be answered with a definite "X" on a calendar. Which reminds me of a comment by the Executive Director of the California Coastal Commission, Peter Douglas, who often said, "Wetlands are never saved, they are always being saved." The process is a thread, not the point of a needle. Thus the decision as to when the book should be written had to be an arbitrary one. My MAC tells me December 21, 2005 was the probable start date.

This book relates the saga of Bolsa Chica, a strip of land located on the coast of Orange County, California, about 40 miles south of downtown Los Angeles, and how through citizen involvement that piece of land avoided becoming another massive waterfront residential and commercial development like so many others like it. What we now call Bolsa Chica was once a Native American winter encampment, then part of a 166,000 acre Spanish cattle ranch. By the late 1800s cattle raising around Los Angeles was on its way out and the Bolsa Chica rancho was divided up into small farms that were to become part of the agricultural boom for which Southern California gained enormous fame. But less than a century later most of those farms had succumbed to the region's insatiable appetite for urban expansion. A few tracts of open space remained, including about 2000 acres of coastal wetland that was part of the original Rancho La Bolsa Chica. Up to 1970 how this area avoided becoming covered with homes can be explained in one word: oil. Once oil was discovered in Bolsa Chica and the wetland began yielding its great mineral wealth, the area became one of the richest oil fields in California. For the next few decades it was far more profitable to pump oil from the ground than to cover that same ground with streets and houses. But the landowners were well aware that the capacity of oil fields is finite and other uses of the property, hopefully equally profitable, must be planned for the future. Much of the Bolsa Chica is coastal lowland, that is, not more than 5 feet above sea level, and in some portions it is actually below sea level. Thus due to its topology, the future of the Bolsa Chica was clearly to be a marina following the tradition of Marina del Rey, the Long Beach Marina, and Huntington Harbour, all rising from similar wetland origins. As the development plans were announced with great fanfare, a small group of local citizens began to raise questions such as "What good are wetlands?" "Are they worth preserving?" and "How can we save the Bolsa Chica Wetland?" The compelling answers led to the formation of one of the most influential, successful, and long lasting grass roots environmental organizations in state history.

And so we follow the story of Bolsa Chica from it prehistoric times through the period when its future seemed headed toward intense development to its present state as a fully functioning coastal wetland.

Huntington Beach, California
David Carlberg

BOLSA CHICA

Its History From Prehistoric Times To The Present
And What Citizen Involvement And Perseverance Can Achieve

1

Bolsa Chica Prehistory

Bolsa Chica Rises from the Sea

Over millions of years of Orange County's early geological history, sea levels rose and fell periodically, inundating large expanses of coastal and inland terrain and then receding, sometimes beyond our present shoreline. Some 1,200,000 years ago the land was uplifted by tectonic activity and over the next million years the shoreline gradually receded approximately to its present edge, leaving behind deep marine sediments many hundreds to thousands of feet thick. Fossils are still being unearthed as open land in Orange County continues to be scraped flat to make way for houses, shopping malls, office complexes, and freeways. For example, in 1999 during the excavation for the Route 174 toll road, some 10 miles from the present coastline, over 30,000 fossils were discovered, including those of seals, sea lions, sharks, and an extinct marine mammal related to manatees. At other locations along the highway route, fossilized remains of a Baleen whale as well as those of numerous land animals such as mammoths, mastodons, and camels have been unearthed. Fossils uncovered in Upper Newport Bay are said to be as rich and varied as those discovered in the famous La Brea Tarpits.

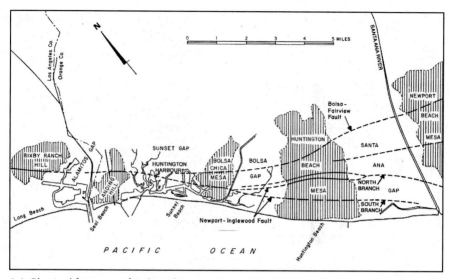

1-1. Physical features of Bolsa Chica environs. The Newport-Inglewood earthquake fault, the cause of the 1933 Long Beach earthquake and still considered dangerous, passes under Bolsa Chica as two branches, the north branch continuing through Los Angeles county to the Santa Monica Mountains. The Bolsa-Fairview fault is thought to be inactive. Also shown are the Bolsa Chica and Huntington Beach mesas and the Bolsa Gap. (Map courtesy County of Orange)

So eventually the present Orange County coastline so familiar to us, including the area of the Bolsa Chica, emerged from the sea for the last time. The Newport-Inglewood fault zone,[1] which passes under Bolsa Chica (Figure 1-1) rippled and rumbled and together with the effects of wind and rain created the low rises that define what we now call the Bolsa Chica and Huntington Beach Mesas. While the Huntington Beach Mesa is relatively flat, the Bolsa Chica Mesa is noted for its two levels or benches (Figure 1-2), the abrupt separation of which, known as an escarpment, generally traces the alignment of

---

1. The Newport-Inglewood Fault Zone consists of a complex pattern of numerous fault lines that extend from an area several miles offshore west of Laguna Beach, through coastal Huntington Beach and continuing through Los Angeles County to the Santa Monica Mountains. It was responsible for the devastating 1933 Long Beach earthquake and caused minor damage to the Bolsa Chica dam. Geologists estimate that earth movement along the Newport-Inglewood fault zone has amounted to about 6 miles in the last 12 million years.

2

1-2. The lower and upper benches of the Bolsa Chica mesa. The drop-off or escarpment between the two benches averages about 20 feet in height.(Photo courtesy County of Orange)

the Newport-Inglewood Fault Zone. It is assumed by geologists that the separation of the two benches was caused by action of the fault.

Rivers and Plains

Rivers flowed throughout the Los Angeles basin, carrying away rain and snowmelt from the nearby mountains and plains. The runoff was rich in sediment that it picked up during the water's rush to the sea. As the flow moved toward the coast and fanned out, its velocity slowed, causing the sediment to accumulated to enormous depths. The sediment layers formed the flat, open plain that makes up much of the present Los Angeles and northern Orange Counties. That sediment provided the rich soil that has been responsible for nourishing the region's abundant agricultural productivity that began in the late 1800s. And of course in more recent times the sediment's convenient flatness made possible the urban sprawl of the greater Los Angeles region.

The Santa Ana River

In Orange County, the principal river that flowed to the sea was the Santa Ana, with a watershed of nearly 3000 square miles. During its history, the Santa Ana River floodplain covered over one third of Orange County before being tamed in 1900 to follow its present, mostly concrete-lined course. The river's headwaters are located in the San Bernardino Mountains a few miles from Big Bear Lake and some 80 miles from its mouth on the border between Huntington Beach and Newport Beach. Due to the river's relatively flat, featureless floodplain, over the course of many thousands of years the Santa Ana River was able to meander all over what is now northern Orange County, its mouth emptying into the sea at various locations along the coast. At times the river merged with the San Gabriel River and even the Los Angeles River far to the west. At other times the river moved south to sculpt a canyon that is now Newport Bay. Some 9000 years ago the river's ocean outfall generally settled on its present location.

In the great flood of 1825, the Santa Ana River deposited huge amounts of sediment into the surf, creating a large sandbar that reached 8 miles down coast, nearly to the present opening of Newport Bay. Then, in the winter of 1883-4, the region received over 38 inches of rain, the greatest amount in recorded history. The ensuing floodwaters of the Santa Ana River deposited yet more sediment that enlarged and extended the sandbar, forming what is now known as the Balboa Peninsula. The newly enlarged peninsula partially blocked the mouth of Newport Bay, preventing waves from the open ocean from entering the inlet. Lacking wave action that would normally carry sediment out to sea, the sediment that washed into the deep bay from land upstream began accumulating, converting the bay into the relatively shallow marshland we presently know. Sedimentation into the bay from upland sources continues to this day, and portions of the upper bay must be dredged periodically. The present, narrow concrete mouth of the Santa Ana River was constructed in its present location in 1900, but remnants of the river's history are seen in the wetlands that still exist on both sides of its mouth, known as the Huntington Wetlands and the Talbert Marsh on the north side and the Santa Ana River Marsh and the Newport Slough on the south side.

Most notably, the Santa Ana River, in its many meanderings, was responsible starting some 15,000 to 25,000 years ago for scouring a break between the present Bolsa Chica and Huntington Beach mesas to form what would eventually become the Bolsa Gap (Figure 1-1) that separates the two mesas. Over the millennia as it emptied into the ocean at Bolsa Chica, the Santa Ana River left behind a layer of plant residue, which in time decomposed to form a deep peat bog that stretches from Bolsa Chica to the present city of Garden Grove. An 1890 survey estimated that the peat bog covered 10,000 acres and was 3 to 30 feet deep. The Bolsa Chica gap remained a deepwater lagoon for additional thousands of years, but eventually sediment from the river transformed the lagoon into the shallow wetland of the present time.

Southern California's First Humans

The first signs of human presence in Southern California appear to go back at least 8500 to 9000 years. Based on the types of hunting, cooking, and other implements found at native settlements, archeologists have established that human activities in the local region covered four major prehistoric time periods, referred to as horizons by most archeologists.[2] Horizon I, or "Paleocoastal," lasted from about 7000 B.C. until about 6000 B.C. and was characterized by the dependence of its human inhabitants on easily acquired shellfish and other marine

---

2. Chronologies of archeological periods differ from region to region. The periods quoted are for the Los Angeles Basin, including Orange County, and the Channel Islands.

sources for food. Starting about 6000 B.C., there was a shift to plants as a food source, defining the period called Horizon II. Seed processing implements such as *manos* and *metates*, collectively known as milling-stones, began to appear during Horizon II, hence this period is also referred to as the "Millingstone" Horizon. Hunting tools were still rare during this period, which lasted until about 1000 B.C. The appearance of small arrow points marked the beginning of Horizon III, ("Intermediate") from about 1000 B.C. to 700 A.D., indicating that hunting of small animals may have provided a major source of food for the first time. It is during this period that the islands off the Southern California mainland, now known as the Channel Islands, were first occupied by humans. That is also about the time period when exotic objects such as certain minerals, pottery, and mollusk shells not originating locally began appearing in Bolsa Chica and Orange County, suggesting the beginnings of trade with distant tribes. Finally, the period from around 700 A.D. to the arrival of the Spanish in the 16th century covers Horizon IV ("Late prehistoric"). Greater reliance on acorns for food is a major characteristic of this period. Acorns provided a rich and easily stored food item that made it possible for natives to end their nomadic existence, establish more stable settlements, and develop higher levels of social organization. The use of bows and arrows, introduced in Horizon III, still had not become widespread. Instead, large projectile points began to appear during this period, suggesting that hunting had turned to larger game, requiring spears that were thrown with the *atlatl*, or spear thrower. However, the bow and arrow did become more common after the arrival of the Spanish and were widely used as a weapon by native insurgents against the European intruders.

Archaeology of Bolsa Chica

It is not certain when humans first walked the ground of Bolsa Chica. Periodic floods by the Santa Ana River no doubt destroyed much of the signs of the earliest human inhabitants of the area. And during

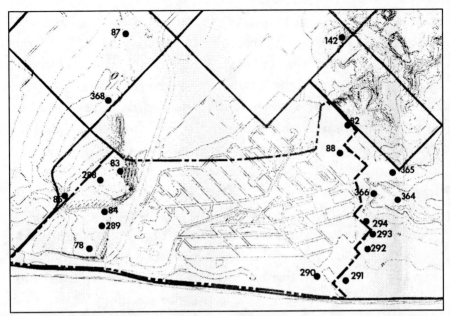

1-3. Approximate locations of some of the registered archeological sites in and around the Bolsa Chica area.(Map courtesy City of Huntington Beach)

more recent times Bolsa Chica has suffered from additional, human-caused devastation of its archeological history. The destruction of middens,[3] dwellings, and other points of archeological interest in and around Bolsa Chica has been from a variety of causes: agricultural and oil activities, coastal defense construction during World War II, amateur artifact collectors, vandalism, and urbanization. There is little information left. Approximately 40 registered archeological sites are presently mapped in and around Bolsa Chica (Figure 1-3). In a 1973 study, it was determined that 60 percent of the sites were either totally destroyed or so badly damaged that their scientific value was limited. The balance was considered damaged but of some scientific value. None of the sites was untouched.

The destruction of archeological sites actually has been a statewide problem that began in the last decades of the 19th century when it

---

3. Middens are trash heaps.

became a popular vogue to display native artifacts in homes and businesses. It has been estimated that tons of relics from coastal California native sites were removed to supply avid collectors in the U. S. and Europe. It was reported that around 1900 a crew from the Los Angeles Examiner carted off three wagonloads of native artifacts removed from several Huntington Beach archeological sites.[4] Museums also contributed to the demand for artifacts. For instance, the Peabody Museum at Harvard University holds a large collection of native artifacts from the Los Angeles Basin and one of the best collections of native California artifacts can be seen at the Musée l'Homme in Paris.

The oldest archeological artifacts unearthed at Bolsa Chica lead to the conclusion that it was inhabited at least as far back as about 8000 years ago. It is believed that the occupants were descendents of bands of Asian nomads who crossed the Bering Sea and migrated down the North American continent on foot or by boat along the west coast. Little if anything is known about these people. It is suggested that many continued their journey all the way to South America. This theory has been strengthened by recent research that demonstrated similarities between the DNA of indigenous people of South America with the DNA of Asians. It is fair to conclude that once Southern California's first tourists arrived, some eventually visited our coastal area, including Bolsa Chica, discovered its inviting climate and rich abundance of food and water and remained.[5]

Of the 39 archeological sites mapped in the Bolsa Chica area, 16 are located on the Bolsa Chica Mesa and 23 on the western edge of the Huntington Beach Mesa that overlooks the Bolsa Chica wetland. All of the sites have been damaged to various degrees and offer limited information about their occupants. What few traces remain of prehis-

---

4. The Examiner was owned by William Randolph Hearst, a man known for a voracious appetite for antiquities.

5. The so-called Mediterranean climate with which Southern California is blessed occurs in only three other places in the world other than the Mediterranean itself. They are central Chile, southwest Australia and the region around Cape Town, South Africa.

toric human occupation consist of millingstones and handstones used to grind seeds and acorns, projectile points for spears and arrows, hammerstones, charmstones, scrapers, drills and other tools for manufacturing items, musical instruments, and ceremonial objects as well as heaps of discarded mollusk shells and animal bones. A number of human burials have been reported, but details as to the identity, age or origin of the remains have not been divulged, due in part to federal and state regulations concerning the handling of Native American burial materials.[6] Some recent action involving the archeology of Bolsas Chica is discussed in Chapter 11.

Cogstones

One of the most remarkable prehistoric artifacts to be uncovered in Bolsa Chica are the so-called cogged stones or cogstones. These are discs of carved stone often with numerous notches around the periphery to resemble gears (Figure 1-4). Some have holes in the centers. The cogstones were made from a variety of materials ranging from relatively soft mudstone, siltstone, limestone, and sandstone to the harder basalt and granite. Steatite (soapstone) was seldom used to make cogstones, in spite of its common use in making cooking pots. Cogstones have been found in about 40 sites around Southern California, principally within the area that extends from the Los Angeles/Ventura County line to just above the Mexican border and inland as far as Cajon Pass and Yucaipa, plus Santa Catalina Island. But the vast majority, over four hundred cogstones, has been reported found in Bolsa Chica alone. They were concentrated in one archeological site on the Bolsa Chica Mesa, which officially is referred to as ORA-83,[7] or the "Cogstone Site." There may be hundreds of other cogstones

6. The Native American Graves Protection and Repatriation Act, passed in 1990, was a better-late-than-never attempt to make up for the centuries of artifact hunting that plagued Native American sites all over the U. S.

7. Official archeological sites in California are designated by a numbering system that shows the county (ORA for Orange County) and the register number.

1-4. Mysterious cogstones found by the hundreds on the Bolsa Chica Mesa. (Photo courtesy The Bowers Museum, Santa Ana, California)

that are unreported. The numbers of cogstones found in Bolsa Chica represent the greatest concentration of cogstones in Southern California and suggest Bolsa Chica was their place of manufacture. This notion is further supported by the discovery of tools at the Bolsa Chica site that could have been used to make the cogstones. Also found at ORA-83 are what appear to be partially completed cogstones that may not have passed quality control and were discarded or were simply left unfinished. Some estimates place the first appearance of cogstones at around 6000 B. C., or sometime immediately after Bolsa Chica's first human occupation. For some unknown cause, the cogstones' manufacture appears to have ceased around 3500 B. C. That means the cogstones that are now in museums, private collections and yet to be found are at least 5500 years old.

Also unknown was the function of the cogstones. They show little signs of wear other than being in the ground for over 55 centuries. The lack of wear supports the theory they were not utilitarian, that is, used for grinding seeds for example, but possibly played some sort of religious or ceremonial role. Theories of what the cogstones were used for abound. Perhaps they represented celestial bodies on a large calendar or star map. This explanation is in line with the claim by some historians that there may have been an astronomical observatory on the Bolsa Chica mesa. If true, it would be the first such site in North America. Others have raised the possibility that the cogstones were game pieces. A few of the hundreds that have been found appear to have been broken and repaired with tar, suggesting that they had some value and were worth keeping even after having been broken and mended. Then the questions are raised, "How were they broken?" "How were they being used when they broke?" The true function of cogstones may never be known, since most had been casually collected, thereby destroying their contextual provenance. That is, to learn how a particular artifact might have been used, archeologists look at what accompanied the artifact when unearthed. Was it part of a human burial? Was it aligned with other artifacts in any pattern or compass direction? Where was it in relation to areas of activities such as food preparation, ceremonial sites, or tool making? Again, there are few answers to these questions.

Another mystery associated with the cogstones was the source of many of the stone materials from which they were made. There are no significant deposits of much of the stone anywhere in the area of Bolsa Chica, leading to the notion that the stone had to be brought in from other areas such as Palos Verdes or the San Joaquin Hills.

ORA-83 is located on the south-east corner of the Bolsa Chica mesa. It is one of the most extensively studied sites in the state, being the object of formal archeological excavations since the 1920s. Much of the site's early archeological studies was disappointing due to damage to the site from farming activities, which scattered artifacts both vertically and horizontally. This made it impossible to determine any degree of context or provenance. Because of the site's potential historical value, numerous attempts have been made to register it with the National Register of Historic Places. All attempts have failed due to the apparent poor quality of the site and the refusal of the land-owner to allow registration. However, more recent archeological exca-vations to satisfy Coastal Commission requirements discovered areas of undisturbed soil. This work yielded an enormous amount of mate-rial, including a number of human remains, which have been reported to be about 4500 to 5500 years old. Much of this new material is still undergoing study.

The Gabrieliños

The most recent Native Americans to inhabit Bolsa Chica, as well as much of the Los Angeles basin, were given the name Gabrieliño[8] by the Spanish. The name refers to the fact the natives lived within the circle of influence of the San Gabriel Mission, which was founded in 1771, two years after the first Spanish land exploration marched through the territory. A variety of other names have been identified with these Native Americans, such as *Kizh* or *Kij*, but they are presently known by their descendents as *Tongva*, meaning in the Shoshonean language, "People of the earth." In recognition of both their connection with the San Gabriel mission and their natural name, we will to refer to Bolsa Chica's last Native American occupants as Gabrieliño/Tongva.

Historians are not certain exactly when the native people who were later to be known as Gabrieliño/Tongva first moved into the Los Angeles basin. What is certain is that they were not the original inhab-itants, of whom nothing is known. By tracing artifacts and languages, some believe the Gabrieliño/Tongva gradually moved into the area in waves between about 1 AD to about 500 A.D. Others believe the migration may have started as early as 1500 B. C. Prior to their move to the coastal areas of Southern California, these natives occupied the

---

8. The Spanish suffix –eño or –iño indicates a person's or object's origins. The title of the popular song by Cuban composer Ernesto Lecuona, *Malagueña*, means "the girl from Málaga. Addition of the *u* allows the *g* to retain its hard sound. A popular Peruvian beer called Cuzcueña, comes from the city of Cuzco.

Great Basin of Eastern Oregon and Nevada and eventually reached the Los Angeles area via the Mojave Desert. The Gabrieliños belonged to a language stock known as Shoshonean or Uto-Aztecan, which is also found in areas of the U. S. Southwest, Mexico, and Central America. The arrival of the Gabrieliño/Tongva into Southern California is thought to have formed a wedge that forced their predecessors to the north (The Chumash) and south (The Juaneños), but they apparently remained good neighbors, sharing many cultural and trade activities with the people they uprooted. In 1994, the State of California in a joint legislative resolution recognized the Gabrieliño/Tongva people as the aboriginal tribe of the Los Angeles Basin. Federal recognition has not occurred, however.

Like the Gabrieliño/Tongva, members of the Juaneño tribe (Acjachemen Nation) still live in the area of their ancestors. Since the Juaneños appear to be the inhabitants of Bolsa Chica immediately prior to the Gabrieliño/Tongva, and perhaps even occupying the area simultaneously, for purposes of resolving issues associated with archeological investigations, the state has recognized both the Juaneños and the Gabrieliño/Tongva as the Most Likely Descendants of the people whose remains have been unearthed in Bolsa Chica. Thus members of both tribes monitor archeological operations.

The Gabrieliño/Tongva eventually occupied much of the present greater Los Angeles basin, including the San Fernando, San Gabriel, and San Bernardino Valleys, much of northern Orange County and the offshore islands of Santa Catalina, San Nicolas, and San Clemente. Based on observations recorded in journals by Spanish explorers at the time, it has been estimated that by 1700 the Gabrieliño/Tongva occupied 50 to 100 settlements scattered throughout the 2500 square miles of the Los Angeles basin. Their total population was estimated to be of least 5000.

While archeological evidence clearly shows Native American occupation of Bolsa Chica on both the Bolsa Chica and Huntington Beach Mesas going back at least 8000 years, it has been debated whether

1-5. Gabrieliño/Tongva village. (Figure courtesy Merryant Publishers. Daniel Liddell, illustrator).

Bolsa Chica was a permanent settlement or merely a seasonal one, that is, one that was occupied only during certain times of the year. There are several bits of evidence that lead one to the conclusion that Bolsa Chica may have been a seasonal encampment for food gathering and processing or other, perhaps religious, purposes. For example, clamshells in a Bolsa Chica midden showed mostly winter markings. If Bolsa Chica had been used year around, clamshells would show both winter and summer markings. Also, most of the bird bones found in prehistoric middens in Bolsa Chica were from migratory species that occurred in the region only during the winter migration season from October to May. It is assumed that during other times of the year the Bolsa Chica inhabitants occupied sites near the foothills of the Santa Ana Mountains where fresh water and seasonal food sources, particularly acorns, were more abundant. In addition to fish, shellfish, and

1-6. Gabrieliño/Tongva plank boat. (Figure courtesy Merryant Publishers. Daniel Liddell, illustrator)

acorns, the natives subsisted on seeds, other food plants, and large and small animals such as deer, bear, dogs, rabbits, and waterfowl.

Prior to the arrival of the Spanish, the life of the Gabrieliño/ Tongva appears to have been relatively stress-free. Food was plentiful, the climate was generally moderate and crime and warfare were rare. The Gabrieliño/Tongva dwellings, called wickiups, were made of reeds that were abundant in the nearby wetlands (Figure 1-5). Due to the mild climate, it is assumed that clothing was generally optional during most of the year, and this was confirmed by written accounts of Spanish explorers. For protection from winter chill, the Gabrieliño/ Tongva wore robes made from rabbit skins woven together.

The Gabrieliño/Tongva were expert boat builders, producing reed boats that were used in lagoons and the near shore for travel and fishing. They also built plank canoes (Figure 1-6) called *te'ats* that were made from hand-hewn boards. The Spanish explorer, Sebastián Vizcaino, who had made contact with Gabrieliño/Tongva on Santa Catalina

Island on his journey through local waters in 1602, commented in his diary on the surprisingly high quality of the natives' plank canoes. The design of the canoes is said to have been borrowed from the Chumash, the Gabrieliño/Tongva's northern neighbors. Since there were no nearby heavy forests, the Gabrieliño/Tongva apparently obtained their wood from driftwood logs or from logs brought down from the nearby mountains. Using bone or antler wedges, the natives split the logs into planks about an inch thick, then fitted the planks together by shaping them with tools fashioned from stone or clamshells. The planks were joined by drilling holes in them with stone drill bits and lashing the planks together with cord made from plant fibers. The holes and joints were then sealed with pine pitch or tar likely brought from what is now known as Brea Canyon where it seeped out of the ground (*Brea* is Spanish for tar). Tar was also used to decorate the canoes.

Plank canoes were unique to the Chumash and the Gabrieliño/Tongva. They were found nowhere else in the New World. Plank canoes were highly seaworthy, and in fact were used for deep sea fishing and for travel to the offshore islands. The Gabrieliño/Tongva traded seeds, nuts, and deer and rabbit skins with the native islanders for shell beads, useful raw materials and manufactured objects. One of the most sought after items was Catalina steatite (soapstone) that was used to make ceremonial objects and utilitarian items such as cooking vessels. Soapstone was highly prized for its ease of carving and its heat resistance, making it ideal for vessels that were used to cook food directly over open fires. Due to its value, if a soapstone vessel broke, larger fragments often were saved and continued to be used for cooking. The Gabrieliño/Tongva did not produce clay pottery until the arrival of the Spanish missionaries in the 18th century, but they were expert basket weavers. Unfortunately few examples of their baskets have survived.

Bolsa Bay was a deep lagoon during earlier times, providing the natives who occupied the Bolsa Chica vicinity with a rich assortment of game, fish, shellfish and waterfowl. However, during a long period when the Santa Ana River emptied into Bolsa Chica, the bay eventually filled with sediment, forming the present shallow wetland. This caused deepwater shellfish species to be replaced by less abundant mud tolerant species, and most varieties of fish probably disappeared entirely. Thus as the ability of Bolsa Chica to sustain a significant human population was reduced, the occupation of Bolsa Chica began to dwindle until by the time of the expedition of Spanish explorer Portolá in 1769, there probably was little if any significant native occupation of the Bolsa Chica mesa and surrounding lowlands. This is supported by the fact there are no specific references to settlements in Bolsa Chica on any maps or village listings in the writings of either 18th century explorers or modern Native American historians. However, sites overlooking the nearby Santa Ana River wetlands were recorded and continued to be occupied during the mission period. One such settlement. called *Lukup*, was described in Spanish journals but present day historians cannot agree on the exact location of that settlement. A few claim the name referred to a village actually on the Bolsa Chica mesa while most historians suggest it was on other sites such as near the present Newland Shopping Center at Beach Blvd. and Adams Street in Huntington Beach or the area of Adams St. and Placentia Rd. in Costa Mesa. All this confusion further points up the dismal state of knowledge of our community's Native American heritage.

2

The Spanish
and the Missions

California's First European Visitors

Once Spain deemed it had conquered "New Spain" (Mexico) in 1521, its attention was turned to the completely unknown and unexplored land to the north called "California"[1] and the possible riches that it may offer. Encouraged by accounts of the enormous amounts of gold and silver being hauled out of South America, Spanish authorities began preparations for exploring further up the west coast of North America in anticipation of additional treasure. Numerous land and sea expeditions to California were launched beginning in 1532. The earlier sea voyages headed north from the west coast of New Spain up the Sea of Cortez (Gulf of California) under the assumption California was an island (Figure 2-1). The supposed island's protected eastern coast seemed the easiest and safest route to follow. When expeditions hit a dead end at the northern tip of the sea, some lingered and explored the mouth of the Colorado River (see Footnote 13) but most turned back south and then around the peninsula that is now known as Baja Cali-

---

1. The exact origin of the name California is not known. The best explanation seems to relate to a popular series of 16th century novels by the Spanish writer Garci Rodríguez de Montalvo that described an exotic island called California ruled by Queen Calafía.

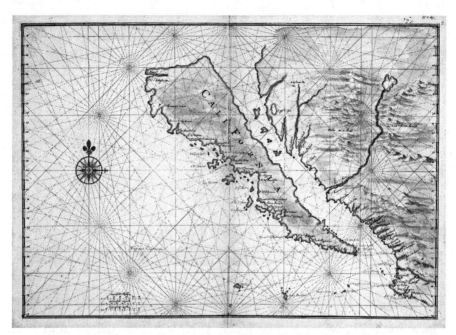

2-1. Map of California as an island published about 1650 by the Dutch cartographer Joan Vinckeboons. California might as well have been an island. Mountain ranges, vast deserts, and unfriendly natives made it extremely difficult to reach the coast from the east for much of the Spanish and Mexican eras. Travel and commerce in the territory depended almost entirely on the sea. (Map courtesy U.S. Historical Archives)

fornia, then northward along its west coast.[2] But all of the early expeditions failed due to bad weather, mutinies, groundings, attacks by unfriendly natives, and unknown causes when ships simply vanished, never to be heard from again. However, land expeditions into Baja California were more successful and in time the Jesuit order managed to establish 21 missions throughout much of the peninsula.

In time a geographical distinction between Baja (lower) California and Alta (upper) California was made. The division was established in

---

2. Many maps of the west coast of North America continued to show California as an island as late as 1715. Some historians suggest that because of the disappointment over the failure to prove the land to be an island, the news was not widely disseminated. As a sign of the indecision of the time, some map publishers even showed California as an island on some maps and at the same time a peninsula on others.

1772 to draw a separation between the lands north of the line under the authority of the friars of the Franciscan order and that of the Dominican order, which had taken over the missions south of the line from the banished Jesuits. A boundary was drawn from the Pacific coast about thirty miles south of the present U. S.-Mexico border across the peninsula to the head of the Gulf of California. The modern border separating the two parts was not established until 1848 through the Treaty of Guadalupe Hidalgo that ended the United State's war with Mexico. It was then that the U. S. acquired California, Nevada, Utah and parts of New Mexico, Colorado and Wyoming from Mexico.

Initial Contact

Eventually Spanish explorers reached the coast of Alta California. Like the unsuccessful explorers before him, Juan Rodriguez Cabrillo, a Portuguese seaman employed by the King of Spain, was under orders from the governor of New Spain to sail up the coast of Alta California to find possible riches. A second purpose for his voyage was to find a direct sailing route between the Pacific Ocean and the North Atlantic. Such a passage, known as the Strait of Anián,[3] had been sought after by the major European trading powers for years. A direct route from the North Atlantic to the Pacific would have avoided the need for ships from Europe to sail around South America or Africa to reach the Orient. Of course the route was never found and in 1728 the Danish explorer Vitus Bering, after exploring the sea that bears his name where Asia and North America almost touch, concluded that the Strait of Anián had been merely a figment of cartographers' imaginations and urged the myth to be laid to rest.[4]

---

3. Also known as the Strait of Cathay. The name Anián apparently comes from Marco Polo's 13th century description of a rich province of China known as Anin.

4. If the Arctic ice sheet continues to melt as a result of global warming as is predicted, a sea route between the Atlantic and Pacific Oceans through the Arctic sea may become a reality.

Cabrillo left New Spain with two ships in July, 1542 and brought his ships into what is now known as San Diego Bay in late September. Cabrillo is usually given credit for discovering California, although he may not have been the first European to set foot in what is now considered the state of California.[5] Continuing northward Cabrillo arrived at the islands of San Clemente and Santa Catalina (as they are now known) on October 4. Cabrillo reported having a brief but friendly contact with the island natives, possibly in Avalon Bay. This was apparently the first encounter the natives of that region had with Europeans. He then sailed for the mainland, a distance of about 22 miles, and again was greeted by friendly natives. It is possible he sailed along the coast of what is now known as Orange County, but unimpressed with the arid look of the landscape, Cabrillo continued northward until entering Santa Monica Bay, where he anchored briefly and had additional contact with natives, then resumed his northward progress. However, on attempting to sail around what is now known as Point Conception, Cabrillo encountered strong north-westerly winds and currents that forced him to spend several days on San Miguel Island, one of Southern California's most remote of its Channel Islands, to wait for better weather.

During Cabrillo's stay on San Miguel Island, he broke his leg in a fall, apparently suffering a compound fracture that became gangrenous. In spite of what must have been a painful injury, Cabrillo ordered his ship to make another attempt to sail up the coast. After once again battling heavy weather, the tiny vessel managed to sail as far north as the vicinity of what is presently known as Fort Ross in northern California before turning south. Oddly, Cabrillo did not discover San

---

5. Historians have long debated this. Just two years earlier, two Spanish explorers, Hernando de Alarcón and Melchior Díaz, independently explored land near the mouth of the Colorado River at the northern extent of the Gulf of California and may have stepped onto soil that is within the present boundaries of California near the town of Winterhaven. A state historical marker commemorating Alarcón's visit is located at that site. In addition, Cabrillo and other explorers recorded accounts of coastal natives reporting seeing bearded men in European dress in interior regions of Alta California.

Francisco Bay, despite his ship passing its opening now known as the "Golden Gate" at least twice, once as his party headed north and again on its return passage. Possibly fog for which San Francisco is famous obscured the Golden Gate from Cabrillo's notice.

Cabrillo did not live to report personally the results of his explorations to the Viceroy of New Spain, for as his ship entered the waters of the Channel Islands on its return voyage, he died of the injury he sustained two months earlier. He is thought to have been buried on San Miguel Island. Before he died, thinking his expedition had failed, Cabrillo requested his officers to retrace their northern voyage, which they did before returning to New Spain. But they, too, failed to discover riches of any kind, the fabled Strait of Anián, or San Francisco Bay.

The Later Voyages

Remarkably, the next known sighting coastal Alta California natives had of Europeans did not occur until more than two generations later when the Spanish explorer Sebastián Vizcaino in 1602 essentially followed in Cabrillo's wake, stopping at Santa Catalina Island (which he named) and other islands of the Channel Island group. Like Cabrillo's men, Vizcaino brought back reports of friendly natives but no riches to speak of. Vizcaino did, however, report the discovery of large bay he named Monterey. So far the only riches found by Spanish explorers had been pearls along the shores of Baja California. Disappointed with the news, the Spanish government was no longer in the mood to pay for any further expeditions into Alta California. It would be almost two centuries before Spanish explorers would return.

The Land Expeditions

Nearly 170 years after Vizcaino's visit, the Spanish king found new reasons to send expeditions into Alta California. Gaspar de Portolá, then governor of Baja California, was ordered to lead a land expedition into Alta California. In spite of the Spanish government's low expectations for any riches in Alta California, Portolá's charge was to establish Spanish presence in the territory to discourage invasion by foreign interests. The Spanish king had received word that European explorers from numerous countries, including Russia, Great Britain, France, and the Netherlands, were eyeing the Pacific Coast of North America.[6] Portolá also was charged with two additional assignments, finding possible safe harbors for Spanish galleons traveling between the Philippine Islands and Spain. It seems pirates were known to lay in wait along the coast for Spanish ships laden with Philippine treasure. Finally, the Spanish king directed missionaries to begin establishing missions throughout the province. The explorers were to travel as far north as Monterey Bay, which Vizcaino had discovered and where Spanish authorities feared foreign interests might use as a landing point (recall that San Francisco Bay had not yet been discovered.). In 1769, four parties set out from the Pacific coast of New Spain, two by land and two by sea. They were to rendezvous in San Diego Bay. To begin their journey, the two land parties first had to be shuttled by boat from New Spain to Loreto on the east coast of the Baja California peninsula. Portolá's land party consisted of two Franciscan Fathers, two servants, 42 natives and a sufficient number of pack mules to carry a six months' supply of food and supplies. A small contingent of soldiers also accompanied the expedition to provide protection against attacks by unfriendly natives. Portolá left Loreto in early March 1769 and reached San Diego Bay on the first day of July. The cost in human lives in those four months is astounding. Due to the harsh conditions on the over 600 mile Baja California leg of the expedition, 23 of the 42 natives that accompanied Portolá's party had ether died or deserted into the inhospitable desert. The other land and sea expeditions also lost a number of men. One ship was presumed lost at sea and never heard from. Overall, the expeditions arrived with half

---

6. Russia eventually succeeded in getting a foothold in California by establishing Fort Ross in 1812, the site of which was purchased from the local natives for three blankets, three pairs of trousers, two axes, three hoes, and some beads.

the men they started out with. In addition, many of the survivors were too ill to continue on the expedition and had to remain at San Diego to recuperate. Housed in makeshift shelters made of sailcloth, at least 60 of the men eventually died as well.

On July 14, Portolá headed north from San Diego on foot and arrived in what is now Orange County on July 23, 1769 at a point a few miles inland from the present city of San Clemente in an area now known as Cristianitos Canyon,[7] part of the Camp Pendleton Marine Base. They pushed northward, following a path more or less parallel to and to the east of the present Route 5, the Santa Ana Freeway (Figure 2-2). It has been speculated that they chose an inland route because numerous wetlands made travel along the coast difficult. The party camped on the bank of the Santa Ana River on the 28th. "A foot deep and a half mile wide," is how Portolá described the river, which he named in honor of Saint Anne, whose feast was celebrated on that date. Nearby was a native settlement the occupants of which may have been those who wintered at Bolsa Chica. A comparison of the artifacts unearthed at Bolsa Chica (and Newport Bay) with those found at the settlement that Portolá encountered appear to support that notion. While Portolá's party never visited Bolsa Chica, they may have spotted it from a distance. In Portolá's journal is an entry describing where some of his soldiers, in scouting on the nearby hills near what is now known as El Toro, reported sighting six islands to the west. The only islands visible from the hills had to be Santa Catalina and San Clemente. It's been assumed that the other four islands were actually prominences now known as the Newport, Huntington Beach and Bolsa Chica Mesas, and Landing Hill in Seal Beach. They probably appeared as islands because of the extensive wetlands that surrounded them.

Portolá's party then continued north through Brea Canyon, the San Gabriel and San Fernando Valleys, setting up camp each evening and eventually reaching the coast around the present city of Oxnard, then

---

7. The name Christianitos ("little Christians") refers to two severely ill native babies who Father Serra baptized.

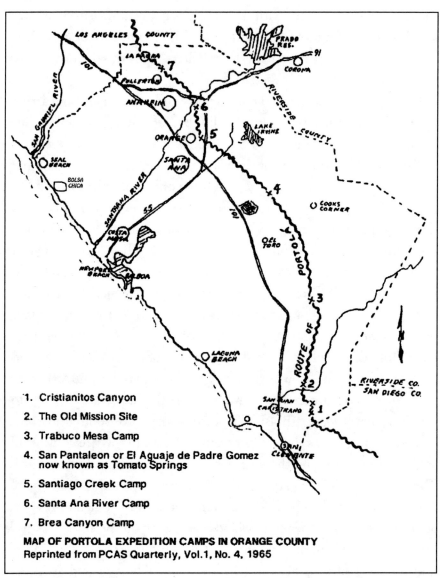

1. Cristianitos Canyon
2. The Old Mission Site
3. Trabuco Mesa Camp
4. San Pantaleon or El Aguaje de Padre Gomez
   now known as Tomato Springs
5. Santiago Creek Camp
6. Santa Ana River Camp
7. Brea Canyon Camp

MAP OF PORTOLA EXPEDITION CAMPS IN ORANGE COUNTY
Reprinted from PCAS Quarterly, Vol.1, No. 4, 1965

2-2. Orange County portion of the route of the Portolá expedition of 1769. Soldiers in Portolá's party may have sighted Bolsa Chica from what is now the El Toro hills. (Map courtesy Pacific Coast Archeological Society)

proceeding up the coast. When the party reached Monterey Bay, they did not recognize it from Vizcaino's 167 year old description. Apparently looking at it from the land, it did not look like a bay, while from

Vizcaino's view from his ship, it did. Instead, Portolá continued north until coming to San Francisco Bay on the 4th of November,[8] at which time the expedition realized its error and returned south, retracing its steps and eventually reaching its starting point, San Diego. By many counts, the trek was a disaster. While the expedition did pinpoint a number of potential mission sites, the explorers assumed they failed to find Monterey Bay. On the verge of starvation, many members of the party deserted. In spite of ample game along their route, which they apparently were unable to hunt, they had to eat their pack mules to survive. But Portolá left his mark on California in many ways. For instance, he is responsible for naming several familiar places in Southern California, such as Santa Margarita, Santa Ana, Carpentaria, and Gaviota, and he certainly must be considered California's trailblazer.

The Missions

Portolá's 1769 discovery expedition through Alta California was followed by further land expeditions. Within two years, two missions were established, one in San Diego and one in Monterey, some 460 miles north.[9] Initially "missions" were nothing more than rough, temporary wooden or brush chapels with thatched roofs and simple altars. It would be a year or more before the padres were able to build the large adobe or stone structures we normally associate with California's Franciscan missions. Missions were one point of the triad of Spain's formula for colonization. The other two points were presidios (forts) and pueblos (townships). These will be covered later. Under the administration of the Franciscan religious order, the missions were charged with converting the native population to Christianity and training the converts to become self-sufficient subjects of the King of Spain.

---

8. Portolá is thus given credit for discovering San Francisco Bay.

9. The Monterey mission was moved to Carmel in 1772, where the San Carlos Borroméo de Carmelo mission church was built.

2-3. The San Gabriel Mission after which the Gabrieliño Native Americans are named. (Drawing by Giana)

Once the first two missions were started, it was the plan of Father Serra, the Franciscan mission system's president, to begin filling in the 460 mile gap between San Diego and Monterey with many more missions. In 1771, Serra ordered a party to find a site near the north end of the gap and one near the south end. The criteria for choosing a mission site were simple: find a location with adequate water and timber, good soil for growing crops and an ample, nearby population of natives to supply labor to build and operate the mission and provide converts. In the summer of 1771 a party set out from Serra's headquarters in Monterey, and within a day's travel chose a site near the present town of Milpitas to establish a mission they named San Antonio de Padua. The party proceeded south to San Diego for provisions, then turned north, eventually stopping at the edge of the Santa Ana River where Portolá had camped on his expedition just two years before. It was the site that Friar Serra had chosen for a mission, but the missionary party was unimpressed with the location and moved further north and west to a site on the San Gabriel River. On September 8, 1771 the mission San Gabriel Arcángel was officially established at a spot near the current intersection of San Gabriel Blvd. and E. Lincoln

Ave. within the city of Montebello. However, no permanent structures were built at that location and during the winter of 1774-75 the missionaries moved the mission to its current location in the city of San Gabriel. Construction of the present stone church building that is just off what is now Mission Blvd. did not begin until 1790 (Figure 2-3).

Generally, each of the California missions was run by a relatively small band of Europeans consisting of one or more friars, usually five soldiers, and if the mission was lucky, a blacksmith or a carpenter. The bulk of the labor needed to build a church and other structures and to keep the mission running was provided by natives, most of whom, at least initially, gladly worked in exchange for trinkets, clothing, tobacco, and food. But the conditions under which the natives worked soon deteriorated.

The San Gabriel Mission and the Bolsa Chica Gabrieliño/Tongva

The circle of influence the San Gabriel mission had over the local Native Americans is thought to have covered roughly the present Los Angeles and San Bernardino Counties and northern Orange County including Bolsa Chica. Thus as mentioned in the previous chapter, the Native Americans within the mission's reach were called Gabrieliños, named after the mission. Since historians have proposed that Bolsa Chica was no longer occupied by significant numbers of natives by the time the Spanish missions were established, few if any natives who may have occupied Bolsa Chica were likely to have been recruited by the mission. They had moved too far away. Alta California Governor Pedro Fages observed that the true area from which pliable converts could be recruited was a circle of less than a 20 mile radius. For natives beyond that boundary, a high rate of escape could be expected and no baptisms were likely to occur, the governor predicted. Bolsa Chica is about 30 miles from the San Gabriel mission and the summer settlement on the Santa Ana river that the Gabrieliño/Tongva may have used was even further.

The Life of the San Gabriel Neophytes

Initially, only limited numbers of natives availed themselves of the California missions' spiritual rewards. In the two years after its establishment, only 73 baptisms were recorded at the San Gabriel mission, and over the next 11 years, about 1000 Gabrieliño/Tongva converts were recorded. This was in spite of the significant numbers of natives in the region, estimated at about 5000 or more, one of the most densely populated concentrations of Native Americans in North America. Understandably, asking the natives to give up deeply held, multigenerational beliefs for the foreign tenets of Christianity was a challenge. For instance, conversion was supposed to save a person's soul from Hell, a place that had no meaning in native lore. While the missions held that conversions were supposed to be voluntary, once a native became a "neophyte" (a convert), his or her life was drastically changed. A convert was required to live at the mission, away from his or her familiar settlement, wear European clothing and eat a strange and (for natives) unhealthy diet. The daily routine of meals, devotion, work, and sleep was laid out like a railroad timetable.

Unmarried male and female converts lived in segregated, crowded, communal accommodations at the missions that were in some respects more primitive than what a native enjoyed in a home village. Notably, the natives' close quarters aided the spread of European infectious diseases, which led to the deaths of significant numbers of natives. Married converts were allowed to live in traditional wikiups or adobe huts near the mission. The harsh conditions prompted at least one out of ten Gabrieliño/Tongva neophytes to bolt and return to his or her village or to flee into the nearby mountains. In some cases soldiers were sent out to round up escapees, who faced harsh physical punishment on their return to the mission. Conditions at the San Gabriel mission were not unique; natives throughout the mission system suffered similar treatment.

Not surprisingly, it was not long before relations between the missions and the natives deteriorated. Acts of violence by Europeans against the natives became commonplace, generating resentment and rage among the normally peaceful, indigenous population. One incident occurred at the San Gabriel mission just a few years after it was established. A soldier raped a native woman, an all too common occurrence. The woman's husband confronted the perpetrator, a skirmish ensued and the soldier shot and killed the husband. Unfortunately the husband happened to be the local tribal chief. It was clearly a divine miracle that the missionaries and solders were able to quell what could have been a bloody episode in retaliation for the loss of the tribal leader.

The growing rage generated by violence against the natives continued to grow, resulting in more frequent acts of revenge. Most violence was directed against the missionaries, since the solders had a variety of weapons to defend themselves. In spite of being grossly out-numbered, mission soldiers often could crush native rebellions by simply threatening to use their guns, for which the natives had great fear and respect. One of the earliest incidents occurred in San Diego in 1775. Several hundred natives stormed the mission, killing three Spaniards including the friar and burning the mission buildings. The natives then turned to the nearby presidio, but withdrew before attacking. Historians note that in this case the heavily outnumbered soldiers at the presidio would certainly have been overwhelmed by the natives despite the solders' weaponry. One account by historian Bill Mason has it that the natives ran out of arrows and had to retreat to their village. As a precaution, Spanish authorities abandoned the mission and did not rebuild it until a year later. Numerous similar incidents continued into the 19th century. In 1812, a small band of natives assassinated the padre at the Santa Cruz mission in retribution for his repeated use of corporal punishment.

The Mission Timetable

Historians point out that Spanish authorities did not intend for the California missions to be permanent institutions. Instead, it was antic-ipated that once the native population had been converted to Christianity and trained in various skills to fend for itself as loyal Spanish subjects, the mission system would be disbanded. The life span for the missions was set at ten years, but while Spain (and later, Mexico) made several attempts to enforce that limit in Alta California, the mission system persisted for over 60 years. The padres insisted that their goals had not been met, even after six decades. In the early years of the 19th century the mission system finally ended cruelly for both missions and the natives. That part of the story will be covered in the next chapter.

The Presidios

Spanish authorities had long feared the invasion of Alta California by foreign forces. This was in spite of the fact the territory did not appear to hold any significant quantities of riches like those of Mexico, Peru, and other conquests. To defend against such invasions, the Spanish established four presidios, or forts, at San Diego, Santa Barbara, Monterey and San Francisco. An additional role of the presidios was to defend the missions against native uprisings, and there were many. Finally, the presidios became a source of colonization of the land. The soldiers attached to the presidios, usually numbering about 20, often had families (native or European) that settled nearby and soon became the nucleus of a *pueblo* or township.

The Pueblos: The Beginnings of Los Angeles

Part of Spain's colonization plan for Alta California was to establish a *pueblo* or settlement near each mission. In 1781 forty four settlers of native, African, and Spanish descent from eleven families were recruited from New Spain to establish a settlement near the San Gabriel Mission. They followed the difficult overland trail from the states of Sonora and Sinaloa, through the deserts of what is now southern Arizona and California, and settled at a site on the present Los Angeles River. Thus was founded *El Pueblo de Nuestra Señora la Reina de Los Angeles de Porciúncula*, known nowadays simply as L. A. The pueblo's first alcalde (mayor) was Jose Vanegas, a native from Jalisco, New Spain (now Mexico). In just six years the population of the little pueblo grew from the original 44 to 141, and by 1821, it was 650.

The San Gabriel Mission Struggles to Survive

Since the San Gabriel mission was at the crossroads of the major north-south travel route (*El Camino Real*[10]) and the east-west overland trail between Sonora and Alta California,[11] the mission became a popular stop-over for travelers and soldiers between New Spain and Monterey. The missionaries found themselves becoming innkeepers in addition to carrying out their religious duties, much to their distress since food and supplies were often scarce.

The early years of the missions were very difficult for the European missionaries. The presumption that the missions could immediately become self-sustaining was overly optimistic. The missionaries found themselves playing the role of Robinson Crusoe, having to improvise for their daily needs and to struggle to find enough food to sustain themselves, the soldiers, the natives whom they were trying to convert, and the many visitors who passed through. To compound their plight, the missionaries initially knew little about agriculture and raising live-stock. In addition, provisions that were supposed to be coming from New Spain were frequently delayed or did not arrive at all. The supply ships from New Spain were small, flimsy craft that were frequently lost at sea. If they made it to Alta California, their crews often suffered from scurvy, malnutrition, and other maladies and had to be housed, fed, and brought back to health by the missionaries before the sailors were able to return to New Spain.

Special items such as tools and other manufactured goods often took a year or more to arrive, for the missionaries' requests had to be sent

---

10. Sections of *El Camino Real*, or The Royal Highway, are presently memorialized by mission bells on curved poles placed along highways in Southern California, such as the Ventura Freeway in the San Fernando Valley.

11. The route from Sonora was known as *El Camino del Diablo*, or the Devil's Highway, due to the unfriendly natives and very harsh conditions that travelers encountered.

to New Spain. From there requests were often forwarded to Spain or occasionally to Cuba or Peru, from which items were shipped. Conditions got so bad that at one point Spanish authorities were on the brink of abandoning Alta California. For all the money being spent in the new province on soldiers and supplies, King Carlos III found himself receiving no return on his investment. However, he felt Spanish presence in Alta California was necessary to counter threats of occupation by foreign explorers, who, as mentioned above, were known to be scouting the west coast of North America.

San Gabriel Mission Fortunes Pick Up

By 1775, the fortunes of the San Gabriel mission had begun to improve and eventually it was to become the richest and most envied of the 21 California missions. This turnaround was due at least in part to the choice of the mission's location. The combination of its abundant water supply, rich soil and nearly constant sunshine supported bountiful crops and lush grazing land. But the majority of the mission's success was due to the forced labor of the natives, without whom the mission would not have survived. The mission's grain and vegetable crops, fruit orchards, vineyards, and livestock grazing fields occupied over 100,000 acres, much of it on Native American land and cared for by native labor.

Though contrary to Spanish edict, the San Gabriel mission began trading with foreign ships in exchange for critical goods such as tools and cloth which they had difficulty obtaining from New Spain. The missions would usually refuse cash for their hides, preferring the goods they so desperately needed. The mission offered hides, tallow, wine, fresh produce, and a few manufactured items such as pottery and candles, providing the mission a significant source of income. But that would soon end.

3

The Rancho Period
En el Rancho Grande

The California *Rancho*

Once the farming and cattle raising operations at the San Gabriel mission were running successfully, the padres found themselves holding a very lucrative monopoly. In spite of an official Spanish government ban on *Californios* doing business with foreigners, Yankee trading ships representing American east coast markets were eagerly received by the padres. The Yankees were equally eager to trade manufactured goods for hides and tallow that were needed to feed burgeoning New England industries. Ships flying the British flag also were seen on-loading hides off California's ports. The mission's cowhides were especially sought after, since political turmoil in South America, the other major center of hide production, had cut off much of that source. But with the introduction of the *rancho* beginning in the late 1780s, the gradual decline of the missions' monopoly was set in motion. While the missions' prosperity continued into the 1800s and peaked during the first quarter of the century, as more and more ranchos were established, competition began to erode the economic power of the missions.

Ranchos were independently operated cattle and farming enterprises that were made possible through immense land grants awarded

35

by the Spanish king and later, by the Mexican government, to private individuals. The king awarded land grants to his soldiers to encourage them to settle in Alta California on their retirement. However, title to the land was not included in the grants, only permission to use the land for raising livestock or farming. Once Alta California came under Mexican rule in 1824, grants that included title were handed out to anyone who qualified, that is, who had the where-with-all to start a farm or cattle ranch and was in the good graces of the local authorities.

In the sparse grassland of the semiarid climate of Southern California, cattle raising required vast amounts of grazing land to sustain the large herds of the *rancheros* (ranch owners). But land was not a problem; there were hundreds of square miles of open land that could be used merely for the asking. California's rancho era was made possible by the availability of almost unlimited amounts of free land, native territorial rights notwithstanding.

The Missions, the Military, and the Nieto Royal Spanish Land Grant

As noted earlier, Portolá's march in 1769 launched the Spanish occupation of Alta California. Expeditions were routinely accompanied by small bands of soldiers to provide protection from attacks by hostile natives. Once a mission was established, a few soldiers were posted at the mission also for protection, as well as to help recruit converts and enforce mission rules. In addition, four *presidios* were built at San Diego, Santa Barbara, Monterey and San Francisco that were manned by larger numbers of solders.

Relations between the mission friars and their military protectors often were strained. It is said that friars relocated at least two missions, Monterey and San Diego, from sites close to the presidios to ones more distant in part to separate themselves from the presidio solders. But the missionaries could not avoid the solders assigned to the missions. A soldier's life at a mission was one of isolation and boredom interspersed with occasional, usually one-sided, battles with native insurgents. The Spanish military men were thousands of miles from their homes and families and communication between them was poor or non-existent. As noted earlier, the soldiers often took advantage of female natives and tended to treat the neophytes harshly. Much to the friars' distress, the soldiers seldom participated in any work around the mission. In addition to their feelings of isolation. the soldiers' rebelliousness also may have been fueled by the fact their meager government pay was often delayed or failed to arrive at all. Out of desperation, many of His Majesty's soldiers eventually deserted, but a few turned to productive pursuits in their spare time such as raising cattle and horses. Three such weekend rancheros were Cpl. José María Verdugo, Cpl. Juan José Dominguéz, and Cpl. Manuel Nieto, all of whom had accompanied expeditions to Alta California under a Lt. Pedro Fages. The three were assigned to the San Diego presidio, but were occasionally ordered to the San Gabriel mission, affording them an opportunity to become familiar with the immense open land that was spread out for miles from the mission in all directions. Then in 1784 they got word that their former squad leader had become governor of Alta California. Recognizing a fortuitous opportunity to cash in on their personal military connection, they sent off petitions to Governor Fages[1] requesting permission to raise cattle and horses on certain unoccupied lands that were located within Mission San Gabriel's sphere of influence.

Verdugo applied for about 36,000 acres around the present Pasadena-Glendale-Burbank area. Dominguéz requested land covering about 75,000 acres extending west from the Los Angeles River to Santa Monica Bay, south to San Pedro Bay and north to about the vicinity of the current city of Redondo Beach. Nieto asked for the land

---

1. In addition to Lt. Fages' military and political fame, he is also noted as a chronicler of nature. His detailed descriptions of the flora and fauna of the Southern California landscape have been invaluable sources of information for present day historical botanists and ecologists.

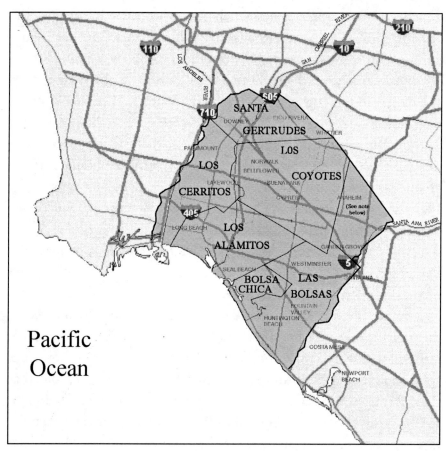

3-1. Boundaries of the Nieto land grant superimposed over a present-day freeway map. The boundaries of the individual ranchos of his heirs are also shown. Note: The governor granted a former soldier and majordomo for Nieto's Santa Gertrudes rancho, Juan Patricio Ontiveros, the triangular eastern-most portion of Los Coyotes along with a large parcel once belonging to the San Gabriel Mission. (Map by the author)

from the San Gabriel River[2] to some 25 miles east to the Santa Ana River and from the shore to the San Gabriel foothills, representing about 300,000 acres. The property included a good portion of what is presently southeastern Los Angeles County and northern Orange

---

2. At the time the San Gabriel River joined with the Los Angeles River near the present city of Downey. Its course did not move to its present alignment, emptying into Alamitos Bay, until the winter of 1867-68.

County, including the area that we now call Bolsa Chica. Governor Fages forwarded the petitions to the viceroy of New Spain and in 1786 the soldiers received word that their petitions were granted, but with a number of stipulations. First, the grants clearly stated that they did not actually transfer title of the land to the petitioners; the King of Spain still owned the land. The grants (or more accurately, concessions) conferred exclusive use of the land to the petitioners to graze cattle, horses, and other animals or to raise crops. In order to retain use of the land, a petitioner must build a house on the land, stock it with no less than 2000 head of cattle, and provide sufficient manpower to prevent the cattle from wandering onto neighboring land. In addition, the petitioner's operations must not encroach on water or timber of any neighboring pueblos, missions, or native settlements.

Apparently Governor Fages and the other bureaucrats who handled Nieto's grant petition did not realize that his request overlapped land claimed by the San Gabriel Mission. The friars complained to Fages and the governor reduced Nieto's grant to about 166,000 acres, still one of the largest grants issued in Alta California.[3] The rancho initially was called Rancho La Zanja (The Irrigation Ditch) but later was referred to simply as Rancho Los Nietos (Figure 3-1). Nieto continued in the service of the king until 1795, running his rancho as an absentee landlord from his assignment at the San Diego presidio. On his retirement he moved into a modest adobe house on his rancho close to the San Gabriel River and near the site of the original San Gabriel Mission, where he raised four children.

Nieto died in 1804 and according to Spanish tradition, his rancho was passed on to his heirs as an undivided estate. That is, his four children, three sons Juan José, José Antonio, and Antonio María, and daughter Manuela, held control of the property as a whole. Oddly,

3. The clash between the missionaries and Governor Fages over the Nieto affair was not the only altercation between the two. Fed up with Fages' general treatment of the missions, Fr. Serra traveled to New Spain and using his apparently considerable influence had Fages removed from office. However, while friction between civil authorities and the missions continued, Fages was able to return to office a few years later for a second term.

historians have been unable to trace what became of Nieto's first wife, Maria Teresa Morillo. She died in 1816, 12 years after Nieto's death. It does not appear that Maria Teresa, from whom Nieto apparently separated, nor his second wife, Maria Theresa Carillo, whom he married around 1795, were included in the family inheritance. While the original Spanish grant was not intended to transfer title of the land to the grantee, as years passed and governments changed, authority by the Alta California governors in dealing with concessions and land grants became considerably more generous. Nieto's heirs were soon to gain full title to the vast land their father had worked.

The Birth of the Republic of Mexico

In 1821, a major political event occurred that had a significant impact on life in Alta California. After 11 years of struggle, New Spain declared its independence from a politically fading Spain. Following three years of internal turmoil a constitutional government was formed and the Republic of Mexico was born. Alta California was now part of Mexico.

Although Alta California was now under Mexican rule, the distant province felt more influence from American immigrants than from any authority or financial support originating in Mexico City. About the only contact Alta California received from the Mexican capital were governor appointments and occasional assignments of soldiers, who were mostly convicts. The new republic began feeling internal financial problems, which meant little or no aid for its struggling Alta California outpost. The arrival of supply ships from Mexico became a rare sight. There is a story that the Presidio at Monterey once ran out of gunpowder, forcing the *comandante* to borrow gunpowder from visiting ships in order to return proper cannon salutes.

The influx of Americans was a growing worry for the Alta California government. To the government's distress, many Yankees tended to flout Mexican laws. Legendary Trapper Jedediah Smith was one such object of distrust. He had been guided from the Colorado Rockies to

California and the San Gabriel mission in 1827 by two native mission escapees. Smith was the first Yankee to travel that route to Alta California. He requested and was denied permission to trap in the Central Valley and was ordered to leave California. He disregarded the order and headed north. He trapped his way to San Francisco where he was arrested. He posted bond and again, ignoring orders to leave the territory, left for the Sierras to continue trapping. His actions were widely known and added strength to *Californios'* distrust of Americans. More on that later.

The first Mexican governor of Alta California was Luis Argüello, who immediately was faced with continuing Native American rebellions, the growing immigration of those assertive Yankees, and the bickering among various political, religious and military alliances, particularly between power groups in Los Angeles and Monterey, the territorial capital at the time. Armed incursions between factions frequently broke out, but they were brief and seldom resulted in casualties. The position of governor of Alta California apparently was not an easy task; during its 25 years under Mexican rule, Alta California changed governors 15 times.

Foreign trade accelerated during Mexico's reign in Alta California, much of it probably involving smuggling, for the new government began imposing heavy tariffs on imported goods. The income was needed to pay for the territory's bureaucracy, since no money was coming from the mother country. Commercial vessels flying flags of at least 22 nations and companies plied the territory's waters. Russian ships were often seen onloading wheat to feed Russia's colonies in Alaska. Nearly 500 Yankee ships alone are reported to have been doing business along the Alta California coast.

The lack of Mexican bureaucratic influence on life in Alta California was especially evident in the resolution of civil disputes. Merchants generally avoided Mexican courts. Instead, throughout the province merchants had developed close ties with one another to the point a handshake or nod was sufficient to seal a transaction. Written contracts were seldom involved[4] and merchants, sometimes competitors, often acted as agents for one another. Business dealings were conducted on an honor system that was seldom violated. The few disputes that did arise were often handled privately and dishonest transactions were simply dealt with by ostracism. Any governmental involvement was usually shunned. Such informalities also were found in dealings with land ownership, which eventually would result in considerable anguish when California became part of the U. S.

The Death of the Missions

The enormous economic and political power of the missions in Alta California had long troubled both the Spanish and the new Mexican government, even as the missions' influence began its decline during the first quarter of the 1800s. Both governments had issued one decree after another declaring the missions' ten year life span had expired, their goals had been met and they were to be secularized. Secularization involved converting the missions into local parishes run by priests rather than Franciscan friars, and disposing of the bulk of the missions' properties, which in most cases were considerable. For many years, the orders were virtually ignored. Then, in 1833, the Mexican congress issued its strongest decree on the secularization of the missions, which Alta California governor Jose Figueroa felt forced to implement. But to lessen the impact secularization would have on the missions, Figueroa allowed the process to extend for a period considerably longer than the Mexican government had intended. To ensure that the process operated smoothly, he appointed commissioners to oversee the secularization of each mission. Unfortunately Figueroa died before many of his plans for a fair and relatively painless secularization process were implemented.

Once secularization was under way, it caused a gradual but significant tearing of the social fabric of the province. Over the next 10 or

---

4. Alta California businessmen had a "built-in happy disregard for all documents of any kind," as one historian put it.

12 years the missions' land holdings were privatized and their Native American subjects were released from mission service. Under secularization, Native Americans were supposed to receive a share of the mission lands, livestock, and other property, but few did. Instead, much of the mission lands, estimated at more than 8 million acres, went to government administrators, including some of the governor's appointed commissioners, or to Mexican *rancheros* who had connections with the government, adding to their already huge holdings. Of the few natives who did acquire some land, many were unable to manage it properly and it, too, eventually fell into the hands of Mexican *rancheros*, sometimes through fraudulent means.

Secularization profoundly affected California's Native Americans in other ways. After living under mission influence for at least three generations, all the while being denied practice of their indigenous social, political, and religious traditions, the natives found they had lost most of their cultural heritage. Once freed of mission influence, with their land confiscated, they had nothing to go back to. Natives who were fortunate enough to know how to ride horses were hired as *vaqueros* (cowboys) to work on the region's many private cattle ranches. But few could ride since under Spanish law, teaching Native Americans to ride horses was forbidden. That was because of the theory that when Native Americans tried to escape mission domination on foot they were easily hunted down by mounted search parties. Since horses were readily accessible, the theory went, those neophytes who could ride usually were able to grab a horse, ride off and avoid capture.

After secularization, the majority of the natives, who could not ride, had to be content with remaining in the region, taking menial positions such as ranch laborers and domestic help. The more fortunate ones, those who were able to practice the skills learned at the missions such as carpentry and boot making, were more readily absorbed into the new regime. Others wandered off into the nearby mountains and deserts to unrecorded fates. All in all, native life after secularization was not much better and probably worse than what existed under the mission system. What little Gabrieliño/Tongva culture that had survived the mission period was all but snuffed out. A few Gabrieliño/Tongva decedents still live in the area and must look on helplessly as their ancestral lands are covered by houses and shopping malls.

The missions themselves also suffered greatly. Their land and livestock were sold or given away. Since there were insufficient numbers of priests to take over the missions as secular churches, many of the mission buildings were abandoned, only to be stripped of furniture, roofs, doors and anything else of value. Some mission buildings became warehouses or livestock barns. Numerous travelers in Alta California recorded their dismay over the conditions of the mission buildings after secularization. On visiting the Santa Barbara Mission in 1834, Richard Henry Dana in his "Two Years Before the Mast" expressed his sadness at seeing the mission in a state of "decayed grandeur."[5] General Stephen Kearney, who led the American military forces in the battle for California's independence from Mexico, tried in 1847 as the territory's first American governor[6] to find ways to reverse the deterioration of the missions, but it was too late. The mission buildings throughout California were already suffering from years of neglect and the ravages of weather, earthquakes, and vandalism. Fortunately, toward the end of the 19th century many of the missions began undergoing restoration, which is continuing to this day.

Nieto Property Is Divided Among His Heirs.

In 1833, the year Mexico began its final move on the secularization of the missions, and after two of Manuel Nieto's sons had died (José Antonio and Antonio María) the remaining family members petitioned Governor José Figueroa to allow a division of Nieto's property

---

5. Soon after, the Santa Barbara mission managed to be rescued from neglect and was the only mission eventually to become a parish church following secularization and the only mission to enjoy almost continuous occupation since its founding in 1786.

6. Technically John Fremont was California's first American governor, but he was deposed by President James Polk 40 days after taking office to be replaced by Gen. Kearney.

Table 3-1. Division of Manual Nieto's rancho among his heirs.

Nieto Heir	Ranchos	Size (acres)*
Juan José (son)	Los Coyotes, Los Alamitos	76,833
Catarina Ruiz (widow of son José Antonio)	Las Bolsas	33,460
Josefa Cota (widow of son Antonio María)	Santa Gertrudes	17,602
Manuela Cota (daughter)	Los Cerritos (Shown as "Los Sierritos" on some maps.)	27,054

*Due to the casualness of early land surveys, acreages were usually quite approximate. Figures may vary widely from survey to survey and from reference to reference. The term *mas o menos* ("more or less") was used often in Spanish land grants, and the practice actually continues today. Rancho period surveyors would often use temporary objects as boundary markers such as trees, animal carcasses, and rivers that frequently changed their courses. Distances were sometimes crudely measured. In Bolsa Chica, surveyors reported that they simply had estimated by eye the distance between two points that were separated by a flooded channel. They obviously did not want to get their feet wet.

A sixth rancho, Rancho Palo Alto, appeared on the governor's partition, which was in the vicinity of Brea Canyon. It was never occupied by the Nieto family and eventually fell into the public domain.

among the heirs so they could each operate ranchos of their own. As you recall, on Nieto's death and according to Spanish custom, his vast holdings were held in common by his heirs. Once the Mexican government took possession of Alta California, to encourage colonization it greatly liberalized the granting of land and the number of land grants accelerated, so that by 1846, about 750 had been awarded compared to about 30 during over 50 years of Spain's domination.

In 1834 the governor obliged his heirs by confirming Nieto's original Spanish grant and in essence declaring that the family now held full title to the land. The governor's decree further allowed the immense rancho to be partitioned into five smaller but still sizable properties (Table 3-1 and Figure 3-1).

Within a month of the governor's decree regarding the division of the Nieto property, Nieto's son Juan José sold his Rancho Los Alam-

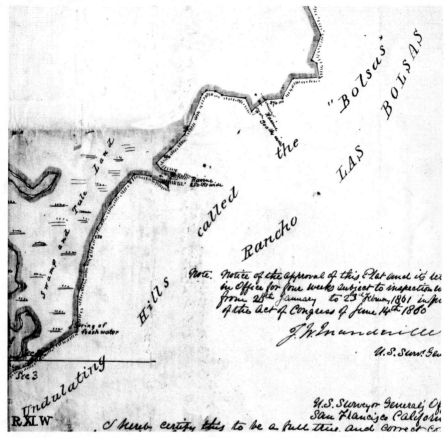

The map contains the following handwritten text:

"Bolsas"

LAS BOLSAS

the

called

Rancho

Swamp and Tule land

Hills

Spring of fresh water

Sec 3

Undulating

R XI W

Note: Notice of the approval of this Plat and its *[text partially illegible]* in Office for four weeks subject to inspection *[illegible]* from 24th January to 23d February, 1861 *[illegible]* of the Act of Congress of June 14th 1860

J.W. Mandeville
U.S. Surv. Gen.

U.S. Surveyor General Of San Francisco Califor*[illegible]*

I hereby certify this to be a full true and correct Co*[py]*

3-2. Detail of the 1858 boundary map of Rancho La Bolsa Chica showing the notation, "Undulating hills called the "Bolsas.""

itos inheritance to Governor Figueroa for a mere $500. Historians suggest that the sale at such a low price was a reward to the governor for approving the regranting of the Nieto property and giving Juan José the largest share.

Ranchos Las Bolsas and La Bolsa Chica

The inheritance Nieto's widowed daughter-in-law Catarina Ruiz comprised about 34,000 acres and extended from the Santa Ana River to Alamitos Bay, and north east to about where the river crosses under the present Route 5 (Santa Ana) Freeway. She called her property

Rancho Las Bolsas and built a small adobe house near the current intersection of Talbert and Gothard Streets in Huntington Beach. The property included all or portions of the present cities of Huntington Beach, Fountain Valley, Westminster, Cypress, Anaheim, Garden Grove, and Buena Park.

What Does "Bolsa Chica" Mean?

There are many accounts where the name Rancho Las Bolsas was derived. One oft repeated theory cites the many embayments or pockets present around the mouth of the Santa Ana River. The claim that *Bolsas* is Spanish for pockets is not correct. Pocket in Spanish is *bolsillo*. The most likely theory of the origin of the name is based on a label on the 1858 map (Figure 3-2) of the rancho that states "undulating hills called Bolsas." According to 18th and 19th century Spanish-English dictionaries, Bolsa is translated as "purse" or "bag" and the low rolling hills that occur along Newland Avenue north of Adams Street viewed from a distance could look like a row of purses. And on the 1834 deseño (see frontispiece), the "undulating hills" are sketched in, looking like a row of purses. For ages, purses were often simple, leather bags tied with a leather thong and hung from one's belt.[7]

Catarina' s brother, Joaquin Ruiz, for many years had been using his sister's rancho to graze his livestock, which in 1831 was reported to consist of about 2400 head of cattle along with 500 horses. In 1841 Catarina decided to grant Joaquin part of her rancho as his own. Joaquin's grant consisted of about 8100 acres, which he named *Rancho La Bolsa Chica*, apparently in reference to the name of his sister's ranch. The most consistent historical explanation is that the name refers to the small, single embayment, now known as Bolsa Bay, which could be referred to as a *bolsa* ("pocket") which as noted above, is an incorrect translation. Considering the possible origin of the name of his sister's ranch, there may be another explanation.

---

7. Hence the origin of the archaic term "cutpurse," for a pickpocket, that is, someone who stole one's purse by cutting the thong from which the purse hung.

Most of Joaquin's ranch was generally flat including several thousand acres of coastal wetlands. However one slight rise separates what are now Huntington Harbour and Bolsa Chica Wetland that is known as Bolsa Chica Mesa. The mesa's upper bench rises almost 80 feet above sea level and appears from a moderate distance as a small hill. Could it be that Joaquin, on a play on the name of his sister's ranch, observed one small "purse" on his horizon and named his ranch Bolsa Chica ("small purse")?

In 1849 Catarina decided to sell a portion of her ranch to Ramón Yorba and his brothers and sisters. Ramón's grandfather was Antonio Yorba, the original grantee of Rancho Santiago de Santa Ana, Catarina's immediate neighbor across the Santa Ana River. She agreed to sell one half of her property, but one half of what? Yorba claimed that the sale should be based on Catarina's original inheritance plus what she inherited from her daughter, Rita, who had died in 1835. Yorba's claim would have actually amounted to two-thirds of Catarina's original holdings. Complicating the question was the uncertainty of the southern boundary of Rancho Las Bolsas. The original Nieto grant described the boundary as simply the Santa Ana River. But part of the river had changed its course during the ensuing years. After much litigation and expense, the courts finally ruled in favor of Catarina and Yorba ended up with the original one half.

In 1854 Catarina Ruiz decided to convey what remained of Rancho Las Bolsas to her daughter, María Cleofa. One year later Catarina died and two years after that the 4 year old State of California finally confirmed Catarina's title to her share of her father's property, 23 years after she had originally applied to the Mexican government for the patent. But just before the title documents arrived, María Cleofa died, leaving her property to her daughter and son-in-law, heaping additional complications and expense onto the question of ownership.

California: America's 18th state.

Meanwhile, Yankee domination of the cultural and financial life of Alta California grew to the point Mexican Governor Pio Pico prophetically warned his subjects in 1841 of the threat of "hoards of Yankee immigrants swarming across the province." Soon Pico's fears materialized as significant political winds were again in motion. In 1846 President Polk declared war on Mexico and after three years of bloodshed, Alta California split from Mexico and one year later became part of the United States. The treaty that ended the war between Mexico and the United States, known as the Treaty of Guadelupe Hidalgo was signed in 1848 and guaranteed that all Spanish and Mexican land grants in California would be honored. However, the land grants soon fell under the force of a new federal law that the U. S. Congress passed in 1851 that was aimed at California. Families, some of whom had held land for over a half a century, suddenly found themselves having to prove the legitimacy of their ownerships. Remember many business deals were concluded with a hand shake. What documentation there was, some over 50 years old, had to be located, expensive new surveys had to be made and attorneys had to be hired to plead before the federally appointed three-man Board of Land Commissioners. Additional costs included translators[8] and travel for the Southern California petitioners and their attorneys, since most of the commission's hearings were held in San Francisco. It was a difficult, expensive, and frequently disheartening time for many founding California families. Land speculators and squatters, sometimes armed with forged documents and hired witnesses, haunted the Land Commission office, waiting to pounce on any disputed ownership that came along, and there were many. While the introduction of the 1851 Land Act was well intended, it proved to be disastrous for a number of long-standing Alta California families.

Many landowners had to borrow money in order to pay the costs of defending the titles to their land to the satisfaction of the Land

---

8. Most of the landowners read or spoke little or no English.

Commission. While there was no government filing fee, attorneys charged as much as $1500 to handle a claim. Initial filings usually took about two years to complete, but the entire process from initial application to final notification averaged 17 years and some applications took 30 years to complete. By 1890 a few applications still had not been confirmed. In its five years of existence, the Land Commission heard about 800 cases of which a little over 600 were confirmed. Of the findings of the Land Commission that were not confirmed, most were appealed in federal courts. That was another $500 to $1000 in legal costs. Locally, normally friendly neighbors were suing neighbors over disputed boundaries, keeping more attorneys busy. With hard cash being scarce, most landowners had to turn to loans to pay for their legal expenses. The going interest rate for loans during the late 1800s was 5 percent compounded per month, a burden that few could sustain.

Bolsa Ranchos Change Ownership

Heavily in debt, Catarina Ruiz' heirs and Ramón Yorba, who together owned Rancho Las Bolsas, and Catarina's brother Joaquin, who owned Rancho La Bolsa Chica, were all eventually forced to sell their property in 1861 to satisfy their debtors. At foreclosure auctions, the winning bidder was Abel Stearns,[9] who for a total of $15,000, became the owner of about 34,000 acres of prime farm and grazing land comprising the original Rancho Las Bolsas and Rancho La Bolsa Chica, which included quite a few thousand acres of wetlands.

---

9. Stearns had a personal familiarity with Bolsas and Bolsa Chica ranches. Stearns prepared a crude map in 1834 (Figure 3-3) to show how the Nieto ranch was to be partitioned. A number of maps prepared by Stearns can be found in historical archives throughout the state.

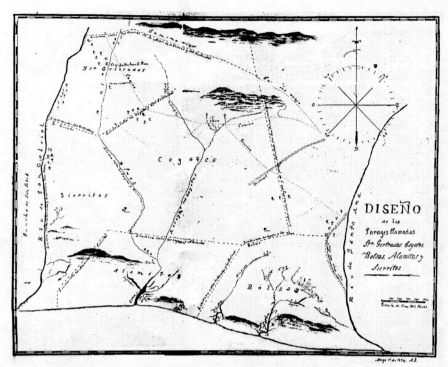

3-3. The 1834 deseño of Rancho Las Bolsas showing drawing of Lomas ("hills") in the vicinity of the "Undulating hills called the Bolsas on the 1858 map. The deseño (plan) for the partition of the Nieto ranch among his heirs that was prepared by Abel Stearns. The date (May 1, 1834) and Stearns' initials are in the lower right corner. (Map courtesy Special Collections Library, University of California, Los Angeles)

4

Abel Stearns:
A Yankee *Ranchero*

The Lure of California

Abel Stearns is undoubtedly one of the most prominent names associated with the early history of Los Angeles and Orange Counties (Figure 4-1). Stearns, one of the few owners of Bolsa Chica, was born in Lunenburg, Massachusetts in 1798. Orphaned at the age of 12, he went to sea and for the next 15 years worked on merchant ships that operated between New England, China, and South America. He immersed himself in the business and traditions of Yankee trading and eventually worked his way up to the position of supercargo, a merchant ship's officer in charge of cargo and commercial affairs. But greater fortunes beckoned Stearns and in 1825 he settled in the newly created Republic of Mexico. During his stay he inexplicably renounced his American citizenship and applied for and was granted Mexican citizenship, which would prove useful many years later.

On hearing of the great business possibilities in Alta California, which was now under Mexican rule, Stearns moved there in 1829. Upon arriving in Monterey, his first thoughts were to own land and become a rancher. He applied to the territorial governor, Manuel Victoria, for a land grant in the Sacramento Valley. While waiting for government approval of his request, he worked as a supercargo for coastal trading

4-1. Abel Stearns. (Figure courtesy Rancho Los Cerritos Museum)

ships that did business with California's *rancheros*. It was his first exposure to the customs of California style cattle ranching. In the mean time his land grant petition raised the suspicions of Governor Victoria. Learning of Stearns' Yankee background and influenced by growing anti-Yankee sentiment, Victoria suspected Stearns of having an ulterior motive in his desire for land and ordered Stearns to abandon his quest and to leave Alta California. After submitting several written pleas to the governor to reconsider, all of which were rejected, Stearns had no choice. He packed his belongings and boarded a ship at Monterey that was headed for Mexico. During a stopover in San Diego while his ship returned to Santa Barbara for additional cargo, Stearns decided not to return to Mexico but instead joined a rebellion against Gov. Victoria. The time was ripe for an uprising, for the unpopular Victoria enjoyed little sympathy or support in the territory. He was considered simply unsuited for the job. The rebellion ended quickly with an armed skirmish in which the governor was wounded and his followers routed. Victoria admitted defeat and sailed for Mexico on the next ship headed south.[1]

A Yankee *Angelino*

Stearns returned to Monterey to try to revive his land grant application but found his paperwork had been lost. Rather than reapply, he gave

---

1. In a bit of irony, the rebels assigned Stearns the task of soliciting money to pay for Victoria's boat fare back to Mexico.

up on the idea of becoming a landowner for the time being and moved to Los Angeles. There he worked as a debt collector and a salesman for a local businessman. Realizing the possibility of a rewarding future in retail trade, he opened a general store in Los Angeles in 1833 at a time the population of the pueblo was less than 1000. Because of his energy, commercial experience, and Yankee acumen, Stearns' business quickly flourished. He began dealing directly with ships from various American and foreign ports that plied the Alta California coast. He stocked his shelves with imported goods by trading in locally produced hides and tallow as well as furs brought in by trappers. Stearns also acted as shipping agent for miners prospecting in the nearby mountains, overseeing the transport of gold to the Philadelphia mint.

Trading ships readily offered manufactured products that were eagerly sought after by the hardy *Californios* in exchange for hides, tallow, and furs. Richard Henry Dana, writing in "Two Years Before the Mast" listed the kinds of products Yankee ships typically traded: "...spirits of all kinds, (sold by the cask,) teas, coffee, sugars, spices, raisins, molasses, hard-ware, crockery-ware, tin-ware, cutlery, clothing of all kinds, boots and shoes from Lynn, calicos and cottons from Lowell, crapes, silks; also shawls, scarfs, necklaces, jewelry, and combs for the ladies; furniture, and in fact anything that can be imagined from Chinese fireworks to English cartwheels."

La Casa de San Pedro

A year after Stearns opened his store in Los Angeles he bought a small house on a barren hill overlooking San Pedro Bay that had been owned by the San Gabriel Mission. He enlarged the building to 4000 square feet to provide space for a store, a storekeeper's residence, and a warehouse. Being on the San Pedro waterfront, it was in a perfect location to serve the many trading ships that anchored just offshore. Stearns called the enterprise *Casa de San Pedro*. Thanks to Stearns' understanding of the overseas merchant business from his years at sea, and being bilingual, the operation was hugely successful. That was in spite of the fact San Pedro was universally considered by most seamen as one of the worst anchorages on the coast, but that was offset by being named the best source of hides on the coast. Word spread among Yankee and trans-Pacific merchants that *Casa de San Pedro* always had a good supply of hides, tallow and other commodities for immediate loading, as well as general provisions for the ships' crews, including local wines, fresh fruits, and vegetables. Before Stearns started *Casa de San Pedro*, ships' personnel had to conduct business with myriads of *rancheros*, missionaries, and trappers, either at the port or sometimes at *ranchos* several miles inland. Dealing with one middleman right at ship's side saved the traders enormous amounts of time and cost. Farmers and *rancheros* would bring their products to Stearns' San Pedro warehouse in exchange for the vast variety of goods brought in by the Yankee clippers.

Abel Stearns' Los Angeles

Stearns became a major figure in the Los Angeles business, social, and political scene. Seeing a need for faster transportation between Los Angeles and San Pedro for ship's crews and passengers from the trading ships, he started a stagecoach line between the two points. He put up the Arcadia Building in downtown Los Angeles, the city's first and largest retail/office building. He spearheaded a campaign for Los Angeles to annex San Pedro,[2] which finally occurred in 1909, several years after his death. During Stearns' early years in Los Angeles he worked as a land surveyor, in spite of having no formal training. As mentioned in Chapter 3, in 1834 he prepared maps of Rancho Los Nietos for the Nieto heirs. Stearns held several municipal offices including *alcalde* (mayor), was a delegate to the constitutional convention when California became a state, and served in the state legislature. On the social front, he married Arcadia Bandini, the young daughter of one of the most prominent families in Los Angeles. Following Spanish custom, the wedding celebration lasted several days and during their

---

2. San Pedro was officially designated as Los Angeles Harbor in 1892.

4-2. Photograph taken about 1875 of Abel Stearns' Los Angeles home, known as *El Palacio* (The Palace) by the local citizenry. Occupying the corner of what is now Main and Arcadia Streets in downtown Los Angeles, its 100 foot ballroom was the site of many festive gatherings. (Photo courtesy Special Collections Library, University of Southern California.)

long marriage, the Stearns' home, referred to as "Stearns' Palace" (Figure 4-2) by the locals, was the site of many lavish social and official gatherings. The Stearns had no children.

Smuggling California Style

During the period that Stearns was closely associated with overseas trading and running a warehouse in the harbor, he was in a position to be involved in smuggling. At least that was the suspicion of Mexican officials in Los Angeles and Monterey. Smuggling was an old tradition in California,[3] due for the most part to the exorbitant tariffs Mexico was charging imported goods. As mentioned in the previous chapter, nearly two dozen nations and companies conducted business with Alta California, no doubt many dealing with contraband.

At the same time that Stearns was having to face smuggling charges, several Los Angeles *rancheros* accused him of dealing with hides from

---

3. Santa Catalina Island was a favorite stopping point for Yankee traders. Before landing on California soil, they would stash most of their cargo on the island, then enter Monterey and pay duties on the small amount of cargo they had, then return to the island to pick up the rest of their goods. Then, with duty receipt in hand, they would head out to Santa Barbara or San Pedro to offload their cargo. Apparently duty officials seldom noticed discrepancies in the ships' documents.

stolen cattle. But Stearns had made so many friends in high places in Los Angeles that all charges were eventually dropped, in spite of the discovery of damning evidence in the *Casa de San Pedro*. However, Stearns continued to have brushes with territorial government authorities. Because of his alleged illegal smuggling activities along with the fact he was American born, Stearns once again raised the distrust of the territorial government and was ordered deported for the second time. In a rerun of Stearns' difficulties with Gov. Victoria some years before, Governor Mariano Chico ordered Stearns to leave the territory on a ship that Chico had personally arranged for the deportation. But as the date of Stearns' departure approached, word reached Chico that his days as governor were numbered. Like Victoria, Chico was a humorless and generally disliked figure. Sensing the powerful public sentiment against him in the territory, it was Chico who boarded the Mexico-bound ship, not Stearns.

Reaching a Dream

Stearns' considerable wealth that he had accumulated from his trade business during its early years allowed him later to take up the role of *ranchero* as well as moneylender. The trading in hides began to decline due to an extended drought beginning in the late 1830s, which caused a drop in the quality of the hides and consequently their prices dropped on the international market. Taking advantage of the downturn in the cattle business and the accompanying drop in land prices, Stearns decided to turn once again to land ownership and ranching. His earliest land acquisition was in 1842 through a debtor's sale: the 28,000 acre Rancho Los Alamitos. He purchased it for $6000 worth of hides and tallow from the heirs of Governor Figueroa, who had died 7 years earlier. As you recall, Figueroa bought the rancho from Manuel Nieto's son, Juan José Nieto, in 1834 for $500. Stearns at last fulfilled his dream of someday becoming a California cattle rancher. Now enjoying the life of a *ranchero*, he lost interest in his trading business and sold the *Casa de San Pedro* in 1845 but retained his retail business in Los Angeles.

After a brief peak during California's gold rush days due to the miners' demand for beef, the mid 19th century saw the cattle business continue to decline for a variety of reasons. Alternating years of floods and droughts and falling beef prices due to the plummeting demand all made life dismal for the *rancheros*. And then there were the costs of satisfying state officials to prove land ownership following California's statehood. Southern California's *rancheros* were forced to turn to loans to get them through the hard times. Stearns had accumulated enough wealth not only to protect him but also to benefit from the times; he become a moneylender. Loans were in the form of cattle, hides, tallow, or cash.[4] At the usual-for-the-time five percent interest compounded monthly, Stearns' loans frequently ended in default. The misfortunes of several *rancheros* gave Stearns the opportunity to fulfill his desire to acquire large tracts of land and the accompanying livestock. Stearns began to realize that land was a more stable investment than cowhides; he began a new phase in his life, concentrating on the acquisition of land. Generally, non-citizens were either prohibited from owning land on Mexico's coast, including Alta California, or given low priority, but U. S.-born Stearns, having received Mexican citizenship many years before, was clear to begin his career as a major Mexican land baron.

Stearns eventually owned a number of properties that ranged from Baja California and San Diego to San Francisco and Sacramento. These were acquired through outright purchase or through loan defaults, land auctions (like Rancho Las Bolsas and Rancho Bolsa Chica) or foreclosure sales. Stearns acquired at least two ranchos in Baja California as grants from the Mexican government. Some properties just fell into his lap. John Sutter (of Sutter Mill and gold rush fame) gave Stearns a lot in Sacramento as a gift merely out of friendship. All in all, by

---

4. The use of cash (usually in the form of silver or gold coins) was relatively rare during these times. Instead the most common form of currency was cowhides, often referred to as "California bank notes."

1862 he owned over 200,000 acres of land, including over 90,000 acres of the original Manuel Nieto grant, along with thousands of head of cattle and horses. Most of Stearns' holdings were in and around Los Angeles County. His land and cattle enterprises were the largest in the region, making him the wealthiest figure in southern Alta California, at least in terms of land and livestock holdings.[5]

The Passing of the California Rancho

Once California gained statehood in 1850, with property ownership came property taxes and other costs. Stearns' income from his fading merchant business was not sufficient to pay the taxes on his vast holdings. Stearns had to depend on income from cattle sales, but as mentioned earlier, the cattle business continued to experience a downward slide. In spite of the declining demand for beef, Stearns' balance sheets remained in the black until the winter of 1862 when the beginning of another extended drought set in.[6] The sparse grass and drying watering holes that followed were not sufficient to support the huge herds of cattle on Stearns' ranchos. The drought continued for several years, causing Stearns to lose thousands of cattle to hunger and thirst, as did most other *rancheros* in the region. It was reported that the region's dry grasslands were strewn with the carcasses of thousands of dead cattle and horses. Like his grazing lands, a major source of Stearns' income had dried up. The state hounded Stearns for back taxes and by 1864 to cover his debts his creditors began seizing what few cattle he had left. Notices began to appear in newspapers

---

5. During this period Los Angeles was still very much part of the wild west as depicted in countless Hollywood films. Most men carried side arms and the town, with a population now about 4000, averaged one murder a week. Cattle rustling and horse theft was a frequent occurrence in the surrounding ranchos. Stagecoach robberies and Native raids on European settlements also were common in the outlying areas of the Los Angeles basin. Stearns was known to have joined at least one posse in pursuit of marauding natives in Cajon Pass.

6. To make matters worse, 1862 was also the year marked by a smallpox epidemic that raged through the Los Angeles area, killing or incapacitating scores of rancho workers (mostly natives) and their families.

announcing sheriff's cattle sales at various Sterns ranchos. Stearns' dream was rapidly fading.

Despite Stearns deep financial difficulties including the loss of his livestock, he was able to retain all of his land holdings except for his first and favorite acquisition, Rancho Los Alamitos. To offset expenses he had taken out a loan using Los Alamitos as security. In 1865 his lender declared the loan in default and forced Stearns to sell the rancho to repay the obligation. Three years later Stearns' fortune turned when he was able to take out another loan against the balance of his ranchos, which enabled him to repay the bulk of his debts and still keep most of his vast land holdings. But with his cattle operations in ruins, Stearns had to come up with a new means of getting financial return out of his nearly 178,000 acres of open land.[7]

In 1868 Stearns turned to a man whom he had met on the ship that brought him from Mexico to California, Alfred Robinson. Now a successful businessman, Robinson and a group of his San Francisco associates agreed to help Stearns through an enterprise called the Robinson Trust. The trust was to take over Stearns' property and to begin selling it off as small parcels for farms and townships. In exchange for the deed to his vast holdings,[8] the trust paid Stearns an advance of $50,000 to liquidate his remaining debts, gave him a one-eighth partnership in the trust, and agreed to pay him $1.50 for every acre sold by the trust. The trust formed The Los Angeles and San Bernardino Land Company, which launched a vigorous and unprecedented (for California) land sales campaign. It brought in a number of aggressive real estate agents to handle land sales. One such agent was a former college math and science teacher and attorney, Robert M. Widney, a man who was to become a well-known figure in Los

---

7. Stearns was not the only *ranchero* having tax problems. It has been estimated that by 1864, over 85 percent of the ranches in the Los Angeles basin were delinquent in paying their taxes.

8. The deed transfer, recorded on June 8, 1869, covered the Ranchos Los Coyotes, La Habra, San Juan Cajon de Santa Ana, Las Bolsas and La Bolsa Chica.

61

Angeles social and political circles.[9] Widney was reported to have ridden over most of the 280 square miles of Stearns' property to familiarize himself with the land he was about to promote. The Southern California land boom was underway.

Stearns' land sales were widely advertised throughout the U. S. and Europe (Figure 4-3). Flyers would be handed out at public events and on steamships headed for Los Angeles, touting the Southern California climate and the rich agricultural opportunities awaiting buyers of Stearns' ranchlands. The ranches were divided into 640 acre tracts, which were further cut up into parcels of 40 to 120 acres, designed to accommodate small farms and fruit orchards. Prices reportedly ranged from $2.50 to $25 per acre. Land sales were good and in one year 20,000 acres of Stearns' holdings had been sold. The timing of the sales of Stearns' ranchos could not have been better. With the Civil War over, former soldiers and their families were looking west for futures in farming. Getting to the west coast was made even easier when the transcontinental railroad was completed to the San Francisco Bay area in 1869, although its extension to Los Angeles wasn't finished until 1876. In a price war, railroads were advertising fares from Kansas City to California for as low as $1.

With the breakup of the giant ranches like Stearns' and others', the age of the Southern California cattle barons had come to a close.[10] For over a century most of the accessible land in California had been held by the missions, and later, by a handful of private landowners. What came next to Southern California eventually was to become Califor-

---

9. Widney arrived in Los Angeles in the same year the Robinson Trust was formed, 1868. Known in business circles as a firebrand, he quickly became a key player in numerous phases of Los Angeles history. He was appointed district judge in 1871, was one of the founders of the University of Southern California, started one of Los Angeles' first street car systems and was a principal designer of Los Angeles Harbor. In a 1903 newspaper ad, he chided Los Angeles business figure Henry Huntington for losing $900,000 in an east coast investment recommended by New York financier J. P. Morgan. "Look to Southern California," Widney wrote, "not New York for profitable speculation."

10. There were exceptions, such as the Irvine Ranch in Orange County

4-3. Undated real estate map depicting parcels of Abel Stearns' ranchos for sale. Shaded areas are parcels that had been sold. Flyers such as this one were distributed all over the U. S. and Europe. (Unknown source)

nia's signature, a vast and diverse agricultural industry consisting of hundreds of independent farmers supplying fruits and vegetables to a rapidly growing population.

Stearns was not a good business partner. Being independent and self reliant since he was 12 years old, he was not about to let a group of businessmen 400 miles away run his business, even though he had signed it away to the trust. For instance, without informing the trust, he would lease some of his land for sheep grazing and make private sales deals with buyers, often undercutting the trust's official prices and conditions. But the trust's sales were good and when Stearns died in San Francisco in 1871 at the age of 73, he had already earned over $155,000 as his share of the trust, a mere two years after he signed over his ranchos to the trust.

The trust continued its sales campaign as the close of the 19th century approached, adding to the fortunes of the trust members, as well as those of Stearns' widow, Arcadia.[11] But one tract had not sold, the apparently unusable and inaccessible coastal marsh that was part of Joaquin Ruiz' Rancho La Bolsa Chica. It remained on the trust's property roll for many years. The area was riddled with peat springs and artesian wells that flowed year around and was thick with willows, sycamores, wild blackberry vines, and grasses. It was the home of wildcats, coyotes, raccoons, rattlesnakes, and ducks, lots of ducks.

---

11. In 1874 Arcadia married Colonel Robert Baker, who owned the 40,000 acre Rancho San Vicente y Santa Monica, which included most of the present city of Santa Monica and parts of West Los Angeles. When Baker died in 1894 with no other heirs, Arcadia inherited his entire estate worth about $8 million, adding to what she inherited from Stearns.

5

Guns and Oil

The Bolsa Chica Gun Club

Just upstream from Newport Bay lies the San Joaquin Marsh,[1] a popular site for duck hunting during the later years of the 19th century. In the 1880s, James Irvine II,[2] who owned the marsh as part of his vast Irvine Ranch, and Count Jasco von Schmidt (Figure 5-1), a prominent Los Angeles businessman and sportsman,[3] started a duck hunting club in the 500 acre marsh. However, as the century was coming to a close, an apparent falling out between Irvine and the club members led Irvine to cancel the club's lease. The hunters found themselves with no place

---

1. The San Joaquin Marsh was converted into a treatment wetland by the Irvine Ranch Water District to remove pollutants in San Diego Creek before it flowed into Upper Newport Bay. A portion of the wetland is now a wildlife sanctuary and is operated by the Sea and Sage Chapter of the Audubon Society.

2. James Irvine I was an Irish immigrant who became a merchant and miner during California's 1849 gold rush at the age of 22. As his wealth grew, he began investing statewide in retail businesses, real estate, and sheep ranching. By 1876 he was able to buy out his partners' 110,000 acre Orange County holdings, which was to become known as the Irvine Ranch. After Irvine's death in 1886, his son, James II, following the trend in the region, began shifting ranch activities from raising cattle and sheep to agriculture.

3. von Schmidt's Los Angeles home is now on the city's list of historical and cultural monuments.

5-1. Count Jasco von Schmidt, founder and first president of the Bolsa Chica Gun Club. (Photo courtesy Sherman Library, Corona del Mar)

to hunt. The displaced sportsmen, mostly Los Angeles and Pasadena businessmen, agreed among themselves that to avoid any future possibility of eviction, the safest thing to do was to own their own hunting reserve. But where?

Prior to the close of the 19th century, over 17,000 acres of wetlands covered the coastline between San Pedro and Newport Beach (Figure 5-2) including at least 2300 acres of wetlands in Able Stearns' 8100 acre Rancho La Bolsa Chica. Like much of California, Bolsa Chica happens to be under the Pacific Flyway, one of the major routes followed by migratory birds in their biannual flights between northern latitudes and tropical America. Bolsa Chica and other nearby wetlands provided millions of migratory and resident birds with opportunities for resting, feeding, and for some species, nesting. Many of the birds that used the region's wetlands were highly regarded game birds, so not surprisingly by 1900 dozens of hunting clubs were established along the immediate coastline. There were 26 hunting and fishing clubs in the Anaheim/ Sunset Bay wetlands alone. In an often-quoted passage from his book, "My Sixty Years In California," local Huntington Beach pioneer Tom Talbert[4] wrote,

"This section of the country along the coast between Long Beach and Newport Beach, south of Westminster was one of the greatest natural habitats for wild life and game birds in the world. Wild ducks, geese, jack-snipe, coots, plover, doves, killdeer, egrets, herons, gulls, pelicans, land birds and waterfowl of every kind and description varied their flights from ocean to swamp, from swamp to grain fields, from grain fields to ocean again, to feast on seafood, grain, seeds, bugs, toads, worms, grasshoppers, and the like. I have seen birds by the thousands so thick in flight as to almost eclipse the Sun. The hours long flight of ducks patterned against a blazing sunset sky was most

---

4. As a teenager, Tom Talbert moved to Long Beach, California with his family from Illinois in 1891 and to Orange County in 1896. By the turn of the century, Talbert was well on his way to become a leading political and business figure in Orange County and Huntington Beach. His imprint on Bolsa Chica remains to this day.

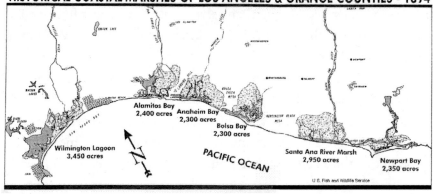

5-2. Historical Coastal Wetlands of Los Angles and Orange counties that existed in 1894. (Map courtesy U. S. Fish and Wildlife Service.)

amazingly spectacular and beautiful. When startled, great flocks of birds arose to circle around and return to their beloved haven."

During the last decades of the 1800s, upland parcels of Abel Stearns' Rancho La Bolsa Chica were selling well to Yankee farmers, but there were no takers for the wetland portions of the ranch; the land was generally considered worthless marshland. However, on hearing of the availability of the Bolsa Chica wetland, von Schmidt and a group of former San Joaquin marsh club members, recognizing the duck hunting potential of the Bolsa Chica wetland, formed the Bolsa Land Company in 1899. The company purchased about 1160[5] acres for $25,000.[6] It then formed the Bolsa Chica Gun Club, which leased Bolsa Chica from the land company for $1 per year. von Schmidt was the club's first president.

---

5. The total acreage of the property was 1740 acres, but about 580 acres of Public Trust submerged land and tidelands was not included in the original sale. Most of the 580 acres was to be acquired later through a state patent. Additional parcels were obtained during the early years of the 1900s.

6. That comes out to be $21.55/acre, which was about the upper range of what good farmland was selling for. Apparently the duck hunters wanted the property bad enough and were willing to pay top dollar for it.

5-3. Photograph of the Bolsa Chica Gun Club building taken about 1900. (Photo courtesy Amigos de Bolsa Chica)

A redwood and cedar hunting lodge, which had been described by a local newspaperman as "The last word in gun clubhouses" (Figure 5-3), was built at the reported cost of $25,000 on the southwestern edge of the lower bench of the Bolsa Chica mesa. The site enjoyed unobstructed views of Bolsa Bay, acres of sand dunes, the blue Pacific Ocean, and Santa Catalina Island on the horizon. In addition, boat-houses, barns, animal pens, workshops, and accommodations for some of the lodge staff members and their families also were constructed about the property. Ponds of various shapes and sizes were eventually dredged out of the wetlands along with channels to provide boat access to the ponds (Figure 5-4). The club held its official opening on October 17th, 1899.

Bolsa Bay Suffers an Ecological Setback.

Historically Bolsa Bay was a true estuary, meaning it was flooded with seawater at high tide but continuously received a considerable amount of fresh water from the Freeman River. The source of the bay's seawater was a natural ocean inlet that was located near where Warner Avenue presently intersects Pacific Coast Highway. The Freeman River collected runoff from the numerous nearby artesian

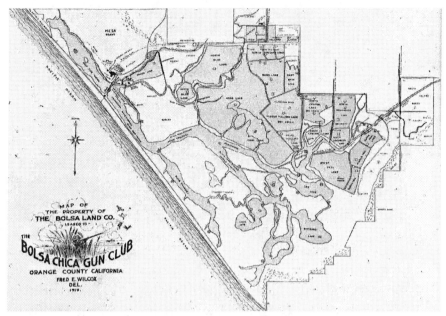

5-4. Map of the Bolsa Chica Gun Club property showing natural sloughs and constructed duck ponds. (Map courtesy County of Orange)

wells and peat springs, from rainstorms, and once the vicinity was farmed, excess irrigation water from surrounding fields, all of which eventually flowed into Bolsa Bay and out into the Pacific Ocean. The influx of fresh water into the hunting reserve was welcomed by the gun club (and presumably the ducks), but the daily tidal currents that moved in and out of the reserve often made duck hunting difficult and not welcomed.

The gun club applied to the state government to allow the club to "reclaim" the wetland under the Swamp and Overflowed Waters Act (SOWA). SOWA was federal legislation originally written in 1850 to allow farmers in various states to drain fresh water wetlands to provide land for farming. Somewhere along the line, SOWA was amended to include tidelands. When California acquired statehood in 1850, it adopted numerous federal statutes, including SOWA. Although some of the reclaimed Bolsa Chica marsh was leased to farmers, the gun club's main purpose of reclaiming the marsh was to improve hunting, not exactly what SOWA was intended for.

In 1899 the Gun Club turned to Tom Talbert for the construction of a dam across a narrow part of Bolsa Bay. The purpose of the dam was to prevent tidal flow from entering the hunting preserve at high tide, but to allow freshwater that accumulated behind the dam to exit at low tide. Talbert solved the problem through the use of flap gates in the dam that opened outward, that is, toward the sea inlet. The cost of constructing the dam was reported to be about $12,000, nearly half the cost of the lodge. It took Talbert three tries before he was able to build a dam strong enough to withstand the forces of the incoming tide (Figure 5-5). The dam was damaged by the 1933 earthquake[7] (Figure 5-6) but it held and in 1959 it was replaced by the Orange County Flood Control District. Once Talbert's dam prevented tidal flow from entering the wetland, the gun club was able to construct duck ponds about the property and enjoy calm hunting waters.

The dam caused a drastic reduction of tidal movement through the ocean inlet. That created a sand bar that quickly built up at the mouth of the inlet and within a year the inlet was blocked. When that occurred, there was nowhere for runoff to flow. The club turned to Talbert to find a way to drain the runoff from Bolsa Bay.

Directly to the north, tidal wetlands that were the southern-most extension of Anaheim and Sunset Bays were separated from Bolsa Bay by a mere hundred yards.[8] Anaheim and Sunset Bays were connected to the ocean by an inlet about four miles north. By using a horse-drawn plow, Talbert's workmen dug a channel across the narrow strip of land separating the two bays, connecting Bolsa Bay with Sunset

---

7. The club building apparently suffered little or no damage from the quake, in spite of it being nearly on top of the Newport/Englewood fault zone, which triggered the quake.

8. In the 1960s the Sunset Bay wetlands were dredged and filled and converted into the commercial/residential development known as Huntington Harbour. The small Environmental Sensitive Habitat Area on the northern edge of the Bolsa Chica mesa known as Warner Pond is all that remains of the Sunset Bay wetlands. The pond was cut off from Sunset Bay when Warner Avenue was constructed.

5-5. Aerial view of the gun club and the location where Tom Talbert built a dam to keep tidal currents from entering the wetland. Talbert's dam was replaced by the Orange County Flood Control District in 1959. (Photo courtesy The First American Corp.)

5-6. Damage to Tom Talbert's dam from the 1933 earthquake. (Photo courtesy Long Beach Public Library)

Bay and providing a route for runoff waters from Bolsa Chica to drain. That channel now flows under the bridge at Warner Avenue and is the source of seawater for the original Bolsa Chica Ecological Reserve that was restored in 1978.

The prevention of seawater from entering the Bolsa Chica wetland led to a shift in the ecology of the wetland. It no longer was an estuary. When the tides drained from Bolsa Chica for the last time, runoff accumulated in pools, creating pockets of freshwater wetlands that supported typical fresh water plants. However, in other spots, when the seawater receded from the wetlands, numerous small saltwater pools remained. As the pools dried out, salt flats appeared. When rain or runoff entered the salt flats and dissolved the salt, a saline environment was recreated. This cycle has repeated itself for over 100 years. Thus in spite of the wetland having been separated from a source of seawater, it still retained some remnants of a saltwater wetland. Plants common in saline environments such as pickleweed, glasswort, and salt grass continued to thrive among the duck ponds and oil wells in many parts of Bolsa Chica. It was the presence of these plants along with other evidence of tidal wetland characteristics that led to Bolsa Chica's wetland designation and its ultimate preservation (See Chapter 11).

Life at the Gun Club

Membership in the Gun Club was limited to 40 with an initial membership fee of $1000 and annual dues of $60. All members were required to be stockholders in the Bolsa Land Company. The club ran annual budgets that ranged from about $25,000 to $60,000, about 90 percent of which was derived from dues, fees, and assessments, and rent from farmers working the club's land. President von Schmidt, reportedly related to the Hapsburgs of European royalty, ran the club under the strict rules of a royal Austrian hunting lodge. The club required its members (men only) to adhere to all federal and state regulations regarding hunting licenses and bag limits. There were strict rules regarding the gauge and type of guns used. Hunting was permitted

5-7. A group of Bolsa Chica Gun Club members pose for a photo on the club's front lawn. (Figure courtesy Honnold/Mudd Library, Claremont Colleges)

5-8. Henry Huntington's Red Cars ran along the shoreline between Seal Beach and Huntington Beach and would let off passengers at the gun club only if they held passes signed by Huntington. (Photo courtesy The First American Corp.)

only during the officially set season, but use of the clubhouse for social functions during the off-season was encouraged. Shooting on the reserve was limited to two days a week, and no one was permitted on the reserve on non-shooting days or during the nesting season. Members could invite guests to the lodge to hunt (again, men only), but visits to the club by children and family members were strictly limited to certain days of the week. As clearly stated in its by-laws, it was a "Man's club" (Figure 5-7).

Shooting at Bolsa Chica was so good that it was not uncommon for members to bag their limit before noon. For those who stayed out on the reserve for the afternoon, gourmet lunches were delivered to the blinds. Not all the members took full advantage of the shooting opportunities at the Bolsa Chica Gun Club. It seems a few of the members, such as Henry Huntington, had joined the club more for the camaraderie and seldom if ever fired a gun on the premises.

Many familiar names appeared on the club membership roster, such as Jonathan Slauson, Jared Torrance, Capt. William Banning, and Henry Huntington, from whom the city of Huntington Beach got its name, and whose red trolley cars were soon to stop just below the clubhouse's front door (Figure 5-8).[9] The club's guest list was even more impressive. The son of one gun club staff member remembers lines of chauffer-driven Duisenbergs, Cadillacs, and Buicks dropping off bankers, industry leaders, sports figures, Hollywood stars, members of the 1932 Los Angeles Olympics Committee, and even royalty. One slim, ordinary looking gentleman observed entering the clubhouse was the Prince of Wales, who two years later would be known as His Majesty King Edward VIII of Great Britain. The future King Gustav of Sweden and the future Pope Pius XII also were guests at the Gun Club, as were Teddy Roosevelt, Herbert Hoover, and George Patton.

---

9. The trolley cars were prohibited from letting off passengers at the gun club stop unless they showed passes signed by Huntington himself. Von Schmidt rode the trolley but never used Huntington's passes. Instead, he reportedly would bribe the conductor to stop at the gun club with boxes of Bavarian creams.

It is said that duck was never served at the Gun Club, but chicken, turkey and pheasant, all raised on the premises, were frequently on the menu. The club took pride in the quality of its dining room, having been able to attract first class chefs, a noted maitre d ' and a superior support staff.

Bolsa Chica Gun Club members could choose to shoot from blinds at ponds that had been constructed throughout the wetland reserve or directly from boats along the wetland's many channels. Boatmen were provided for each hunting party. Dogs were not allowed on the reserve; instead, schoolboys in hip boots were hired to retrieve downed birds. And, as a change of pace, club members could fish in ponds or Bolsa Bay that had been stocked with black bass.

Not all of the Bolsa Chica Gun Club property was used for hunting. About 500 acres were set aside for growing grains to attract the water-fowl and other sections were leased to farmers. Barley was commonly grown on the Bolsa Chica mesa and crops such as celery were scattered along the foot of the Huntington Mesa. The club raised its own chickens, turkeys, and pheasants for the dinner tables and kept up to four cows to supply milk and cream. There was also a small garden for providing fresh vegetables.

Farmers vs. Gun Club

Due to its prominent membership, the gun club was a center of Southern California wealth and power, occupying land surrounded by struggling farmers. Before the gun club was established, farmers, fishermen, and others used the Freeman River to get through the Bolsa Chica wetland by boat to access the shoreline. When the Gun Club blocked the route with the dam, the farmers protested. They formed an organization called the Westminster Farmers' Club, and filed a lawsuit against the gun club. The suit was in defense of the farmers' right to use the river for commerce and navigation, a right that was protected under both state and federal constitutional law–the Public Trust. The farmers pleaded their case at state and federal levels, even writing to President Theodore Roosevelt, but the gun club members had the upper hand, using all the influence and power at their disposal. The gun club convinced War Secretary Elihu Root that the Freeman River was nothing but a drainage ditch and not subject to the Public Trust. Root ordered the Los Angeles office of the Army Corps of Engineers, who was entrusted with enforcing the Public Trust and was sympathetic toward the farmers, to back out of the controversy. In addition, in a lengthy letter to the gun club president, the club's attorney urged the club to put up additional barriers along Freeman River to prevent passage of the locals and make it appear to the courts that the entire water course was non-navigable and not protected under state or federal laws. In 1903 the county grand jury entered into the battle and sided with the farmers. Counter suits and armed threats were exchanged between both sides over several years, but in the end, the farmers lost.

During the early decades of the 1900s, local hunters were able to boat from Anaheim Bay into Outer Bolsa Bay through the opening that Tom Talbert plowed and which Warner Avenue now spans. Since Outer Bolsa Bay was Gun Club property, the hunters were considered poachers and often shooed away by gun-toting guards. To keep out trespassers, the Bolsa Land Company proposed to build a new dam at the opening, but the company's legal counsel advised them against the idea. The company would have to explain the reason for the new structure, and if it stated it was to keep boats out of Outer Bolsa, it would be an admission that the bay was navigable and that would jeopardize its tideland patent, which was based on the club's claim that the tideland was not navigable. The Gun Club eventually let the idea pass and instead depended on its guards to prevent trespassers from hunting in Outer Bolsa Bay.

The Beginning of Huntington Beach

While Bolsa Chica was not part of the City of Huntington Beach, the city has had a far greater influence on Bolsa Chica's destiny than has the county. Essentially all of the activist groups focusing on Bolsa Chica, both pro-development and environmental, began in Huntington Beach. On official levels, city staff, commissions, committees, and the city council have spent numerous hours debating various aspects of Bolsa Chica. Thus Huntington Beach's history is intertwined with Bolsa Chica.

In 1901, a land investor, Philip A. Stanton, purchased 1500 acres of coastal property a few miles down the coast from Bolsa Chica for $100,000, or about $67 an acre, from Robert J. Northam, Abel Stearns' ranch manager.[10] Northam had purchased the property in 1897 from the Robinson syndicate and apparently made a considerable profit on the sale since the trust was selling most property for not more than $25 an acre. Stanton formed the West Coast Land and Water Company and subdivided about 10 acres of the land into lots between what is now First and Sixth Streets and two blocks inland from Ocean Avenue (Pacific Coast Highway). Intending to turn the enterprise into a west coast version of New Jersey's Atlantic City, Stanton named the township Pacific City. But due to lack of easy transportation to the town, land sales were slow and within two years Stanton sold the property to another group of investors headed by J. V. Vickers, a wealthy land investor with holdings in Arizona and California, including Santa Rosa Island. Vickers, recognizing the need to get tourists to the town, approached Henry Huntington with an interesting proposal. If Huntington would agree to extend his Pacific Electric carline from Long Beach to Pacific City, the owners would change the town's name to Huntington Beach and Huntington would receive a substantial financial interest in the town's development company to be named The Huntington Beach Company. Huntington accepted the offer.[11]

---

10. Robert Northam was the nephew of Edwin R. Northam, one of the partners of the Robinson Trust.

11. Huntington undertook a similar arrangement with the city of Huntington Park in 1902.

On July 4, 1904, the city celebrated the arrival of the first Pacific Electric Railway "Red Cars." The city was incorporated in 1909.

Big Oil Enters the Picture

By the end of the 19th century, the two images most often associated with Southern California by both residents and visitors were orange trees and oil derricks. In 1876 Standard Oil Company (then known as the Pacific Coast Oil Company) opened the first commercial oil field in California near Valencia in northern Los Angeles County, and by 1901 there were over 900 oil wells operating around the Los Angeles area. Orange County saw its first successful oil well in 1882 near the town of Olinda.[12] By 1894 the newly formed Union Oil Company had established a richly successful oil field in the Brea-Olinda area.

While the Bolsa Chica wetland received an abundant supply of fresh water from the Freeman River, that water, mostly farm runoff, could not be used for drinking and cooking. Early in its beginnings, the gun club had a well dug near the clubhouse as a possible source of potable water. However, the water was so saturated with natural gas it could not be used. Instead, the gas was separated from the water and used for cooking and lighting in the clubhouse and outbuildings. The club had to have its drinking water piped in from inland sources. Apparently no one in the club at the time recognized the significance of the presence of natural gas under the clubhouse.

Similar experiences were reported in nearby Huntington Beach, where farmers were hard pressed to find gas-free water to irrigate and wash their crops. There was so much gas in the water that their pumps simply could not pump it. So, like the operators of the Bolsa Chica Gun Club, Huntington Beach residents separated the gas from the water and used it as fuel. In the early 1900s, a popular demonstration shown to Huntington Beach visitors was to fill an empty milk bottle with water from the kitchen tap, seal the bottle until the inevitable gas

---

12. The 12 acre Olinda Historic Museum and Park in Brea provides public trails among original oil wells dating back to the 1890s.

bubbles rose to the surface, then open the bottle and place a lighted match above the opening. The muffled pop and bright yellow flash usually prompted applause and requests for encores. Residents speculated that the gas might indicate the presence of oil beneath the city.

By 1916 the talk of the possibility of oil beneath Huntington Beach had reached officials of Standard Oil Company, who had been considering drilling for oil in Newport Beach just across the Santa Ana River from Huntington Beach, but decided against it. Standard sent its petroleum geologist to Huntington Beach, who after seeing the gas in the city's well water and being familiar with the geology of the area, went back to his office and convinced his superiors that the Huntington Mesa was THE place to drill for oil. It is said that this is the first time in oil industry history an oil field site was chosen on the sole advise of a professional petroleum geologist.

Standard Oil Company officials approached the Huntington Beach Company, who owned much of the city, and acquired a lease for the mineral rights on 500 acres around the vicinity of Golden West and Clay Streets. In August of 1920 an exploratory well began producing a modest but encouraging 70 barrels of oil a day. The well was named Huntington Beach No. 1. The oil company moved its drilling equipment north to the upper edge of the Huntington Mesa within the Bolsa Chica Gun Club property. There, operating under a lease from the Gun Club, on November 6, 1920, as the drillers hit a depth of 2549 feet, a gusher blew the well connections off with a roar heard for miles around. The sound attracted thousands of spectators, who had to be held back to a safe distance, according to a newspaper account. Within 24 hours, an estimated 20,000 barrels of oil had covered the ground around the well. Once the well was tamed, it yielded 2000 barrels a day of thick, black oil. The well was named Bolsa Chica No. 1

The news spread fast. Standard Oil Company and a number of independent oil operators quickly began filling empty lots in much of downtown Huntington Beach with oil derricks and storage tanks. Before oil was discovered, the Huntington Beach Company was

5-9. Oil derricks in the 17th Street Townlot District of Huntington Beach sprang up almost overnight in spite of the city's desire to reserve the area for upscale residences. (Photo courtesy The First American Corp.)

struggling to sell lots in the city. Once oil began flowing, the company realized the significance of the discovery and turned its sales offices into lease offices. Oil leases that had started out at $25 to $50 per acre became $1000 per acre. When the city ran out of empty space, oil drillers bought and then either moved or tore down over 300 houses to make room for more oil wells. The parcels between 17th and 23rd streets, known as the 17th Street Townlot District, were especially impacted by the oil boom. The Huntington Beach City Council had prohibited oil drilling in the area to set it aside as a choice residential area. But then a wealthy Newport Beach entrepreneur, Charles O'Conner, convinced (some say bought) the public to approve a ballot measure that urged the city council to rescind the drilling prohibition. The council complied and wildcatters quickly moved into the 17th Street District (Figure 5-9).

Within a few years, the city's population rocketed and Huntington Beach became one of the leading oil producing regions in California. Oil workers occupied nearly every available living space in the new oil boomtown, often using the same beds in shifts. The influx of oil workers coupled with the elimination of houses to make room for more oil wells created a severe housing shortage that jeopardized the city's hopes for a growing tourist trade. By the end of 1923, 232 wells had been drilled throughout the city, producing over 33 million barrels of oil and 41 million cubic feet of gas for the year.

But the initial boom did not last. Within less than ten years, the oil pool below the city began showing the effects of the high concentration of wells within the small area of Huntington Beach and production began to drop off. The oil companies began looking toward the beach and beyond to tap into the vast oil pools thought to exist under the state owned tidelands, which by law extended from the mean high tide line to three miles out. Those pools could be tapped by drilling wells in the sand or mounted over the water on short piers. But to preserve the state's beaches for recreational use, the state had prohibited drilling on its beaches or offshore.

To get around the law, Standard Oil leased a narrow strip of land from the Pacific Electric Company that was between Pacific Coast Highway and the bluffs, overlooked the beach below (Figure 5-10). The bluffs, now a popular city park, extend from the southern edge of Bolsa Chica to about 17th Street. The edge of the vast oil pool that lay under state tidelands extended beneath the bluffs, allowing Standard Oil to tap into the pool without a state oil lease or payment of royalties. Envious of Standard's ruse and wanting to get their share of the tideland oil, Huntington Beach independent oil companies clamored to reverse the state law that prohibited drilling on city beaches. The independents got Huntington Beach city officials to propose state legislation to give the city ownership over tidelands and water out one mile from shore. If successful, the city could then lease the tidelands to the independent oil companies, opening the door to oil wells on its

5-10. Standard Oil Company's oil wells on the bluffs overlooking the beach, making it possible to tap into the state-owned offshore oil pool. (Photo courtesy The First American Corp.)

beaches and in shallow water just off shore. Not wishing to share tidelands oil pools with other companies, Standard Oil successfully used its considerable political clout to prevent any attempts by competitors to open the beaches and nearshore waters to oil drilling. At least two bills giving the city ownership of its nearshore waters passed both houses handily but were pocket vetoed[13] by two different governors. The independent companies then sought other ways that would allow drilling on city beaches and nearshore waters, including getting two initiatives on a state-wide ballot to reverse the prohibition of drilling

13. When a governor refuses to act on a bill within a certain period of time, it is considered "pocket" vetoed.

on beaches. Both measures failed, reportedly due to Standard Oil's considerable resources to influence voters.[14]

Meanwhile, oil production in the Huntington Beach city lots had been falling off through the late 1920s, but in 1931 it inexplicably turned around and continued to rise. This anomaly attracted the attention of state officials and curious, they began spying on the independent drillers. They discovered that the Huntington Beach independent oil companies had invented a drilling technique that was to revolutionize the oil industry: slant drilling. The independents found if they used a tool known as a whipstock, they could make their drill pipes follow a huge arc that passed under the beach, allowing them to tap into the state tideland oil pool. Like Standard Oil, the independents were avoiding the prohibition of drilling on the beach and evading the payment of royalties to the state. By 1933, a new oil boom shook the seaside town. Seeing a rich new revenue source, the state struck a deal with oil companies to allow them to continue slant drilling into tideland oil pools provided the companies paid royalties to the state. However the state maintained its position prohibiting drilling on beaches. Slant drilling is now a common practice for many of the wells located in Bolsa Chica and elsewhere.

Bolsa Chica (Finally) Joins the Oil Boom

The Signal Gasoline Company was begun in 1922 as a producer of gasoline from natural gas.[15] In 1928, the company decided to enter oil exploration and production and changed its name to the Signal Oil

---

14. The Bolsa Land Company also was active in opposing any attempts to open tidelands to oil drilling. Their stated reason was concern for property values if oil wells were allowed to rise along their frontage, but it also may have been due to their relationship with Standard Oil Co.

15. Citrus farmer Sam Mosher started the Signal Gasoline Company and built a plant near Long Beach on Signal Hill (hence the company's name). The plant separated the highly volatile liquid petroleum fraction that accompanied the natural gas that was normally allowed to escape into the atmosphere during oil extraction. The liquid was sold to refineries, who blended it with their gasoline.

& Gas Company. Speculating that vast pools of oil lay beneath the Bolsa Chica wetlands, Signal as well as other oil companies tried to convince Bolsa Chica Gun Club members to lease a major portion of the lowlands for oil production, but club members refused their offers, preferring to see the hunting reserve continue operating undisturbed by the clatter and roar of drilling equipment and oil pumps. This was in spite of Standard Oil Company's spectacular gusher at the south end of Bolsa Chica in 1921, described earlier. The Bolsa Land Company was well aware of the oil potential under the wetlands, for it had hired a geologist in 1924 to determine the extent of oil beneath Bolsa Chica. The geologist predicted that there was a considerable amount of oil under the wetland and recommended the gun club allow drilling immediately before surrounding oil operators could tap into the pool. In spite of the geologist's report, the club continued to refuse offers to drill in the wetland. The club, however, had already agreed in 1920 to allow Standard Oil to begin oil production on the Bolsa Chica Mesa. The club was given a $100,000 bonus for signing the lease and a 16 2/3 percent royalty. Standard's wells apparently were far enough removed from the central wetlands to not interfere with the club's primary purpose, shooting ducks.

However, by 1940, the economic states of many club members had been bruised by the stock market crash of 1929 and the depression of the following decade. The possibility of collecting additional oil royalties was just too inviting to ignore. The club turned to Standard Oil, who had been working the Bolsa Chica Mesa, to offer the lowland for drilling provided the oil company agreed to raising the royalty it was paying club members from 16 2/3 percent to 25 percent. Standard's geologists surmised that since production on the mesa seemed to be fading, its operation must have depleted the oil pool under the lowland. Moving oil operations to the wetland did not seem economically feasible and the company let its drilling lease expire in July of 1940. Meanwhile Signal Oil personnel were more optimistic and had offered the club a 36 percent royalty plus 50 percent of net profits

5-11. Bolsa Chica Wetland criss-crossed with raised service roads connecting hundreds of oil wells. (Source unknown)

for permission to drill in the lowland. A lease was signed in June of 1940 for 22 wells on 110 acres of wetlands. In 1943, a second lease was signed, expanding Signal's operation to an additional 900 acres of lowlands. Since this lease was close to the beach, Signal also was able to take advantage of the slant drilling technique developed just down the highway from Bolsa Chica and tap (legally) into offshore state oil pools. Some of those wells are still operating on a 25 acre parcel immediately adjacent to Pacific Coast Highway.

Finding Bolsa Chica

Before the Signal oil lease could be finalized, the exact boundaries of the Bolsa Chica gun club property had to be confirmed. Because historically wetland properties were not considered particularly valuable, little attention was paid to their exact boundaries. But since the state and federal governments had begun claiming mineral rights to tidelands (which included parts of Bolsa Chica), knowledge of exact boundary lines became critical. Signal discovered that the last and somewhat precise boundary determination for Bolsa Chica was carried out in 1858 by U. S. Deputy Surveyor Henry Hancock to confirm Catarina Ruiz' grant of the Rancho La Bolsa Chica to her brother, Joaquin.

Signal Oil surveyors found they had to retrace Hancock's 85 year old boot steps. In Hancock's field notes, he described placing a three inch hemlock stake one foot underground to mark the starting point of his survey. The oil company men estimated where the stake might have been placed and began digging around the area. About six feet from the estimated location they found remnants of a wooden stake that matched Hancock's description. Working from there, the surveyors were able to come up with a sufficiently accurate boundary map of the gun club holdings which satisfied all concerned.

Oil Dominates Bolsa Chica

The impact of oil drilling in the Bolsa Chica wetland has been both beneficial and destructive. It was beneficial in that the enormously lucrative oil revenues that came out of the wetland that lasted over 30 years prevented most of the area from becoming overrun by urbanization that had surrounded it on three sides. But what little wetland character Bolsa Chica managed to retain during its life as a hunting reserve was nearly destroyed by the oil operations. Because of its high groundwater level, often rising and flooding the wetland, the oil company had to construct a network of raised roads and drill pads, obliterating much of the wetland's natural islets and sloughs (Figure 5-11).

Drilling in the Bolsa Chica wetland began in August of 1940 and within seven months, 19 wells were producing oil. One of the remarkable things about the Bolsa Chica oil field was the absence of the familiar wood and steel derricks that were seen by the hundreds in the oil fields a few miles south. There was a serious steel shortage leading up to and continuing through the war years, so Signal had eliminated the need for using the tall derricks by operating a portable derrick

5-12. One of two "Panama Mounts" on the Bolsa Chica Mesa that were used during WWII for placement of 155 mm coastal defense guns. (Photo courtesy Fort MacArthur Museum)

to drill and service its Bolsa Chica wells. The rig, which cost Signal $30,000, could be moved from well to well as needed. While common in Texas and Oklahoma oil fields, this was the first time such equipment was used on the Pacific Coast.

War Comes to Bolsa Chica

When Japan entered World War II in 1941, the threat of an attack from the west became a real concern. Due to the presence of several likely targets in the immediate area, the ports of Los Angeles and Long Beach and the Huntington and Bolsa Chica oil fields, the U. S. Army chose the Bolsa Chica Mesa as an ideal site for a coastal defense battery. As visitors to Bolsa Chica can attest, a splendid view of the ports can be had at the Bolsa Chica Mesa overlook. The army acquired over 600 acres of Bolsa Chica from the club owners. The gun club was evicted from the lodge, which was turned into the site headquarters. Underground reinforced concrete bunkers, tunnels, trenches, water towers and other support structures were constructed all over the Bolsa Chica Mesa. The largest of the two bunkers was 600 feet long and 200 feet wide. Its walls were 4 feet thick and its ceiling was 16 feet thick. An observation tower, disguised as a water tower, was built near the beach.

To arm the site as quickly as possible while more permanent batteries were being built, in 1942 two 155 mm field guns on Panama mounts were placed on the edge of the lower mesa, just below the Gun Club. The circular concrete mounts can still be seen just north of the mesa overlook (Figure 5-12). Further up on the mesa the installation of two

6 inch long range gun emplacements was begun in 1943 and completed the following year. Construction of mounts for two 16 inch guns also was begun in 1943, but the guns were never installed.

Return to Peacetime at the Gun Club

Following the end of the war, the artillery guns and other structures were removed and the property was returned to the gun club owners, but the Panama mounts and the bunkers remained. It is reported that the club had to spend a considerable amount of money renovating the club building following the Army's departure. Use of the gun club was resumed for a short time, but interest in the facility and the hunting reserve waned and the building was soon abandoned. It has been speculated that the ecological balance of the wetland had been so disturbed by the presence of the oil production activities that duck populations were too meager to continue hunting in Bolsa Chica. Farming activities on the property continued, however. In the late 1960s the lodge burned down and its ashes reportedly were bulldozed into the wetland below. The last major signs of the army's presence, the bunkers, remained through the 1990s. Over the years various possible uses of the bunkers were suggested, such as nightclubs, restaurants, or living quarters for the homeless, but nothing ever materialized. In spite of measures to prevent public access into the bunkers, locals managed to enter the structures for impromptu beer parties and other pursuits. Left behind on the bunker inner walls had been 50 years of untouched graffiti art, which provided rich material for cultural historians and photographers. The larger bunkers were destroyed in 1999 to clear the way for a residential development, but the smaller ones still remained a magnet for young explorers as of this writing.

By the 1950s there were more than 200 owners-in-common of Bolsa Chica, consisting of a few original gun club members and the heirs of deceased members. Whenever new drilling leases or other actions affecting the owners had to be approved, the oil company complained that it had to deal with the over 200 landowners and their more than

200 attorneys. To streamline their relations with the oil company, in 1963 the owners decided to form six separate corporations, each owning a specific portion of Bolsa Chica. The corporations were named Bolsa Grande, Bolsa Huntington, Bolsa Laguna, Bolsa Los Patos, Bolsa Mesa, and Bolsa Pacific.

Over the years a number of individual oil companies and consortiums have held the mineral rights in Bolsa Chica. In 1974 Signal sold its oil rights to Burmah Oil Company. Subsequent oil operators in Bolsa Chica were: Aminoil from 1974 to 1976; Phillips Petroleum from 1976 to 1984; SWEPI (Shell Western E&P, Inc.) from 1984 to 1986; and AERA Energy, (previously known as Cal Resources and owned by affiliates of Shell and Exxon-Mobil) from 1986 to the present (2009).

From 1941 until the Bolsa Chica property was sold in 1970, the gun club heirs earned about $130 million in oil royalties, which after taxes amounted to about $64 million. That figure could have been considerably lower if Bolsa Land Company tax advisors hadn't realized when the royalties first began rolling in, the company would be subject to an excess profits tax. The Bolsa Land Company was quickly dissolved as a corporation in 1941 and all oil royalties went directly to its former stockholders, who became tenants-in-common and who by filing separate tax returns collectively saved about $40 million.

The multitude of gun club members and their heirs retained the surface rights of Bolsa Chica until 1970, when they sold their interest for $28,620,000 to a land development subsidiary of Signal Oil and Gas, known as Signal Landmark.[16] A new and extraordinary phase in the history of Bolsa Chica was to begin.

---

16. Since the 1970 purchase of Bolsa Chica by Signal Landmark, due to a series of acquisitions, spinoffs, and other corporate moves, the ownership and/or development and/or management of the property has been under a number of names such as Bolsa Chica Co, Henley Properties Inc, California Coastal Communities Inc (its registered name with the SEC along with its 60 subsidiaries), Koll Real Estate Group (KREG), and Hearthside Homes Inc. For the sake of simplicity and clarity, throughout the book we will use the name "Signal."

6

Wetlands, tidelands and submerged lands

"Mud is beautiful." – Rim Fay

Whenever water and land meet, any of a variety of specific habitat types may be created. What habitat exists in a particular location can have both biological as well as legal and economic implications. And as you will see, there are sometimes differences of opinion as to what specific habitat is present in a given location at a given time.

Bolsa Chica's Aquatic Beginnings

For tens of thousands of years Bolsa Chica was an estuary, meaning a wetland that was fed by both seawater and fresh water. During rising tides, it was flooded by seawater through a natural ocean inlet, the last known location of which was near the present intersection of Warner Avenue and PCH. Fresh water was provided at various times by the Santa Ana River, from dozens of peat springs and artesian wells in the surrounding area (part of which was aptly named Fountain Valley) that flowed to the sea through the Bolsa Gap, from rain runoff, and once the adjacent land was occupied by farms, from their irrigation overflow. Where the seawater and fresh water mixed, brackish water resulted, that is, water that is less salty than seawater but more so than spring water.

Then in 1899 Bolsa Chica was converted from an estuary into a fresh water marsh when the gun club cut off the wetland's seawater source with a dam. Within a relatively short time, that action drastically changed the wetland's ecology, but not entirely. With its supply of seawater blocked off, the Bolsa Chica was soon dominated by fresh water runoff. However, pockets of salinity remained, supporting saltwater wetland plants for several decades thereafter. When Signal Oil hired the Dillingham Environmental Company to conduct a biological survey of Bolsa Chica in 1970, the company came back with astonishing results. In spite of suffering the effects of being cut off from the sea for 70 years and existing as an oil field for 30 years, Bolsa Chica was in relatively good health. For example, the survey found 168 plant species growing in Bolsa Chica, 98 of which were native species including some typical marine wetland types. And in a survey spanning 12 months, 141 species of birds totaling over 60,000 individuals were observed feeding, resting and nesting among the service roads and oil wells. Most of the species were birds commonly found in coastal wetlands. While the numbers of wetland species and total numbers of individuals were below what would be expected in a healthy wetland, the old and battered Bolsa Chica wetland still had a heartbeat.

Bolsa Chica's Wetland Evolution

During Bolsa Chica's long history, portions of it went through several phases: river mouth, estuary, fresh water wetland and finally, marine wetland. How do these terms differ? To start out, a short definition of a *wetland* might be useful. A survey of wetland definitions among several governmental agencies reveals a multitude of responses. Those specific definitions will be covered later in this chapter, but for the time being, a wetland can generally be defined as land with soil that is periodically flooded or saturated with water often enough to support the growth of plants normally associated with saturated soil, and at the same time to inhibit plants that are intolerant of saturated soils. Thus knowledge of soil types and plants typical of wetlands is but one of the requirements to identify a wetland. However, not all wetlands have plants growing in them. Mud flats, for example, are saturated by water but are frequently devoid of plants. They are still considered wetlands. In addition, plants that are "normally associated with saturated soil" are sometimes found in areas that are not declared wetlands. Thus it's pretty clear that identifying wetlands is much more complex than it appears on the surface.

Depending on character and location, wetlands can exist under a number of names, such as swamps, bogs, fens, marshes, estuaries, wet meadows, prairie potholes, vernal pools and tidelands. They can be freshwater wetlands, marine or saltwater wetlands, and (brackish) estuaries. We'll only cover those types of wetlands that are or were found in Bolsa Chica.

Coastal Wetland Ecology – Life with Seawater

Before we get into some of the specifics of the Bolsa Chica wetland, it would be useful to discuss a little bit of the ecology of marine wetlands, that is, the relationships between the plants, animals, and the habitats that characterize coastal wetlands.

Marine wetlands are dominated by seawater, which has a salt[1] concentration of about 35 parts per thousand (ppt) or 3.5 parts per hundred (percent). While this salt concentration is not considered particularly high, it is sufficiently high to be unsuitable, actually fatal, for drinking by most animals including humans and for irrigating most plants. That is because of the effect of salt water on the cells of animals and plants. Water is absolutely necessary for the life of cells. Remove the water and cells die. Water acts as a necessary solvent to allow the thousands of chemical reactions in the cells to proceed, as well as being a by-product of respiration. In addition, water aids in the

---

1. The term "salt" is used in a very general sense here. We normally associate "salt" with ordinary table salt, or sodium chloride. And while sodium chloride makes up about 98 percent of the salts in seawater, the rest consists of salts of magnesium, potassium, calcium, and a host of other elements, including gold.

transport of nutrients and waste products in and out of cells, and for higher forms of life it helps maintain a constant body temperature.

Water enters cells through a process known as osmosis. The process is based on the principle that water molecules tend to pass through a cell membrane from the side that has a lower concentration of salts to the side that has a higher concentration. Thus water enters cells because the interior of most cells contains a higher concentration of salts than the fluid in which they are suspended[2] and nature constantly tries to equalize things. By moving water from a lower salt concentration to a higher one, the salt concentration on the outer side of the membrane should become higher and the concentration within the cell should become lower. Thus, theoretically at least, the salt concentrations on either side of the membrane should eventually become equal.

So when we drink a glass of freshwater or when we water a plant with freshwater, the water will enter the cells of our intestine or the plant's roots because the salt concentration in the cells is slightly higher than that of the freshwater. If we drank seawater or watered our house plants with seawater, which has a higher salt concentration than that within the cells, it would soon prove fatal in both instances because our (or the plants') cells would pump water out and they would soon become dehydrated.

But coastal wetlands are relatively rich in healthy plant life. In light of what we just said about the effect of salt on plant cells, how is plant life possible in the presence of seawater? Over the millions of years of their evolution, marine wetland plants have adapted to the salty environment by developing several mechanisms that protect them from the high concentrations of salt that would kill most other plants. Called halophytes, they are dependent on a salty environment so much as they have become tolerant of high salt concentrations. Whereas the roots of ordinary plants are able to exclude salt (actually only the sodium portion of the salt molecule), marine wetland plants take up salt into

---

2. Salinity in typical animal cells runs just under 10 ppt. Huntington Beach tap water is pretty standard municipal water, having a salinity that varies from about 0.2 to 0.6 ppt.

their roots along with the water, but then get rid of the excess salt in their tissues in various ways. Cord grass and salt grass, both found in Bolsa Chica, excrete salt through special glands on their leaves. The sparkle of sunshine off of salt crystals can often be seen on the plants' leaves. Pickleweed, a perennial that is relatively abundant in Bolsa Chica, gets rid of its excess salt by accumulating it in its stems. At the end of the growing season, the stems fall from the plant, taking the excess salt with them.

All wetland plants have to survive in soils that are frequently if not constantly saturated with water. Although we have just stated how water is absolutely necessary for life, too much of a good thing can be fatal. Oddly, the roots of plants are more like animal cells in that they require oxygen. That is because, unlike plant leaves that utilize light energy through photosynthesis to power their metabolism, roots are devoid of such a source of energy. Roots thus must depend, like animal cells, on oxidative metabolism for their survival. In oxidative metabolism, cells derive energy from certain chemical sources such as sugars and use oxygen as a final step in the process. Water-saturated soils lack oxygen because the water fills the spaces between soil particles and excludes air. It's often been said that more houseplants are killed by over-watering than by under-watering. So how do wetland plants survive in water saturated soil? Wetland plants have evolved a system in which oxygen is captured by the upper parts of the plant and delivered to the roots to support their metabolism.

Of course there are, in addition to plants, many animals associated with the oceans that are able to survive in the presence of salt water, and interesting adaptations have occurred there as well. For example, there is a group of sea birds known collectively as "tubenoses" (albatrosses, shearwaters, and petrels) that spend long periods of time at sea. These birds have salt glands in their bills that extract salt from their blood, making it possible for these birds to drink seawater. Thus in spite of its noxious salt content for most living things, seawater provides a hospitable home for a number of plants and animals.

Tides

Another environmental influence that coastal wetland plants and animals must deal with is the movement of the tides. A body of water acts like any other object and is subject to the pull of gravity. Over the period of a day and at any particular location, sea levels rise and fall due to the combined effects of the gravitational forces of the Sun and Moon on the water. These effects are manifest in the periodic movements of the tides. When the Sun and Moon are aligned in a certain way relative to a particular spot on Earth, such as Bolsa Chica State Beach, their combined gravitational effect causes the sea to rise and we witness a high or flood tide. As the Sun and Moon take up a different alignment over the next six hours or so, the sea recedes at Bolsa Chica to its lowest level, known as low or ebb tide. Sometime later, a new alignment of the Sun and Moon results in another flood tide, usually at a height somewhat different from the earlier high tide. The difference is because the alignment of the Sun and Moon is not exactly the same as it was at the earlier high tide. The high-low-high-low daily tidal cycle continues each day but each flood and ebb tide occurs a little bit later than those of the previous day, that is, the daily cycle does not coincide with normal clock time. That is because the Moon's rotation around the Earth is slightly out of synch with the Earth's rotation about its axis. This situation results in the Moon arriving to a particular point in the sky not quite an hour later each succeeding day. During the course of a year, the alignments of the Sun and Moon relative to the Earth vary considerably so that, for example, there are times when the Sun and Moon are lined up 90 degrees from one another in relation to the Earth. When that occurs, their gravitational forces nearly cancel one another's and the difference between high tide and low tide is slight. The tides we observe during these times are known as neap tides. At other times, around the summer and winter solstices, May and June and in November and December, we see so called

Zonation

High Tide

Low Tide

Subtidal Channels are important habitat for fish and feeding habitat for diving birds.

Mudflats are rich in invertebrate life for Shorebirds. Algal mat grow here also.

Low Marsh is good habitat for cordgrass, insects, herons and egrets and the clapper rail

High Marsh supports pickleweed and patches of cordgrass. A good habitat for Savannah Sparrow and Clapper Rail

6-1. Zonation in a coastal tidal wetland. (Drawing courtesy Amigos de Bolsa Chica)

spring[3] tides, which occur when the Sun and Moon are on opposite sides of the Earth. In spring tides, the differences between high and low tides are the greatest. Spring tides accompanied by storms have frequently caused flooding in Bolsa Chica and surrounding communities due to the combined heights of the high tides and the high waves generated by the storm. And runoff from heavy rains often exacerbates the flooding. Other factors that affect the timing and magnitude of the tides are the bathymetry or the depths of the immediate off-shore areas, and the Earth's rotation around the Sun. In spite of all these interacting factors that influence the times and magnitudes of the tides, they can be predicted with amazing accuracy.

Tidal Zones

Biologists have designated various areas or zones along a coastline according to their relationship with the average heights of the tides (Figure 6-1).

---

3. In this context, "spring" does not refer to the season, but indicates the tides that "spring" or "jump up."

The area along a coast that is most affected by the tides is what is referred to as the intertidal zone. Whether a sandy beach, a quiet bay, or a rocky coastline, it is the area that is bounded by the high tide line and the low tide line, that is, the area that is on average wet during high tide and dry during low tide. For a number of reasons, the intertidal zone of a sandy beach or the "mud flat" of a coastal wetland is of special interest to biologists. Intertidal zones frequently contain the richest variety of organisms, providing important feeding grounds for shorebirds and other coastline inhabitants. This is most evident when seeing large numbers of birds feeding along the edge of the shore during low tide. Another reason the intertidal zone is so interesting is the way intertidal plants and animals have adapted to the wet/dry cycles during the tide's daily phases, as well as how they survive the constant pounding action of waves on exposed shores during high tide. For example, in rocky intertidal zones, certain animals such as mussels and barnacles are able to withstand sun-drenched dry periods during low tide and violent wave action during high tides, while others such as clams and scallops cannot. Mussels and barnacles have evolved powerful adhesives to hold them fast to rocks and other solid surfaces such as wharf piles and boat hulls.[4]

And so various plants and animals of a coastal wetland find themselves under a variety of conditions relative to the tides. They can be…

- inundated all the time (living below the lowest tide line)
- Inundated during the two high tides in a day and left high and dry at other times (living in the intertidal zone)
- Only inundated during high spring tides, and relatively dry the rest of the year.

---

4. Such natural adhesives have attracted the attention of medical researchers who see uses of the adhesives in surgery and dentistry.

It is this variety of conditions that is partly responsible for the enormous biological diversity that is characteristic of coastal wetlands.

Estuaries

The estuary is one common type of coastal wetland in which seawater, driven by the tides, enters the wetland and meets freshwater that flows from inland sources. While once a true estuary, Bolsa Chica lost that distinction in 1899 with the building of the gun club dam. The outer Bolsa Bay portion of the 210 acres of the original Bolsa Chica Ecological Reserve that was restored in 1978 might be considered estuarine, receiving freshwater in the form of urban runoff from the Wintersburg-East Garden Grove Flood Control Channel (henceforth referred to as the Wintersburg Channel) and seawater from Anaheim Bay through Huntington Harbour. However, true estuaries are usually fed by fresh water on a continuous basis, while the flow from the channel varies considerably from season to season.

The Benefits of Coastal Wetlands

As will be covered in the next chapter, coastal wetlands are frequently targeted for marinas, harbors, and other water-oriented development. There are a number of reasons why coastal wetlands must be preserved in their natural state. Coastal wetlands perform a multitude of functions, some of which are:

- **Protection from Flood and Storm Waves.** Urban drainage systems are usually designed to convey storm water to a nearby river, lake, or ocean. During most storms, a drainage system operates smoothly and runoff is handled expediently. In highly urbanized areas such as Southern California where much of the land is covered with impermeable surfaces, runoff can quickly exceed the capacity of drainage systems, causing water to back up and flood neighborhoods and commercial districts. Thus during intense storms when the outflow of a drainage system cannot keep up with the volume of water that pours off the watershed, a nearby wetland can act as a safety valve that would avoid flooding by collecting and storing the excess storm water until the outflow is able to catch up.

The 2005 experiences with hurricane Katrina in the gulf coast point out the fact that the coastal wetlands in that area that had been lost through various human interventions could have provided a buffer from waves and storm surges that so devastated New Orleans and adjacent regions. As ocean waves pound sea walls and levees, their enormous energy is released in the instant they make contact. The physical strength of the structures is the only factor preventing the sea from breaking through and flooding the land. In contrast, when sea waves pass over a coastal wetland, the energy of the waves is dissipated harmlessly over a long stretch of space and time.

- **Wildlife Habitats.** As early as the 1700s, Americans recognized that wetlands offered rich habitats for game birds and other animals. Four major flyways cross the U. S. along which tens of millions of birds migrate between northern regions of North America and tropical America and points in between each year. Wetlands offer many of these travelers their only opportunities for resting, feeding, and for some species, nesting. Resident species, that is, birds that live year around in a given habitat depend even more on the existence of stable, well functioning wetlands. But in spite of this knowledge, early Americans continued to drain our wetlands, and the practice continues to this day.

- **Improvement of Fisheries.** Numerous fish and shellfish species important to commercial and sport fishing spend at least some of their lives in wetlands. It has been estimated that about $20 billion are earned by coastal wetland-dependent fisheries each year in the U. S. California halibut spend their first one or two years in coastal wetlands, and several other popular sport species such as striped bass, sand bass, yellowfin croaker, and diamond turbot frequent coastal embayments like Newport Bay and the newly restored Bolsa Chica wetland.[5] In addition, small fish species such as top smelt, slough anchovy, and deepbody anchovy, on which larger fish as well as birds forage, are usually plentiful in these habitats. In a survey conducted two years following the wetland's restoration, 41 species of fish were identified in Bolsa Chica. With the amount of seafood imported into the U.S. reaching 70 percent of our consumption, one way of reversing the trend is to acquire and restore more of our coastal wetlands.

- **Improvement of Water Quality.** When freshwater runoff flows through a fully functioning wetland, the microorganisms, plants, and animals in the wetland work together as a purifying filter so that the quality of the water that exits the wetland is considerably improved over what entered it. Particulate matter is trapped by plant roots and dissolved pollutants such as nitrates and phosphates are incorporated into the tissues of plants and microorganisms or converted into forms less damaging to the environment. And the slowing effect of the water flow by plant roots provides greater time for chemical, biological, and physical purification to occur and for the lethal effects of sunlight to kill pathogens in the water.

Both natural and artificial wetlands (known as constructed wetlands) are being used more and more by various agencies to improve water

---

5. In 2007, the Amigos de Bolsa Chica received the Sustainable Fisheries Leadership-Coastal Habitat Conservation Award from the National Oceanic and Atmospheric Administration for their work in preserving the Bolsa Chica Wetland.

quality before releasing urban runoff into a lake or ocean. The Irvine Ranch Water District, which serves a 118 square mile sector of heavily urbanized Orange County, California, has constructed a series of artificial wetlands to treat its runoff before draining it into the Pacific Ocean. The City of Huntington Beach is considering diverting urban flow from the Wintersburg Flood Control Channel through a series of wetlands constructed in the city's Central Park before using it for irrigation or allowing it to drain into the Bolsa Chica wetland. The Wintersburg Channel is a major storm channel with a watershed of 27 square miles of Orange County. Wetlands can even purify sewage. The city of Arcata, California, utilizes a series of enhancement marshes to treat partially treated sewage. The wetland's effluent meets EPA discharge standards most times of the year, when precipitation is not excessive.

- **Recreational Opportunities.** Because they attract birds and other wildlife, wetlands are prime destinations for bird watchers, wildlife photographers, and artists. Where allowed, hunting and fishing in wetlands attract additional visitors. All in all, local businesses like hotels, restaurants, gas stations, and other visitor-serving establishments benefit from the presence of nearby wetlands.

- **Foundation of the food chain.** Coastal wetlands are phenomenal food factories, producing many times more organic matter than a corn or wheat field. There are several reasons for that. Runoff from nearby land brings a continuous stream of nutrients to feed the wetland plants. Turbulence due to the tides helps to distribute the nutrients throughout the wetland and also aerates the water. The organic richness of the wetland is derived primarily from decomposing plant and animal remains in the water. Add to that the waste released by birds, fish, mammals, and other animals that inhabit the wetland. These mate-

102

rials are consumed by microorganisms (bacteria, fungi, algae, protozoa) that provide food for larger organisms, which in turn are devoured by yet higher forms such as worms, insects, and shellfish, which are then eaten by birds and fish, and on up to larger animals, including humans.

The process just described, while usually referred to as a food chain, is in reality of complex food web. A chain implies a linear progression of consumers from the smallest to the largest. The fact is, the so-called chain actually has innumerable side branches, forming a complex network or web of predators and preys.

Delineation of Wetlands

Because of the growing awareness of the ecological value of wetlands, approaches had to be established for their protection. But ways of identifying, or delineating, wetlands had to be established before they could be preserved. On a federal level, wetlands are protected under the Clean Water Act. In California it is the 1976 California Coastal Act, part of the State Public Resources Code, that covers wetland protection. Section 30231 of the Public Resources Code requires "... the maintenance and restoration (if feasible) of the biological productivity and quality of wetlands..." Section 30233 limits the filling of wetlands to certain identified priority uses and requires mitigation for any authorized filling of wetlands. In implementing the law protecting wetlands, it is first necessary to be able to identify or delineate the boundaries of the wetland. This becomes especially critical when a piece of land that appears to be wetland is threatened with development. The difference in the worth of a piece of land that may be wetland and subject to protection versus one that is not can be enormous. The evidence supporting a wetland designation must be strong enough to stand up in court, where such action often ends up.

Section 30121 of the Public Resources Code defines wetland as...

"Lands within the coastal zone which may be covered periodically or permanently with shallow water and include saltwater marshes, freshwater marshes, open or closed brackish water marshes, swamps, mudflats, and fens."

The U. S. Fish and Wildlife Service uses a slightly different definition:

"Wetlands are lands transitional between terrestrial and aquatic systems where the water table is usually at or near the surface or the land is covered by shallow water."

While the Environmental Protection Agency and the U. S. Army Corps of Engineers use yet a different definition:

"Those areas that are inundated or saturated by surface or ground water at a frequency and duration sufficient to support, and that under normal circumstances do support, a prevalence of vegetation typically adapted for life in saturated soil conditions. Wetlands generally include swamps, marshes, bogs and similar areas."

None of these definitions is complete enough by itself to aid in the delineation of a piece of land as wetland. That requires identifying certain parameters or criteria that are characteristic of the particular parcel. For purposes of delineating wetlands, three frequently used parameters are:

1) Vegetation (Does the land support predominantly hydrophytes, that is, plants that prefer saturated soil?),

2) Substrate (Is the ground predominantly undrained, that is, "hydric"?) and

3) Hydrology (Is the ground saturated or covered by shallow water at some time during each year's growing season?).

To determine if a given parameter points to a parcel as a wetland, certain "indicators" must be present. Indicators are physical, biological, and chemical features that can be observed in support of a parameter. For instance, hydric soils, because they are saturated with water, become anaerobic, that is, lack oxygen, which can be detected with appropriate chemical analysis. In addition, anaerobic conditions provide opportunities for the growth of so-called anaerobic bacteria, which can produce hydrogen sulfide, detected by the unmistakable odor of rotten eggs when the soil is disturbed.

How many of the three parameters must a plot of land exhibit in order to be designated a wetland? Surprisingly, it depends on the agency that is doing the delineation. The Army Corps requires all three parameters, supported by indicators, while the California Coastal Commission and the U. S. Fish and Wildlife Service require only one parameter.

Also needed by the scientific personnel who are responsible for delineating wetlands (known as delineators) are methodologies, that is, guidelines for conducting field studies of a potential wetland. Such guidelines include techniques on identifying and mapping vegetation and soil types, references to field guides and other useful publications.

Tidelands and Submerged Lands

Tidelands are a specific type of wetland that is subject to the ebb and flow of the tides. Generally it means the area between the mean low tide line and the mean high tide line. Mean tide levels are values averaged over the 17 year natural tidal cycle. Land below the mean low tide line is referred to as submerged land. The mouths of rivers and bays consist of tidelands and submerged lands, providing navigable passage for watercraft involved in trade and fishing. The 600 acre newly restored Bolsa Chica wetland consists of submerged land rimmed by tideland, receiving seawater from the ocean inlet but no significant freshwater except for rainwater that falls directly into the wetland.

How much wetland was present in Bolsa Chica was probably the most contentious issue in the attempts to develop the Bolsa Chica wetland. Partly due to differences in definitions of wetlands and partly due to the enormous economic ramifications of the designation, it is not surprising that it took nearly three decades for the issue to be resolved.

The Legal Side of Tidelands, Submerged Lands, and Wetlands

Tidelands and the Public Trust

As we defined earlier, tidelands are those areas between the low and high tide lines, whether they occur in a wetland, a river mouth, or on a beach. Since tidelands are found along coastal areas of seas and lakes, they represent a separation between dry inland areas and deep water. That is, people have to cross a tideland to get to the water to fish, ship goods, or travel by water from one point to another. The ability of the public to have access across tidelands for commercial uses like fishing and shipping has been so vital that it has been protected by law as far back as the 6th century. In 530 AD, Roman Emperor Justinian ordered his legal experts to compile all the laws that govern human pursuits. Among the most important items on the list were those involving commercial ventures that used waterways for transportation. These activities required access across tidelands. To prevent individuals from controlling the use of these vital passageways, Justinian ordered a proclamation that public access to the navigable portions of rivers, lakes, and seas via tidelands could not be denied and that the government holds an easement on these lands as a Public Trust. This concept, known as the Public Trust Doctrine, is reflected in the Magna Carta,[6] the Constitution of the U. S. and the laws of many states, including California. Sections 4 of Article 10 of the California constitution provides:

"No individual, partnership, or corporation, claiming or possessing the frontage or tidal lands of a harbor, bay, inlet, estuary, or other navigable water in this State, shall be permitted to exclude the right of

---

6. Clause 33 of the Magna Carta reads. "All fish-weirs [traps] shall be removed from the Thames, the Medway, and throughout the whole of England, except on the sea coast." Fish weirs often extended the entire width a river, blocking the passage of boats. Clause 33 has been interpreted by historians as the prohibition of anything that would prevent free public use of a river for navigation.

way to such water whenever it is required for any public purpose, nor to destroy or obstruct the free navigation of such water; and the Legislature shall enact such laws as will give the most liberal construction to this provision, so that access to the navigable waters of this State shall be always attainable for the people thereof."

Even if a tideland is sold or given to a private interest, the Public Trust remains in effect in the form of an easement.

Legislative action and the courts have interpreted and refined California's tideland laws. In some cases these decisions have resulted in a weakening of tideland protection. For example, in one case, the California Supreme Court determined that a tideland could be filled if the area was part of a harbor project, was relatively small, and had been deemed by the legislature as not being useful for navigation. Considering that the last two criteria could be somewhat subjective, it is no wonder so many tideland disputes have ended up in court.

Prior to the 1960s, the Public Trust Doctrine was looked upon by most as some quaint, esoteric page in maritime law. As environmental activists began challenging government agencies throughout the 1960s and into the 1970s over tidelands protection at such places as Ballona Creek, Upper Newport Bay, and Bolsa Chica, the picture began to change. The Supreme Court case cited above and others spurred interest in the Public Trust Doctrine and the protection of tidelands. The 1970s was an age of increased environmental awareness, major catalysts of which included the establishment of Earth Day in 1970, followed by the passage of the Clean Water Act in 1972.[7] As evidence of the growing concern for tideland protection, a two day conference on the Public Trust Doctrine was held at the law school of the University of California at Davis in the fall of 1980. The event attracted 600 attendees. Held 10 years earlier, it probably would have drawn but a fraction of that figure.

---

7. http://www4.law.cornell.edu/uscode/33/ch26.html

The Variable Public Trust Doctrine

So it is clear as practiced, the Public Trust Doctrine is not fixed. The courts have recognized that times change and the public's uses of tidelands change, resulting in decisions that have strengthened tideland protection. For example, in a California Supreme Court 1971 ruling in a case known as Marks v. Whitney, the court said "Public Trust easements are traditionally defined in terms of navigation and fisheries. Public Trust easements have been held to include the right to fish, bathe, swim, to use for boating and general recreational purposes the navigable waters of the state and to use the bottom of the navigable waters for anchoring, standing, or other purposes...."[8]

However, the public's right to use tidelands under the Public Trust land is not unlimited. For example, if an activity that is allowed under the Public Trust might be a safety hazard to the public, such as heavy equipment loading and unloading freight at a wharf, access can be denied. But tidelands areas that are off limits for the public must be minimized. In a landmark case in Chicago in 1892, the Illinois Central Railroad petitioned the state legislature to grant the company use of nearly the entire Chicago shoreline for its commercial activities. The state refused and the rail company sued, the case going all the way to the U. S. Supreme Court. The Supreme Court backed the state's position, but agreed that granting limited shoreline use to the company was acceptable provided some public access was assured. While activities that are allowed in tidelands must somehow be related to the sea, the courts and regulatory agencies often have permitted uses such as restaurants and conference centers because, as the argument goes, they bring people to the shore.

Congress passed the Submerged Lands Act in 1953[9] that transferred ownership of the land from the mean low tide line out 3 miles to indi-

---

8. The public's access to ocean beaches up to the mean high tide line has been a contentious issue in California and a major crusade of the state's Coastal Commission for many years.

9. http://www4.law.cornell.edu/uscode/43/ch29.html

vidual states. Prior to that time, the federal government had claimed ownership of all coastal submerged lands, arguing that such lands were the federal government's responsibility for the defense of our shores and the carrying out of foreign relations, which outweighed the interests of the individual states. But congressional representatives of the coastal states successfully convinced their inland colleagues that the states had a greater and more direct interest in what occurred off their immediate shores than the federal government. The act, however, did reserve defense, regulation of navigation, and other related aspects to the federal government.

Submerged lands cannot be sold or transferred to private entities, although they can be leased for various purposes such as oil extraction, piers or floating docks. When California challenged Signal on the state's ownership of submerged land in Bolsa Chica in 1970, it was determined that there were 63 acres of submerged lands in the wetland. The figure was rounded up to 70 acres and was included in the acreage the state acquired under the 1973 boundary settlement.

7

The Bolsa Chica
Wetland in Jeopardy

*"Eventually we are all drawn to the water's edge, in recreation,
contemplation, sustenance or profit." - Jean-Michel Cousteau*

Wetlands and Marinas

The human need to travel across bodies of water for transportation,
hunting, fishing or trading no doubt led to the invention of the raft,
made of reeds, logs or inflated animal skins tied together. The desire
for more speed prompted the development of the more streamlined
canoe, variously made from a hollowed-out log, a light frame covered
with birch bark or animal skins, or wooden planks. Sometime during
human history came the discovery that travel over water could be an
enjoyable pastime as well as being practical. That led to the eventual
birth of the pleasure boat industry and the need for marinas.

Marinas are commercial developments that cater to pleasure and
commercial boat owners and provide facilities for building, launching,
storing (on or off the water), living on, maintaining, and repairing
boats. There are over 11,000 marinas serving an estimated 20 million
pleasure boats in the U. S. used by nearly 80 million people who annu-
ally spend $23 billion on boats, accessories and related expenses. With
nearly 900,000 boats, California ranks second only to Michigan in the

number of registered pleasure craft. With a reported deficit of about 20,000 boat slips in California in the early 70s, and boat owners clamoring for space to berth their boats, great pressure was placed on local and state officials to provide marinas and related support facilities. And obviously marinas must be at or near the water's edge, whether the ocean, a lake or river, occupying large amounts of scarce and expensive shoreline property.

Since marinas offer interesting and pleasing vistas, it is not unusual to see restaurants, hotels, office buildings, and residences occupying prime locations that overlook the view, justifying elevated rents. Thus considering the demand for marinas and the magnitude of financial gains possible, marinas have always been strong attractions for investors and land developers.

In contrast to states on the east and gulf coasts, California's ocean shoreline is not blessed with a lot of natural, protected harbors in which to place marinas. The bays of San Francisco and San Diego are two magnificent exceptions. A protected harbor is one that due to its natural shape protects moored boats and docks from the effects of ocean currents, swells, and storm waves, an essential feature of a good marina. Lacking such protected harbors, California has built numerous marinas in artificially protected harbors, often by simply constructing a breakwater around a section of open water. Examples are marinas at Santa Barbara, King Harbor/Redondo Beach, and Dana Point.

The same technique has been used to form major commercial harbors. Los Angeles Harbor, once considered in the 19th century as one of the worst anchorages on the west coast, is now, along with adjacent Long Beach Harbor, the fifth busiest harbor in the world, thanks to a protective nine mile long breakwater that separates the harbors from the open sea.

Another approach to creating a marina is to find a large piece of low-lying land somewhat inland of the shore and construct an artificial harbor. This is accomplished by scooping out soil to make deep water ocean entrances, channels and boat slips and using the soil to fill the rest of the project to provide dry land for buildings. That requires moving an enormous amount of soil, but there are natural areas where nature has already done much of the scooping: wetlands.

The Loss of Wetlands

In Chapter 6 we described the many benefits of wetlands and the moves to provide for wetland protection and preservation. But the need for commercial shipping facilities and the popularity of boating and waterfront housing and businesses in California's mild climate have led to the destruction of much of the state's wetlands to make way for harbors and marinas. How much of California's wetlands have been lost due to development? No one really knows exactly. Several figures have been tossed out that vary from 40 to 95 percent. Different state agencies quote different figures, and in some instances the same agency has been known at different times to report different figures. The problem is that an accurate and comprehensive inventory of the state's historic wetlands has never been carried out. Thus it is impossible to determine how much we have lost if we don't know how much we started out with.

In addition, erroneous conclusions have been reached when figures for coastal wetlands are lumped with inland wetlands, such as those in the San Joaquin Valley. Over eighty five percent of the valley's wetlands have been filled, so when their loss is added to the loss of coastal wetlands, the figure can be misleading when it is applied to coastal wetlands alone. There are some exceptions to the lack of information regarding the fate of California's wetlands. Certain areas, such as the Los Angeles and Orange counties coastline, have been more carefully studied and a good history of the area's wetland losses have been determined by the U. S. Fish and Wildlife Service (Figure 5-2). In addition, the California Environmental Resources Agency[1] has amassed historical and current data into a coastal wetlands inventory for all of Southern California (covering from Point Conception to the

---

1. http://www.ceres.ca.gov/wetlands/geo_info/so_cal.html

Mexican border), bringing greater clarity to the question of coastal wetland losses in that region of the state. The agency estimates that Southern California has lost about 70 percent of its 46,800 acres of historic wetlands.

Lack of accurate information concerning specific coastal wetlands has occasionally resulted in some costly errors. For example, after the state purchased a piece of property in Newport Beach in 1970, it was subsequently determined, through the discovery of a 1878 surveyor's map, that the state had spent $2 million on a strip of tideland that was already protected under the Public Trust.

Wetland Protection

In contrast to tidelands, which can be more precisely defined, America's wetlands in general and those around the world have not been afforded the same level of protection from destruction. Historically, that is, since the European colonization of North America, wetlands were considered as worthless, mosquito-infested wastes of good land and therefore commercially exploitable. Wetland habitats culturally have long been associated with mystery (will o' the wisp, Virginia's "Great Dismal Swamp"), danger (quicksand, poisonous snakes, toxic or odorous gases, "The Swamp Thing," "Creature from the Black Lagoon" etc.) and disease (swamp fever). For these reasons, throughout human history, all types of wetlands (estuaries, fens, swamps, bogs) have been held in relatively low esteem and even feared.

Popular literature has certainly helped fuel the negative reaction toward wetlands. Authors as diverse as William Shakespeare and Jack London have used fens and swamps as embodiments of evil. For instance, in Shakespeare's *The Tempest*, Calaban and Prospero are exchanging insults and Calaban says, "As wicked dew...from unwholesome fen drop on you...!" London, in his book, *"Before Adam,"* wrote, "Of our wanderings in the great swamp I have no clear knowledge. My memories of what occurred invariably take the form of nightmare. For untold ages, oppressed by protean fear, I am aware of wandering, endlessly wandering, through a dank and soggy wilderness, where poisonous snakes struck at us, and animals roared around us, and the mud quaked under us and sucked at our heels."

In America, the questionable reputation that swamps and related places hold probably originated with the Pilgrims, who found swamps common throughout New England. Because the swamps were frequently dark and heavily wooded, one could not see very far into them, making them menacing and seldom penetrated. And besides, the swamps were thought to be full of evil Indians. In the Southern colonies it was no different, except swamps also were associated with escaped slaves and such areas were to be cautiously avoided. The threatening image of wetlands started to wane in the mid 1800s when artists and photographers discovered the beauty of wetlands. But even so, among some, suspicion and disdain toward wetlands has continued even into the 21st century.

In our country's early years, the more adventurous entrepreneurs ignored the myths and saw the commercial value of wetlands. If they were freshwater wetlands, they were drained and converted into productive farmland or open for lumber harvesting. The draining of swampland was made easier by a series of federal legislative acts that began in 1855. As pioneers moved westward, more and more of America's wetlands were drained, filled and logged or planted with crops. Much of California's San Joaquin Valley was once covered with wetlands for nearly its entire length. Today barely 15 percent of the valley's wetlands remain, the rest having been drained and filled to make way for farms, fruit orchards, highways, and housing. As America's international trade grew, coastal wetlands were dredged for much needed harbors. By the 19th century, the loss of America's wetlands accelerated as mechanization and more efficient drainage techniques came into play, such as the advent of steam-driven dredges.

Beginning in mid 19th century, the federal government launched a series of new programs, known as the Swamp Land Acts of 1849, 1850, and 1860,[2] that actually encouraged farmers to drain wetlands and even offered to share in the costs. As the middle of the 20th century approached, the U. S. was losing wetlands at an average rate of 550,000 acres per year. But about that same time, an awareness of the ecological value of wetlands began to emerge. Ironically, in 1934, while the government was supporting the destruction of our wetlands, congress passed the Migratory Bird Hunting and Conservation Stamp Act[3] as a means of raising funds to acquire and restore wetlands, one of the first attempts by the government to reverse the loss of wetlands. In spite of the increased demand for harbors and marinas, wetland destruction actually slowed, and by the mid 1980s, the rate of wetland loss was nearly cut in half, to 290,000 acres per year. By the 1990s, annual losses amounted to just under 59,000 acres, and by 2004, net wetland acreage in the U. S. was reported to have increased by 32,000 acres.

However, these figures include all types of wetlands, freshwater and salt water combined. If one looks just at coastal wetlands, which make up about 5 percent of America's wetlands, losses continue. Between 1998 and 2004, over 28,000 acres of coastal wetlands in the U.S. were reported lost, mainly due to navigational needs and commercial and residential development, including marinas.

In California, losses of coastal wetlands roughly paralleled national trends. For instance, as we saw in Chapter 5, in 1900 there were an estimated 17,000 acres of coastal wetlands between San Pedro and Newport Harbor. By 1970 this figure was down to about 4000 acres, a loss of 75 percent. Greatest losses occurred in the San Pedro-Wilmington area due to harbor expansion, and at the mouth of the Santa Ana River, where much of the wetlands was drained and filled for residential development and industrial plants for electric generation and sewage treatment. Wetland acreage at both these areas was reduced by over 90 percent. Fortunately much of the remaining wetlands around the Santa Ana River mouth have been acquired and either have under-

2. http://water.usgs.gov/nwsum/WSP2425/history.html

3. http://www.fws.gov/laws/lawsdigest/mighunt.html

gone restoration or are undergoing restoration. The passage of tighter federal controls regarding the filling of wetlands and especially the establishment of the California Coastal Commission have essentially halted much of the loss of marine wetlands in the state. Provisions in the California Coastal Act prohibit the filling of coastal wetlands, but do provide for exceptions. The Act requires that whenever a wetland is filled, the loss must be mitigated in some fashion.

The California Coastal Act and the Coastal Commission

Awareness of the value of coastal wetlands continued to rise in the public's mind in the 1960s. Much of that awareness was triggered when Southern California environmentalists watched helplessly while the 2100 acre Ballona Wetlands were nearly totally obliterated by the construction of Marina del Rey. The anguish continued when Christiana Oil Company, with little concern for environmental values, turned 850 acres of Sunset Bay wetlands into what is now known as Huntington Harbour. But about the same time, government action in California made its first significant progress in the protection of some of its wetlands with the establishment of the Bay Conservation and Development Commission (BCDC) in 1965, which set restraints on the filling of San Francisco Bay tidelands and wetlands.[4] It was clear California needed statewide legislation to protect its entire 1100 mile coastline. For several years, in spite of pressure from environmentalists and others, the state legislature repeatedly failed to pass a coastal protection act that would do for the California coast what the BCDC did for San Francisco Bay. Finally, citizens' groups launched a coastal protection initiative that took only two months to qualify for the November, 1972 ballot. Known as Proposition 20, the initiative passed by an 800,000 vote margin in spite of opposition by both business and labor interests, civic organizations, and most of the state's major daily newspapers. The act established regulatory bodies that would eventu-

---

4. Joe Bodovitz was the first executive director of the BCDC and was to play a pivotal role in the preservation of the Bolsa Chica wetlands (see Chapter 9).

ally become the California Coastal Commission, which oversees local coastal planning within a defined coastal zone through Local Coastal Programs ("LCPs"). LCPs were to be part of the general plans for the state's 73 coastal counties and cities. The LCPs must incorporate the policies of the California Coastal Act, a milestone document that the state assembly drafted in 1976. More on LCPs will be found in Chapter 10.

The Law and Bolsa Chica.

One might say the legal history of Bolsa Chica began in 1786 when the Spanish king through his representatives in New Spain granted Corporal Manuel Nieto the use of an immense spread of land that included Bolsa Chica. Jumping ahead to 1874, Joaquin Ruiz received word from California's Board of Land Commissioners confirming his ownership of the 8100 acre Rancho La Bolsa Chica, granted to him by his sister, Catarina. However, following Public Trust Doctrine, the grant excluded any land within the property that was considered tide- and submerged land. As you recall, financial difficulties forced sale of the rancho in 1854 to Abel Stearns, who in turn deeded it to the Robinson Trust. The trust then sold about 1160 acres to the Bolsa Land Company in 1899. The Bolsa Land Company then leased the land to the newly formed Bolsa Chica Gun Club.

It was not long before the gun club members found themselves in somewhat of a quandary. Before they were dispossessed, the club members had been hunting in the still waters of the San Joaquin Marsh, while in the Bolsa Chica estuary they had to contend with the troublesome ebb and flow of the tides. They had to find way of taming the strong currents that flowed in and out of their hunting grounds four times a day. Besides, the kind of ducks that were most sought after preferred fresh water wetlands. As described in Chapter 5, the gun club came upon the idea of building a dam across a narrow portion of Bolsa Bay. But that would have been contrary to state and federal law; the gun club did not own the tidelands according to the

Public Trust, a fact that was clearly specified in the Joaquin Ruiz grant. According to state law, such Public Trust protections are passed down to subsequent owners. Clearly the dam would interfere with the public's access to the sea by way of the Freeman River, which was the major watercourse that flowed through Bolsa Chica.

There was, however, a way of getting around the Public Trust. It was possible for an individual to acquire title to tidelands by applying to the state for a patent. Patents are grants issued by the state that transfer title of public lands to private parties provided the land is used in some way that benefits the public as defined in the Public Trust, such as for a harbor. That is, the state is supposed to retain easement rights over the tidelands while the private party uses the tidelands for public use. Surely the gun club had no intention of opening its hunting reserve as a public harbor, but members of the gun club applied for a patent nevertheless.

Horace Dobbins, a member of the gun club, filed for a patent on 528.82 acres of state tidelands in Bolsa Chica in 1899. Without any apparent question concerning the true objective of the patent or whether it even complied with state law pertaining to tideland protection, the patent was granted. Dobbins immediately conveyed his interest in the patent over to the Bolsa Land Company, an act in itself which appears to be contrary to the law pertaining to tideland patents. The granting of tideland patents is supposed to be limited to private citizens for very specific benefits.

Once the dam was built, the waters of the wetland were calmed and the gun club was able to construct numerous diked ponds to attract migrating ducks. The building of the dam was a critical turning point in the overall ecology of the Bolsa Chica wetland. As described in Chapter 1, the Bolsa Chica wetland had been an estuary for many thousands of years. By cutting off its source of seawater, it soon began to lose the functions and characteristics of an estuary.

When local farmers realized that their passage to the ocean was blocked by the gun club's dam, they complained to the Army Corps of Engineers and several levels of government. However, the farmers' battle failed because they could not provide enough convincing evidence that the Bolsa Chica tidelands had provided benefits under the Public Trust, that is, could be used for commerce and navigation. Their testimony was countered by witnesses on the gun club's side that swore one could not float a boat on the Freeman River.

Wetlands in Jeopardy

The conversion of the Bolsa Chica lowland into an oil field beginning in 1940 was the principal factor that prevented the area from becoming urbanized in later years. The quantity of oil and gas that came out of Bolsa Chica's muddy wetland proved to be one of the most abundant in the state. Any thought of shutting down the wells to allow Huntington Beach's urban sprawl to creep into Bolsa Chica, was, for the time being, out of the question. Oil production out of Bolsa Chica remained high for a number of years. But oil pools do not last forever. In spite of the development of new techniques to squeeze more oil out of the ground, oil company executives began to prepare for the day when the costs to operate an oil pump and to transport and process the oil are more than the value of the oil. As the mid 60s approached, that day seemed near for the two major companies operating in Bolsa Chica, Signal Oil and Gas Company and Standard Oil Company, both vying for the privilege of turning Bolsa Chica into another Marina del Rey. Since it already had long enjoyed an oil lease on the gun club lowlands, Signal had its foot in the gun club door and was able to purchase the Bolsa Chica from the 300 heirs of the club members in 1970. The company's plan to turn Bolsa Chica into a marina was merely following a pattern that had been established all along the nearby coastal area for years. Some local examples:

Marina del Rey – once a wetland
San Pedro/Wilmington - once a wetland
Alamitos Bay - once a wetland
Huntington Harbour – once a wetland

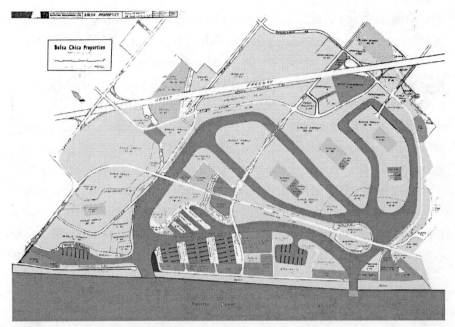

7-1. Development plan for Bolsa Chica proposed by Standard Oil Company in 1965. Two navigable ocean inlets would lead to a network of channels serving several thousand boat slips. Light gray areas would contain about 15,000 residential units. Darker areas are schools, parks and commercial areas. The wetland would be completely obliterated. (Map courtesy Huntington Beach Co.)

A marina in Bolsa Chica was not the only proposal for the area's future. Orange County has other plans for it. In its master plan, the county had envisioned an airport in Bolsa Chica, with raised runways extending out into the ocean. The state Parks and Recreation Department quickly squashed that idea, not wanting to ruin a beautiful beach the state had just purchased and renovated. So Bolsa Chica as a marina seemed to be its destiny. Marina plans for Bolsa Chica had become known to the citizens in the surrounding community many years before Signal's purchase of the area. For example, the Army Corps of Engineers had been authorized in 1945 and again in 1964 to carry out a study of the feasibility of constructing a marina in Bolsa Chica. In addition, the gun club had hired two engineering companies in the 1960s to study the feasibility of a marina/residential complex in the wetland. Other interests released plans in the mid 1960s calling for extensive marina, commercial, and residential development that would fill from 70 to 100 percent of the wetland, depending on the developer. In 1961 Edward Valentine, a San Marino investor, announced plans to extend Huntington Harbour into Bolsa Chica. In 1964, a plan designed by Signal Oil Company's rival, Standard Oil Company, showed the marsh as being completely obliterated with intense development, which included about 15,000 residential units (Figure 7-1). Local citizens feared the worst in the face of the development juggernaut that would severely impact the surrounding neighborhoods that consisted mostly of single family homes. In addition to the social impact of a marina development, the destruction of a rare and endangered natural resource was also on the minds of many local citizens. Action was clearly necessary.

Signal Oil Company Plans for Bolsa Chica and the 1973 Agreement

When the heirs to the gun club sold Bolsa Chica to Signal Oil and Gas Company in 1970, rights to the tidelands presumably went with the title, owing to the Dobbins patent. Through state records the wetlands could be traced down from Manual Nieto to Catarina Ruiz to Joaquin Ruiz to Abel Stearns to the gun club and finally Signal. Secure that its title to all of Bolsa Chica was unclouded, the company began a series of neighborhood "show and tell" meetings to present its plans for development in Bolsa Chica. In addition, the company went before the Huntington Beach Planning Commission and City Council to lay out their plans for the historical wetland.

When the state attorney general's office was made aware of Signal's plans for Bolsa Chica, it immediately stepped in to notify the oil company that the state held legal interest in about 526 acres of submerged lands and tidelands under the Public Trust. Specifically the state's position was that it retained its easement over the tidelands in Bolsa Chica, and in addition, the gun club's patent did not include title to 63 acres of submerged lands, for which by law the state retained title. As a result of the state's action, Signal found itself unable to obtain clear title to the property, meaning its development plans were at least temporarily on hold. Naturally Signal disputed the state's claim, arguing that specifically the Bolsa Chica tidelands (and certain islands that had formed in the tidelands in the ensuring years) were legally Signal's as a result of the gun club acquiring them through the state patent in 1899. Signal met with state officials in October of 1970 to discuss its options. The state pressed its position. In a letter from California State Attorney General Evelle Younger to Lindell Marsh, attorney for Signal Properties, Younger states, "…we believe that your contention appears to be without any basis, in fact or in law." While the state was prepared to go to court over its claim, it was agreed that litigation would have led to a lengthy and costly battle. A more practical approach was to negotiate a settlement that was generally beneficial for both parties.

A special task force was formed to resolve the issue of Bolsa Chica, which was the first time in state history that such a comprehensive approach had been utilized to settle what was considered a "boundary dispute." That is, what was state property and what was Signal property in Bolsa Chica?

The Task Force included representatives from the State Lands Commission, the Attorney General's office, Fish and Game Department, Department of Navigation and Ocean Development, and the Department of Parks and Recreation. In addition to resolving the boundary dispute, the Department of Resources asked the Task Force to prepare a conceptual plan for the development of the public benefits of Bolsa Chica in those portions that were to be gained as a result of the negotiations. Public benefits were envisioned to include 400 acres of restored saltwater marsh, a public marina to accommodate at least 500 boats together with launching ramps and parking capacity for 200 trailered boats. In reviewing these goals, it became clear the plan could not be met easily considering the configuration of the tidelands and submerged lands that the state claimed to have an interest in. The

123

7-2. Bolsa Chica in 1901. The dark areas show the extent of the historic tidelands. (Source unknown)

526 acres consisted of a myriad of narrow, finger-shaped channels and sloughs (Figure 7-2) that would have been a nightmare to manage if the state intended to restore it as a wetland wildlife reserve. Instead, it was decided to consolidate the 526[5] or so acres into a single rectangular parcel immediately adjacent to Pacific Coast Highway (Figure 7-3) in place of the unmanageable channels and sloughs. That aspect of the agreement constituted the *land exchange* part.

The negotiations between the state and Signal also were concerned with a "boundary settlement" which was to determine how much land the state actually owned or held in the Public Trust. Since oil activities in Bolsa Chica had altered much of its topography, attempts to locate the exact margins of its historical tidelands were generally unsuccessful. For instance, Signal had surveyors study the tideland patterns in the relatively pristine Seal Beach Navy Weapons Station with the possibility of extrapolating their findings to Bolsa Chica. The results

---

5. Includes the 63 acres of submerged lands,

124

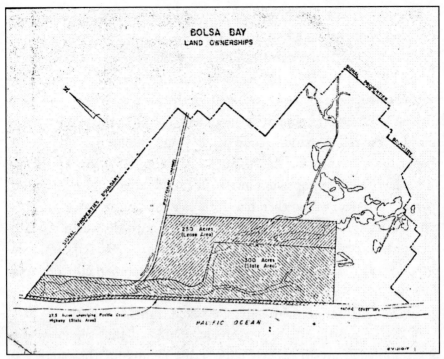

BOLSA BAY
LAND OWNERSHIPS

230 Acres
(Lease Area)

300 Acres
(State Area)

27.5 Acres underlying Pacific Coast
Highway (State Area)

PACIFIC OCEAN

7-3. Map of the 1973 boundary settlement between the state and Signal. The 530 acres that the state claimed to fall under the Public Trust was consolidated into the shaded, rectangular portion shown. The 300 acre shaded portion was deeded to state, the remaining 230 acres was to be deeded to the state if an ocean entrance were constructed at state expense. (Map courtesy State Lands Commission)

were less than satisfactory, eventually forcing opposing sides to come up with a compromise.

After nearly two years of negotiations, the state and Signal reached a settlement, which was approved by the State Lands Commission in January of 1973. The agreement is officially known as the "Boundary Settlement and Land Exchange Agreement Regarding Lands in the Bolsa Chica Area, Orange County, California." While it appears that Signal conceded to the state's claim of 526 acres of tidelands, it was not going to give in totally to the state. Signal was willing to give up 300 acres, plus 27.5 acres of the Pacific Coast Highway right of way, but hold back the balance with conditions.

The state was to be given a rent-free lease on the balance of the 526 acres that the state had originally claimed, or 230 acres (rounded up from 226), that were immediately adjacent to the 300 acre parcel. A major condition of the agreement was that if within 14 years the state constructed a navigable ocean inlet that would serve the property owner's waterside residential development as well as the public marina and the restored marsh, the state would be given title to the 230 acres. The state was to provide the cost of construction of the inlet, and the funds had to be appropriated in the state budget within 10 years, i.e., by 1983. The state would then have title to a total of 557.5 acres of Bolsa Chica. The agreement was subsequently amended to extend the time the state was to construct the opening to 1990, provided an appropriation was obtained by 1986. The 63 acres of submerged lands were consolidated into 70 acres for which the state as owner of the land was to receive royalties on the oil and gas taken from the parcel.

A key ingredient in the agreement stipulated that Signal was to be exempted from all other Public Trust claims for the balance of the company's lowland holdings in Bolsa Chica, covering almost 800 acres. The agreement caught the attention of the newly established Coastal Commission staff. It interpreted the agreement as a free pass for Signal with regards to coastal protection regulations. In a report to the commissioners, the staff wrote, "Subsequent development of Bolsa Chica is no more exempt from the Coastal Act than subsequent private development pursuant to a previously conceived public redevelopment plan." The state attorney general agreed, affirming that the 1973 agreement did not exempt Signal from any other local, state or federal regulations, including the Coastal Act.

Grass Takes Root

Convinced of the economic benefits of Signal's massive marina development at their doorsteps, local business interests, many local residents, and the city of Huntington Beach itself were all supportive of the plan. The city sent a delegation to Sacramento during the early stages of the discussions between the state and Signal the voice the city's support of what was eventually to be known as the 1973 agreement. But as time passed, there was a decided change in the wind.

As details of Signal's development intentions in Bolsa Chica spread, a growing number of citizens became concerned about the planned development in the wetland. Initially, at least, the concern was not so much from an ecological point of view, but from questions about the legality of the 1973 agreement, the fear of the impact a Marina del Rey-like development would have on traffic, utilities, schools and other aspects of the city's infrastructure, and the public financial costs. In the early 1970s four Huntington Beach citizen groups had begun to focus their attention on Bolsa Chica: the League of Women Voters, the American Association of University Women, the Huntington Beach Environmental Council,[6] and the Friends of Bolsa Chica.

The League of Women Voters was a national organization that spun off from the National American Women Suffrage Association, the force behind the passage of the 19th amendment to the U. S. Constitution, which gave women the right to vote. From its inception in 1920, the LWV limited its membership to women, but in 1973 LWV members voted to accept men into their organization. One of the major goals of the LWV was to offer voters unbiased, nonpartisan information about the electoral process, candidates for office and issues that affected its members. And so when plans for the development of Bolsa Chica became known, the Huntington Beach LWV chapter took on a study of the issue of the possible future of Bolsa Chica for the purpose of enlightening its members and the general public. The leader of the Bolsa Chica study group was the first male member admitted into the chapter, Herb Chatterton.

The second organization that focused its attention on the future of Bolsa Chica was the Huntington Beach chapter of the American

---

6. Now known as the Environmental Board

Association of University Women (AAUW).[7] Also a national organization, the AAUW was founded in Boston in 1881 by a small group of women college graduates to encourage more opportunities for education and employment for women. The organization provides fellowships and grants for education and community-based projects. One of the projects of the Huntington Beach AAUW branch in 1970 was to examine the pending development in Bolsa Chica. The study was motivated by one of the national AAUW organization's study themes, "The Human Use of Urban Space."

The Huntington Beach Environmental Council was formed in 1970 by action of the city council. Some of its members were professionals in areas of ecology, chemistry, and geology and could see many of the negative aspects of the development plan for the wetland. While the official city position continued to support the marina plan for Bolsa Chica, a number of the environmental council's members began to question the plan as private individuals.

The Friends of Bolsa Chica was an organization of veterinarians that had been focusing its concern on the Bolsa Chica since 1969, particularly the fate of wildlife in the Bolsa Chica. The organization was an outgrowth of the Wildlife and Ecology Committee of the Southern California Veterinary Medicine Association.

The Huntington Beach AAUW and LWV often offered joint public programs on Bolsa Chica. For instance in January of 1974 the two groups sponsored a workshop that featured speakers from Signal Landmark, the city of Huntington Beach, the state departments of Fish and Game and Parks and Recreation and the Regional Coastal Conservation Commission (the predecessor of the Coastal Commission). The workshop was well attended, resulting in the dissemination of information about the impending impact of Bolsa Chica's future on the surrounding community.

---

7. The Huntington Beach chapter has subsequently merged with the Fountain Valley and Westminster chapters.

As these organizations dug deeper into the plans for Bolsa Chica, more and more questions concerning the development began accumulating. While the first feelings of apprehension over the wetland's development were almost entirely based on its impact on the city's infrastructure, ecological concerns began to surface. Most of the LWV and AAUW members who were involved in the early studies of Bolsa Chica had little or no background in biology or ecology, but spouses and others, who subsequently became aware of the results of the studies, did. An enormously potent stone in the foundation of the movement to save Bolsa Chica emerged from these connections: the public's increased understanding of the ecological benefits of wetlands and the need to preserve Bolsa Chica.

Bolsa Chica Undergoes its First Restoration

Under the 1973 agreement, the state was given title to 300 acres of Bolsa Chica lowlands consolidated in a more or less rectangular parcel adjacent to Pacific Coast Highway. Considering the presence of producing oil wells on part of the 300 acres, it was decided to restore only about 210 of the 300 acres. Levees were constructed around the area to be restored and the flap gates in the dam that had prevented free movement of tidal seawater between outer and inner Bolsa Bay since 1899 were permanently opened. The restoration of the Bolsa Chica Ecological Reserve was completed in 1978 (Figure 7-4).

Was the 1973 agreement wrong?

Legal opinions regarding the validity of the 1973 agreement between the state and Signal Oil were understandably mixed. Presumably with the support of their legal advisors, both the County of Orange and the City of Huntington Beach officially supported the agreement. But some attorneys who specialized in Public Trust issues strongly took issue with the agreement. Public Trust Doctrine was an esoteric specialty that few attorneys were familiar with, and for private citizens even less so. The conclusion reached by many as the 1970s wound

7-4. Amigos de Bolsa Chica co-president (with wife Rhoda) Ken Martyn speaking at the opening of the Bolsa Chica Ecological Reserve, November, 1978. (Photo courtesy Amigos de Bolsa Chica)

down was that the 1973 agreement's legality could only be determined in the courts. But who would challenge the State of California and a major oil company?

8

The Amigos Emerge

Grass Continues to Grow

After attending numerous Bolsa Chica workshops and study sessions sponsored by their organizations, members of the local chapters of the AAUW and the LWV continued to question the development plan for Bolsa Chica that had been presented by Signal at community functions. In time it was agreed among members of the groups that the area should not be developed but instead be preserved and restored to its natural state. Initially the primary concern was not strictly environmental but on the impact the marina development would have on Huntington Beach's infrastructure, its streets, schools and the like. There was also the feeling that the financial burden on taxpayers would not be cost-effective. The public's responsibilities in the agreement involved the construction of a marina and the associated public works, the navigable inlet, the deepwater channel, the rerouting of Pacific Coast Highway (an alternate plan that avoided an expensive, high bridge over the inlet) and other infrastructural improvements. One estimate placed the public improvement costs of the marina plan at nearly $230 million, which presumably would have to come from a combination of federal, state, local and special district funding sources. Members of the LWV felt that any public funds expended in the marina would be better spent on the city's parks and open space plan.

The LWV was poised to oppose the marina plan, but its structure prohibited it from launching a campaign to save the wetland, especially if it involved legal action, and it was pretty clear the battle was headed to the courts. Initially some of the members of both the LWV and AAUW, as individuals, tried to lobby their state representatives to have the 1973 agreement reversed, saving Bolsa Chica from development. They were soon followed by citizens unaffiliated with the groups, but their pleas generally fell on deaf ears. An agreement that took two years to hammer out was not going to be reversed based on the arguments of a handful of residents. But perhaps if a new organization were formed for the sole purpose of fighting the loss of Bolsa Chica, it might carry more weight. Beginning in the fall of 1975, a small group of Huntington Beach residents, mostly made up of the members of the LWV and AAUW who had participated in the Bolsa Chica studies a few years earlier, began meeting to discuss the formation of such an organization. Some of the participants in these discussions were Linda Moon, Ruth Bailey, Charles Falzon, Ken and Rhoda Martin, Nancy Donaven, Herb Chatterton, Shirley Dettloff, Fred and Lynn Bolding, Charlene Bauer, and Margaret Carlberg. The organization would spearhead a campaign to preserve and restore the Bolsa Chica wetland. Being neophytes in advocating the preservation of anything, the Bolsa Chica activists looked for other, similar battles to act as models.

The Battle of Back Bay

About a decade earlier, a similar scenario had played in nearby Newport Beach. An area known as Upper Newport Bay was earmarked for waterfront development by the Irvine Company, which owned most of the surrounding upland. The problem for the company was that the shoreline of Upper Newport Bay consisted of tidelands surrounded by steep cliffs, leaving little flat, developable land at water level. As things stood, it would have been impossible to carry out the company's plans for a massive waterside development because it did not own the tidelands. As you recall, tidelands are constitutionally protected from development, but an exception might be arranged. The company approached Orange County officials in 1963 with a proposal involving a land exchange. The company asked that it could acquire 157 acres of tidelands along the bay's edge in exchange for about 450 acres of property elsewhere in the bay. In the plan, a deep, mid-bay channel would be dredged, the spoils of which would be used to fill the bay's tidelands to provide dry land on which the company's development would be constructed. In addition the channel would provide a deep water route to the lower bay for the many boats that would be moored in the development, as well as carry runoff from San Diego creek to the ocean via the lower bay. The creek is a major storm channel, which presently drains some 154 square miles of Orange County. The dredging, incidentally, was to be at the county's expense.

By law, such land exchanges must be financially balanced in favor of the public. According to Irvine Company figures, the trade would be something like plus $10 million on the county's side, but a subsequent study by an independent assessor found the deal to be at least $100 million in the Irvine Company's favor, due to the company acquiring almost 7 miles of prime waterfront property in the deal. Of the 450 acres the county was to receive, well over half of it was part of the bay that was to be dredged to supply spoils for filling the tidelands. Only about 54 acres or 13 percent of the 450 acres was usable waterfront property. In spite of the heavily one-sided transaction, county officials agreed to the land trade, as did the State Lands Commission.

News of the land trade reached a Newport Beach couple that lived near Upper Newport Bay. Frank and Frances Robinson (Figure 8-1) had often visited a nearby beach on the upper bay with their children. The prospect of losing the beach to development plunged the couple into an extraordinary campaign that ultimately saved the entire wetlands of the upper bay. They formed the Friends of Upper Newport

133

8-1. Newport Beach residents Frank and Frances Robinson, who successfully fought the filling of Newport Back Bay wetlands (in the background) for a waterside development. The Robinsons provided invaluable advise to the Amigos de Bolsa Chica in its early years. (Photo courtesy Jay Robinson)

Bay and soon found themselves toe to toe against the largest and most influential power in the county, the Irvine Company. Undaunted, the Robinsons and two other couples[1] filed a lawsuit in 1963 challenging the constitutionality of the land trade. Their arduous and expensive efforts paid off in 1973 when the courts ruled in their favor. In 1975 almost 900 acres of Upper Newport Bay, including the tidelands that the Irvine Company had planned to fill, were dedicated as a state ecological reserve. The Friends filed a second lawsuit a few years later questioning the Irvine Company's claim of ownership of three islands in Upper Newport Bay. This time the Friends of Upper Newport Bay lost, but with a political spin. The judge ruled against them, not neces-

---

1. They were Harold and Joan Coverdale and Wesley and Judith Marx. Wesley Marx, a prominent author, has written several articles and books on the health of the oceans such as prescient "The Frail Ocean," first published in 1967.

sarily because of the lack of merit of their case, but because a ruling in favor of the plaintiffs would have placed in jeopardy the ownership of some of the most expensive property in California, Newport Beach's Balboa and Lido Islands, which had been formed by the same natural forces that made the islands in Upper Newport Bay.

The Amigos de Bolsa Chica Appears

The battle of Upper Newport Bay caught the attention of the Bolsa Chica advocates. They invited the Robinsons to advise them on how to approach the drive to save Bolsa Chica. That the Robinsons' counsel was an enormous inspiration for what was to follow is probably an understatement. The affable couple attended Bolsa Chica study sessions of the LWV. They started out by stressing how important it was that the people involved in the fight to save Bolsa Chica form an independent organization whose sole mission was the preservation of that valuable resource. The idea fermented through the fall of 1975, as plans for a new group solidified. Following the inspiration of the Friends of Upper Newport Bay group, members of the budding Bolsa Chica organization decided to call themselves the Friends of Bolsa Chica. Unfortunately that name already had been adopted by another group. "Since the name Bolsa Chica is Spanish, why not make the organization name all Spanish?" suggested Huntington Beach resident and Amigos co-founder Ruth Bailey, who was to serve as the city's mayor a few years later. Amigos de Bolsa Chica was immediately adopted as the name of the group.

The Amigos de Bolsa Chica held their first public meeting on the evening of January 15, 1976 at Huntington Beach's City Hall. The principal order of business was to elect officers. They were: President, Herb Chatterton; Vice President, Linda Moon; Treasurer, Rhoda Martyn; Secretary, Nancy May (Donavan). One of the first acts of the Amigos was to appear before the February 3, 1976 meeting of the California Coastal Zone Conservation Commission. On its agenda was a proposal to urge the state to purchase a number of parcels of open space, one of which was Bolsa Chica. Linda and Wally Moon, representing the Amigos, emphasized the need to act immediately in light of the imminent threat of development. Several other Huntington Beach citizens spoke in favor of the state's acquisition of Bolsa Chica.

At its meeting later in the year, the statewide commission included 560 acres of Bolsa Chica lowlands on its number one priority list for purchase. In the week following the commission resolution, the Orange County Board of Supervisors passed a motion by Supervisor Harriett Wieder, whose district included Bolsa Chica, to support the commission's action. The motion, however, urged the state to limit the amount of wetland acquired in order to set aside some property for private development to occur. In a letter to the board of supervisors, the Amigos objected to the resolution, preferring to see no development in the lowlands at all, a position that the organization continued to advocate.

Unfortunately later in the year the commission dropped Bolsa Chica from its priority list, saying that the wetland was not ready for funding. In spite of the setback, attempts to find ways to purchase the Bolsa Chica wetland continued, but each time they failed, due principally to lack of sufficient funds to meet the property owner's price. In 1977, newly elected state assemblyman Dennis Mangers was able to get a line item placed in the state budget in the amount of $3.6 million for the purpose of purchasing 923 acres of Bolsa Chica lowlands. An additional one million dollars was identified from local sources. Signal refused the offer, claiming that the value of the property was closer to $36 million, or ten times the state's appraisal.

The Robinsons returned to Huntington Beach several times to advise members of the newly minted Amigos de Bolsa Chica. One of their important lessons was how to establish and take advantage of relationships with local and state agencies. When discussing issues either face to face in private offices or in public testimony, keep it impersonal. Don't ever say a nearby marina will ruin your property values or spook your dog. Talk about the loss of benefits to the community when a wetland is filled for a marina and detail the public costs in dollars. Point out the ecological values of a wetland. Bring in biologists and geologists to back up your statements. While Robinsons' instructions to the members of the Amigos emphasized a strictly non-emotional approach to dealing with the bureaucracy of environmental planning, a strategy the Amigos took to heart, it did not mean the Amigos lacked emotion. There was a great deal of emotion among the Amigos members that energized their perseverance and which ultimately led to their unprecedented success. But that is getting way ahead of the story.

Another lesson that the Robinsons related was to keep close contact with governmental officials and their staff at all levels. Meet with them regularly. The Robinsons once remarked that to their surprise, while county supervisors and other county and state officials and their agencies had generally supported the Upper Newport Bay land trade, the Robinsons often would encounter staff members who were sympathetic to the couple's cause and even risked their jobs by feeding them inside information. Frances Robinson remembered a conversation she had with a State Lands Commission staff member early in the campaign to save Upper Newport Bay. He urged the Robinsons to take the question to court. "You'll win," he said.

Frank Robinson called them "glitches," no doubt from his aeronautical engineering background. Glitches are tactics that are totally legal and ethical that one takes advantage of during the permitting process of a development project. Such projects must go through a series of permit hearings by various levels of government, local, state and sometimes federal. By law most public hearings by agencies at all levels must allow for oral and written input by interested parties, whether governmental agencies, organizations, or private individuals. Thus at each step there is an opportunity to delay the process with a meticulously researched and well-planned and executed presentation devoid of any emotion or personal comments. The presentation must be sufficiently convincing with facts and figures to cause the process to be put on hold, usually until further information is gathered to corroborate the information presented in the glitch. At best the glitch may even cause the project to be denied or greatly modified in the opponents' favor, but at least any delay in the process gives opponents more time to study testimony presented by the proponents of the project and prepare rebuttals with additional materials.

On the advise of the Robinsons, beginning from its start as an organization, the Amigos launched its campaign of educating the public on the benefits of preserving the Bolsa Chica wetlands. To inform the community of the Back Bay's natural attractions, the Friends of Upper Newport Bay had been holding regular walking tours, using knowledgeable guides to point out features of the area. Emulating the Back Bay experiences, in 1976 the Amigos began leading groups on tours of the Bolsa Chica, which it found to be an ideal outdoor classroom. College professor Peter Green lectured visitors on the biology of the wetland. Dr. Green and his wife Cathy set up microscopes for visitors to see for themselves the immense diversity of life that is normally beyond the reach of the human eye. Professor Robert Winchell and wife Grace explained the unique geology of the area. Presentations on the birds, history, and politics of Bolsa Chica were accompanied by illustrations and maps. The Amigos' monthly public guided tour tradition has been operating uninterrupted for over 30 years, in addition to the organization's program of private tours for schools and other groups.

Another tactic to spread the word about Bolsa Chica was the publication of a newsletter, the Tern Tide. Beginning as a single sheet, it has evolved into an informative, multipage publication. The Bolsa Chica and the Amigos' campaign to save the wetland has attracted the news media and through the years the issue has been among the top newspaper stories in terms of column inches devoted to it. In addition, articles about the wetland have appeared in Orange Coast, Sunset, Bird Watchers' Digest, and many other magazines.

The Amigos' first major fund raising event was held on the evening of December 4, 1976 at the home of Ruth and Jerry Finley. The event was called "Bolsa Bash"[2] and the cost was $2.50 per person. Over 100 attended.

The U. S. Army Takes Up Bolsa Chica

In 1945 the U. S. Army Corps of Engineers was authorized by congress to investigate the need for a coastal recreational harbor in the Anaheim Bay/Bolsa Chica area. But when approached by the Corps, the gun club members, showed little interest in the idea. The club members response caused the Corps to put off any significant action until 1965 when attention to a marina in Bolsa Chica was beginning to grow among local boat owners and business interests. The Corps was initially charged only with determining the feasibility of a navigable inlet to serve a small boat harbor in Bolsa Chica, work that was sponsored by the County of Orange. The state Department of Boating and Waterways picked up sponsorship of the Corps study in 1972. Eventually the Corps came up with 9 alternative development plans for the wetland that ranged from an 1800 berth marina, conforming to the general plan of the 1973 agreement, to a non-navigable inlet serving a large restored wetland. In 1976 the Corps studies expanded to include details of the Bolsa Chica wetland restoration. However, by 1978, when the Corps became aware of the wide lack of consensus between the landowners and members of the community as to how Bolsa Chica should be developed, the Corps dropped funding for the Bolsa Chica studies from its 78-79 and 79-80 fiscal year budgets. However, the County of Orange reestablished sponsorship in October of 1979 with the goal that the county would promote the idea in the community that a marina would be a great improvement for the wetland.

---

2. The name was inspired by Friends of Newport Back Bay's annual Back Bay Bash.

The 1978 Study Group

By early 1978 Signal recognized that there was growing opposition to its plans for Bolsa Chica in the surrounding community. The company proposed[3] the formation of a study group for the stated purpose of bringing all the interested parties together to exchange information and to reconcile any differences that existed as to how Bolsa Chica should be developed. The "interested parties" essentially consisted of every federal and state and local agency that had ever dealt with or would potentially deal with Bolsa Chica, plus the Amigos and any other organizations that the core members of the group approved of their joining. The group core members included the State Lands Commission, the Attorney General, Department of Fish and Game, and the Amigos. The first meeting of the group was held in April of 1978.

Signal hired the firm of EDAW Inc., a widely regarded environmental planning and design company, to come up with a set of alternative development plans for the study group to review. The plans generally were to fit around the basic design that had come out of the 1973 land trade agreement as well as other concepts that were proposed by the members of the group. As you recall, the 1973 plan provided for 530 acres for a public marina, open waterways and restored wetland and the balance of the property, about 900 acres of lowlands and 200 acres on the Bolsa Chica mesa, to be developed exempt from the Public Trust.

The EDAW staff sketched out about 20 plans for the group's consideration and comments. Most of the versions generally consisted of various modifications in the location, orientation, and other details of the marina, namely the inlet, Pacific Coast Highway, residential and commercial centers and so on. Members of the group were invited to submit plans, some of which departed from the 1973 model to various

---

3. Signal apparently did not want it to appear that the study group was their idea, so the company arranged for its attorney to contact the attorney general, who then initiated the first meeting of the group.

degrees. The Amigos presented a plan that consisted of no marina development and a totally restored wetland. Through a process of elimination, most of the plans were dropped and features of others were combined in even more iterations. Eventually EDAW was to present a report detailing the conclusions of the group. During this time, EDAW hired the engineering firm of Moffatt and Nichol to prepare a report on the design and cost aspects of the development of Bolsa Chica that would include some of the alternative plans submitted by members of the study group. Joining EDAW's efforts in the Bolsa Chica study was Williams-Kuebelbeck and Associates, who produced additional economic evaluations of the alternative plans.

While not a member of the study group, the California Coastal Commission, through staff members of the South Coast Regional Commission, had been monitoring the progress of the group. It became clear to the Coastal Commission by June of 1978 that the direction of the study group appeared to be headed toward planning a marina development in the wetland without consideration of the California Coastal Act or any other state and federal environmental regulations. Mel Carpenter, Executive Director of the Coastal Commission, in a letter to the group questioned the purpose of the group, since it was not following the usual planning guidelines required for a development in the coastal zone. If the group was in fact a planning body, to comply with state guidelines, the group must review a much wider range of alternative plans, including a no project alternative.

A couple of months after the study group was formed, the Amigos commented in a letter to the study group that the group's purpose was not, as initially claimed, just for exchanging information but appeared to be a planning body. Most discussions were steering toward Signal's original marina plan, wrote Jeff Fillbech, Amigos Vice President. In addition, discussions by Signal's consultants were heavily favoring the marina plan. The Amigos remained in the group for a few more months, but in January of 1979 the organization resigned from the study group. One month later, the Amigos filed a lawsuit against the state and Signal, aimed at the 1973 agreement. Since the state was a defendant in the Amigos' lawsuit, the state was compelled to order its agencies to drop out of the group and the effort, which had cost Signal over $200,000, rumbled to a halt. In examining the group's wreckage, Lindell Marsh, Signal's attorney, proposed that the study group failed primarily because it lacked a formal structure that would have committed members to stick it out to the end. A formalized structure was in fact introduced early in the process but apparently was rejected by the group.

In early 1979, the county board of supervisors attempted to resurrect the study group, calling it the Bolsa Chica Planning Task Force. Invitations to participate were sent out to all parties connected with Bolsa Chica, including the Amigos de Bolsa Chica, which had just filed the lawsuit over development in Bolsa Chica. In a June, 1979 letter to Supervisor Philip Anthony, Amigos president Dave Carlberg declined the invitation, expressing the organization's disappointment in the way the 1978 study group was steered toward the developer's plan while ignoring input from state and federal experts and community opinion. If the EDAW report that came out of the study group was to become the major resource document for the preparation of the upcoming Bolsa Chica Local Coastal Plan (LCP), Carlberg continued, the LCP would become a public document biased in favor of a private developer, subverting the LCP process.

Legal Action is Launched

Almost from the very beginning of the Amigos de Bolsa Chica, it was clear that the Signal marina juggernaut could not be stopped and the only real chance of achieving the goal of preserving all of the Bolsa Chica wetland was through legal action. To prepare for a lawsuit, research was initiated to collect information that would counter the state's contention that it was constitutionally free to trade away tidelands in the manner it did in Bolsa Chica in 1973. Beginning in August of 1976, Amigos attorney Gretchen Hoad began training members in doing title research. As documents, maps and other data were collected from libraries, governmental agencies, and private archives, another detail of the land trade began to emerge. It appeared that, based on the acreage it was supposed to hold title to in Bolsa Chica, the state had been short changed in the oil royalties that it was entitled to.

So in 1979, the Amigos de Bolsa Chica took on a major oil company, Signal Oil and Gas Company and affiliated companies, and several agencies of the state of California by filing a lawsuit against them. The major points of the lawsuit were the following:

1. In developing the residential parcels on the east edge of Bolsa Chica, Signal was filling tidelands in violation of Sections 3 and 4 of Article 10 of the California State Constitution, which establish a Public Trust over all state tidelands that existed as of 1879.

2. The 1973 Land Trade Agreement was void because it violated Sections 3 and 4 of Article 10 of the California State Constitution as well as Section 6 of Article 16 of the state constitution, which prohibits the state from giving away state property to private interests. That refers to the state relinquishing title to tidelands in Bolsa Chica over which the state held an interest.

3. Public Resources Code 6307, on which the 1973 agreement was based, was unconstitutional because it ignored the Public Trust Doctrine. Section 6307 contradicts the constitution by allowing tidelands to be conveyed to private interests without regard to the Public Trust.

4. The lawsuit requested a full accounting of the oil revenues due the state in view of the acreage for which the state held title.

Section 6307 allows tidelands to be traded away provided six conditions are met, many of which did not appear to be fulfilled in the 1973 land trade. For example, one condition reminiscent of the Newport Back Bay lawsuit, states that the monetary value of the land received by the state must be equal or exceed the value of the land passed to the private interest. The state received 327 acres versus about 600 acres of protected wetlands that the state conveyed to Signal. Was the land

143

trade equitable? There appears to be no easy answer. There is no widely accepted method to assess the *ecological* value of undeveloped land such as that in Bolsa Chica. When comparing the *market* value of the 327 acres the state acquired, which includes 1.25 miles of frontage on a major state highway, with the value of Signal's 600 acres, a different picture might emerge. However, the state never considered using the 1.25 miles of coastal property for anything other than a restored wetland. Does that change the picture?

It had not been determined exactly how many land trades involving tidelands like that of the 1973 Bolsa Chica agreement had been consummated by the state since Section 6307 had first been enacted in 1968. When queried, all state officials would say was, "too many to count." A rough estimate at the time of the filing of the Amigos' lawsuit put the number at nearly 200 but the total number of acres associated with the land trades is unknown.

In October of 1979 a Superior Court ruled in favor of Signal's contention that there was nothing constitutionally wrong with the 1973 agreement. Undeterred, the Amigos filed an appeal in 1980. Amigos' attorneys continued working on pretrial details such as answering attacks on technical aspects of the lawsuit, one of the most critical of which was the question of the timeliness of the lawsuit. It was claimed by the state, Signal and other defendants that the statute of limitations had expired for questioning the constitutionality of Section 6307 as it applied to the 1973 agreement. The Amigos claimed that statutes of limitations did not apply to questions of the Public Trust. An appellate court disagreed with the Amigos' position in 1983, stating that the statute of limitations for challenging the 1973 agreement ran out in 1977. The loss in the appeals court, however, left the door open for the Amigos to carry their appeal to the State Supreme Court. The Audubon Society, the Sierra Club, and the League for Coastal Protection then entered the case as "friends-of-the court."

In the mean time, the Amigos continued their public education programs with free tours of the Ecological Reserve and other outreach

8-2. In a demonstration of the width of the navigable channel proposed by Signal's marina plan, the Amigos de Bolsa Chica organized a "Hands Across the Sands" public display. About 600 people lined up between the banners that marked the beach area that would be lost. (Photo courtesy F. Scott Nickerson)

events. For example, in August of 1985, the Amigos organized "Hands Across the Sands," a public demonstration at which nearly 600 people lined up along Bolsa Chica State Beach, hand in hand, to show how much beach was to be taken up by a Marina del Rey-type opening for Signal's marina plan (Figure 8-2).

After four years of waiting, the Amigos was informed that the State Supreme Court decided not to hear the case and advised that the case be returned to the County Superior Court. Back to square one. In 1987 the Amigos refiled its case, which was followed almost immediately by a countersuit by Signal, claiming the Amigos' lawsuit was "frivolous and without merit." The countersuit was dismissed by the court, making it possible for the Amigos to continue its legal battle to preserve the Bolsa Chica wetland. Was the organization headed back to the courtroom?

9

The 1980s (continued)

The 1980s was a watershed decade for Bolsa Chica. Support was mounting for the total preservation and restoration of the wetland not only among private citizens but also from the local and state agencies that had jurisdiction over it. Even the State Lands Commission, which supported the 1973 agreement, was now opposing the marina development in Bolsa Chica. This was the decade of the Amigo's lawsuit battle that was filed in 1979 against Signal, other oil companies, and the State. And it was the decade of the Bolsa Chica Planning Coalition, an extraordinary alliance of all of the principal parties in the Bolsa Chica saga that represented a giant step toward total wetland preservation.

The Orange County Planning Process and the Coastal Commission

This might be a good time to consider the county's planning process as it applies to projects within the coastal zone.[1] As required by the

---

1. The Coastal Zone was defined in the Coastal Act of 1976 as that strip of land and water "extending seaward to the state's outer limit of jurisdiction, including all offshore islands, and extending inland generally 1,000 yards from the mean high tide line of the sea. In significant coastal estuarine, habitat, and recreational areas it extends inland to the first major ridgeline paralleling the sea or five miles from the mean high tide line of the sea, whichever is less, and in developed urban areas the zone generally extends inland less than 1,000 yards." To avoid bisecting individual parcels, the zone may vary considerably.

Coastal Act, all governmental bodies that have jurisdiction over development in the coastal zone must have in place a Local Coastal Program (LCP).[2] An LCP acts as a guideline to assure cities and counties in planning future developments in the Coastal Zone that the projects conform to the Coastal Act. A complete LCP actually consists of two documents, a Land Use Plan (LUP) and an Implementation Plan (IP). The purpose of an LUP is to define the nature of development in specified areas. The IP describes how the development in the LUP will be implemented by, for example, zone changes. Once an LCP is generated it must go to the California Coastal Commission for certification. When an LCP is certified, permitting authority for most development in the coastal zone is transferred to the local jurisdiction, which then is required to follow the LCP in its approval of projects. However, jurisdiction over projects within tidelands, submerged lands, and other Public Trust lands remains with the commission. Any changes in an LCP must go back to the commission in the form of an amendment for review and approval.

While the Coastal Act recommends reviews of LCPs every five years, there is no legislative power to enforce the provision. Our understanding of such issues as beach erosion, water quality, and the relationship between wetlands and uplands has changed drastically. Any oversights or errors in LCPs certified many years ago cannot be corrected unless a local jurisdiction volunteers to do so.

Since Bolsa Chica is in an unincorporated Orange County island,[3] its planning generally has been processed through the county, which is referred to as the "lead agency." Once an applicant submits a development plan for a specific project to the Orange County Environmental Management Agency (EMA), the preparation of a number of planning

---

2. As of 2007, 65 percent of the state's 74 cities and counties had a fully certified LCP, covering about 90 percent of the coast.

3. The City of Huntington Beach has annexed small, developed portions of the Bolsa Chica mesa and in 2008 it hired a consulting firm to study the feasibility of annexing all of Bolsa Chica. As of this writing, no decision had been made.

documents is begun, including an LUP. When an LUP is completed, the County Planning Commission then reviews it and if approved, it is sent to the Board of Supervisors. Once the supervisors give their blessings, the LUP is forwarded to the Coastal Commission. An IP may accompany the LUP, but it is not necessary. However, the LCP is not considered complete without an IP and one eventually must be submitted.

The completed LUP is subjected to a review by the coastal commission staff, which prepares a (often lengthy) report for the commission that includes a summary of the project, pertinent sections of the coastal act and other information that support the staff's recommendations for the commissioners as to whether the LUP should be certified, certified with modifications, or denied certification. The commission may accept all of the staff recommendations, some, or none. If modifications are attached to the certification, the project is returned to the county board of supervisors to approve the modifications. Once certification is completed, the applicant goes back to the county to prepare documents that lead to actual construction.

While ideally the planning process as described above normally follows a nice, linear path that ends with a shovel striking the earth, the path to Bolsa Chica was more like a spider web. The entangled events that marked Bolsa Chica's planning route started in 1973 with the boundary settlement, which was supposed to establish ownership in Bolsa Chica. This was followed in 1979 by the Amigos' lawsuit, which questioned that ownership. While the lawsuit froze the clearing of any titles to the property and hence actual construction, Signal continued working on the details of a development plan that essentially was based on the concept that came out of the 1973 Agreement. That is, the plan included about 500 acres of restored marsh, waterways and other water features while the balance of the property, about 900 acres, would be developed as a waterfront residential and commercial zone exempt from Public Trust regulations.

In 1980 Signal began offering a series of workshops at various locations in and around Huntington Beach to introduce the public to the company's development plans for Bolsa Chica. The county Environmental Management Agency followed with similar presentations.

SB 493

While the 1973 agreement was supposed to give Signal a certain degree of immunity from regulations under the Public Trust, the company still had the Coastal Act to answer to. Early in 1980 the Coastal Commission had designated the Bolsa Chica lowlands as wetlands, which set the stage for a battle over the Coastal Act's impact on wetland protection. Signal chose to avoid a direct battle. The company, through its lobbyist, John Knox, persuaded State Senator Paul Carpenter to submit a bill, Senate Bill 493, in June of 1981 that would remove the Coastal Commission's constitutional authority to certify Signal's Bolsa Chica plan and give it to the county. That is, whatever plan the county would authorize for Bolsa Chica would automatically be deemed to comply with the Coastal Act in the complete absence of any commission oversight. Signal's early feelings of insecurity were well summed up by a quote by its spokesperson, Wayne Clark, in the June 12, 1981 Orange County Register, "I think it's obvious that the coastal commission is of a mind to reject any county's local coastal program…" In addition, three months later, Stewart Case, Executive Secretary of Citizens for Ocean Access and Recreation,[4] is reported to have claimed he overheard a coastal commission staff member remark, "The Bolsa Chica will be developed over my dead body."

---

4. Citizens for Ocean Access and Recreation was one of many organizations supported by Signal to gather public backing for their plans in Bolsa Chica. A similar organization, Friends of Bolsa Chica Marina/Marshlands, appeared briefly in the spring of 1983, and another, Citizens for Bolsa Chica Marine Park, emerged in 1987, all promoting the virtues of Signal's marina plan. In 1980, the Orange County Coast Association weighed in with an alternative marina plan for Bolsa Chica that was designed by architect and yachtsman Bill Ficker.

For over a year SB 493 went through several amendments and in August of 1982 it was heard before the Assembly Energy and Natural Resources Committee. The hearing "was shaping up to be a showdown between the Coastal Commission and the Amigos de Bolsa Chica on one side, versus the major land owner Signal Landmark and Orange County on the other side," as Huntington Beach Independent writer Roger Bloom described it. The Amigos' intense lobbying efforts paid off and the bill was defeated in the committee by a vote of 6 to 4.

The Bolsa Chica LUP

When the county's Land Use Plan for Bolsa Chica went to the Board of Supervisors in December, 1981, the county planning commission had recommended increasing the restored wetland from 400 acres to 450 acres.[5] The board increased the size of the marsh to 600 acres, "if economically feasible." The supervisors approved the plan in January of 1982 and in April submitted it to the Coastal Commission. The plan envisioned 600 acres of open waterways and restored marsh, 3,200 residential units on the mesa and 2,500 units on 335 acres of lowlands, a 75 acre 1,800 slip public marina served by a 700 foot wide navigable ocean inlet, and 30 acres of commercial uses such as a neighborhood shopping center and two or more hotels and restaurants. The county also submitted two alternate plans spanning two possible development extremes: one consisting of total development in the lowland but preserving the original 300 acre ecological reserve fed by a non-navigable inlet, and a second alternative plan with only 110 acres of residential development in the lowland, 1100 acres of restored marsh and a non-navigable inlet.

The Costal Commission staff found eight areas in the county LUP that raised substantial issues, and the commission added one more concerning the treatment of archeological sites. Following extensive input from the public both in support and opposition to the plan, the

---

5. The 400 acre figure apparently came from the conceptual plan for the public benefit portion envisioned in the 1973 agreement.

commission voted to continue discussion of the LUP to its June, 1982 meeting.

Discussion of the Bolsa Chica LUP was continued from the commission's June meeting to July, then was scheduled for further consideration at its November session. One of the major flaws in Signal's plan that continued to vex the commission was the amount of wetland that the company was proposing to preserve. The Coastal Act is very clear concerning the protection of wetlands and the question before the commission was just how much wetlands was in Bolsa Chica. The county ignored the definition of wetland from the Coastal Act and instead invented its own. In the mean time, Signal's PR machine was hard at work attempting to sway public opinion in support of Signal's position on the amount of wetlands in Bolsa Chica. In July, Signal's PR representative, Wayne Clark, wrote in a letter to the editor of the local newspaper, the Huntington Beach Independent, "Bolsa Chica is not a wetland. It's a vacant lot with less environmental quality than… many other vacant lots in Huntington Beach."

But by early November, there was still no clear agreement between the commission staff and the county staff on three issues: public access to shoreline areas in the marina, flood and seismic safety standards, and how much wetland was to be preserved. The latter point was probably the most critical sticking point. Lacking an agreement, the commission had no choice but either to continue the item once again or simply deny the plan and allow the county to take its time resolving the various issues. County development director Bob Fisher explained to the commission that psychologically it would be better for the county to pull the plan from consideration rather than have it carry the stigma of being denied. Fisher asked to withdraw the document and the commission granted the request.

The Bolsa Chica Habitat Conservation Plan.

The standoff between the Coastal Commission and the County of Orange and Signal regarding the extent of wetlands in Bolsa Chica was attracting considerable attention in Sacramento, so much so that it was determined that some independent force had to break the logjam. As a result, the legislature passed and the governor signed Senate Bill 429 in 1983 that added Section 30237 to the Coastal Act.[6] Section 30237 authorized the Department of Fish and Game and the Coastal Conservancy[7] to prepare a Habitat Conservation Plan (HCP) for Bolsa Chica. The Conservancy's role was to prepare the HCP based on Fish and Game's determination of the extent of wetlands in Bolsa Chica. As SB 429 stipulated, either the county or the landowner formally had to request the preparation of the HCP. In October of 1984, the county submitted its petition for the preparation of the document.

The purpose of the HCP was simple: hammer out a solution for the dispute over how much wetland acreage was to be preserved in Bolsa Chica. The resolution of the question was far from simple. The Conservancy found itself trying to achieve three goals for a solution which would conform to the Coastal Act. The plan had to...

- satisfy the county's objective of providing public water-oriented recreational opportunities,
- preserve local community character, and
- ensure that the developer receive an adequate return on its investment.

The answer to the question that the HCP was to come up with had at its core the interpretation of Section 30411 of the Coastal Act. This section defines the exception to the rule that wetlands are not to be filled. The exception is that if the Department of Fish and Game finds

---

6. The section was repealed in 2004.

7. "The Legislature created the Coastal Conservancy [in 1976] as a unique entity with flexible powers to serve as an intermediary among government, citizens, and the private sector in recognition that creative approaches would be needed to preserve California's coast and San Francisco Bay lands for future generations. The Coastal Conservancy's non-regulatory, problem-solving approach complements the work of the Coastal Commission.. " From the Coastal Conservancy's website.

a particular wetland to be so severely degraded that it would require major restoration to fully function, funding for the restoration could come from the proceeds of a boating facility developed in an area of not more than 25 percent of the wetland. The remaining 75 percent could then be restored.

Fish and Game determined that 1000 acres of Signal's lowlands were severely degraded wetlands and required major restoration. Thus 250 acres (25 percent of 1000) could be developed into a marina and the remaining 750 were to be restored. Adding to the 750 were the 268 acres of wetlands out of the 300 acres of state owned lowland that were not severely degraded to arrive at a final total of 1018 acres of wetland to be restored in Bolsa Chica. In contrast, the county, using its own definition of degraded wetland, found only 842 degraded acres, which using the 25 percent rule, comes to 621 acres of wetlands that must be restored. And then Signal's own consultant found only 453 acres of degraded wetlands. The Conservancy disagreed with all of the above determinations and in spite of the mandate of SB 429 that required the use of Fish and Game's figures, the Conservancy argued that Fish and Game should have included the state's wetland acreage in calculating the amount of wetland to be restored, that is 1000+268 or 1268 x 75 percent or 951 acres. Was anything about Bolsa Chica ever simple?

And so in its final analysis the Conservancy proposed the restoration of 951 acres of wetlands while the county LUP called for 621. In other details regarding the wetlands, the preparers of the HCP, the Department of Fish and Game and the Coastal Conservancy, surprisingly, supported Signal's proposal to fill the Warner Pond ESHA[8] and to relocate the eucalyptus ESHA from the Bolsa Chica mesa to the Huntington Mesa. That is, "relocate" meant cutting down the trees on the Bolsa Chica mesa and replanting other trees in Harriett Wieder Regional Park on the Huntington Mesa. Both actions seemed to be contrary to the Coastal Act. While the Department of Fish and

---

8. Environmentally Sensitive Habitat Area, an zone that has unique or special ecological value and is afforded extra protection due to its vulnerability to harm by human activities.

Game's report that accompanied the HCP agreed to the destruction of the two ESHAs, it questioned the feasibility of adequately mitigating the loss of the ESHAs as well as some other plant communities that were destined for destruction. The department also expressed doubts whether many of the assumptions regarding the phasing out of oil activities and other details of the restoration were doable. In spite of Fish and Game's cautionary appraisal of the HCP, the department joined the Conservancy staff in supporting the general concept of a marina and a navigable inlet as described in the HCP. The Conservancy staff enthusiastically referred to the marina as becoming a possible "world class harbor." The HCP did include some changes to Signal's original plan. To accommodate the increase in the required wetland acreage to be restored, the HCP recommended reducing the marina commercial and residential areas by 126 acres and cutting the public marina by 800 slips.

One of the key features of the Bolsa Chica plan was the relocation of Pacific Coast Highway around the development. That, it was argued, would avoid the cost of a high bridge over the navigable inlet. Such a bridge would be necessary to accommodate the passage of large sailboats in and out of the marina. The realignment of the highway sparked a loud reaction from nearby residents, some of whom lived within 175 feet of the new highway alignment. An organization known as Citizens Against the Rerouting of Pacific Coast Highway (CARP) had formed to protest the plan. A reported 300 residents appeared at the August 6, 1984 Huntington Beach City Council meeting to protest, and the council responded by issuing a resolution opposing the rerouting.

The LUP was resubmitted to the Coastal Commission in November of 1984 with the HCP attached. The commission certified the LUP but with modifications, citing numerous inadequacies in both the LUP and the HCP. The major concern on this occasion was the question of whether the navigable inlet was "the least environmentally damaging feasible alternative" in achieving the restoration of the wetland. The

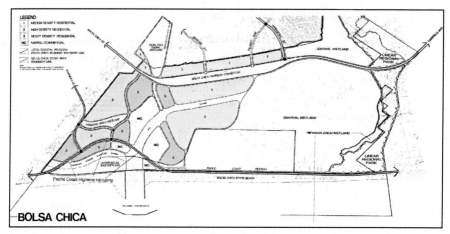

9-1. Signal's Marina Plan consisting of a navigable ocean inlet, a public marina, 1000 acres of waterways and restored wetland surrounded by a mix of medium to heavy density residential units. (Map courtesy County of Orange)

determination of the inlet's feasibility was still under study by the Army Corps of Engineers and was not yet complete. The county responded that there was no other alternative.

In the mean time, the Amigos' intense efforts to steer development of Bolsa Chica to a totally restored wetland attracted the attention of the Sea and Sage chapter of the National Audubon Society. The highly regarded organization awarded the Amigos its 1985 Conservation Award, which it shared with the Bolsa Chica Land Trust.

The county eventually accepted the commission's modifications and the LUP, known as the "Marina Plan," was certified in January of 1986 (Figure 9-1). The plan consisted of fewer boat slips (1,300 compared to 1,800) but more than what the HCP recommended. The LUP also included dry storage for 400 boats and more public facilities such as launching ramps and public parking were added. Visitor serving facilities included a motel, seven restaurants and 85,000 square feet of retail space. The longer rerouting of Pacific Coast Highway was eliminated and replaced by a shorter detour that took advantage of the elevation of the Bolsa Chica Mesa's lower bench, thus reducing the cost of a bridge. One of the more controversial features of the plan was the so-called Bolsa Chica-Garfield or Cross-Gap Connector, which consisted of extensions of Bolsa Chica Street and Garfield Avenue that would loop across the lowlands and connect. The amount of wetland acreage that the wide right-of-way would destroy was the major point of opposition to the connector road. The Marina Plan included the restoration of 915 acres of wetlands and a 600 foot wide navigable inlet which the state had agreed to construct by 1987[9], according to the 1973 boundary agreement.

On at least two occasions during the period Signal was attempting to get its Bolsa Chica LUP certified by the Coastal Commission, once in 1984 and again in 1985, Signal Senior VP William R. Allen responded to the commission's action with a threat of legal action against the commission, claiming that the 1973 agreement had given Signal immunity toward any further compliance with the Coastal Act, that the commission's action was a breach of the 1973 agreement that the state had signed, and the commission had violated Signal's civil rights. Signal was not going to relinquish any more acres of designated wetlands in spite of the HCP claim of the presence of 951 acres. But eventually Signal agreed to the preservation of at least 1000 acres of wetlands and other concessions. It was said at the time that the inclusion of the additional public, coastal dependent facilities in the marina was what clinched the certification in 1986.

In spite of the improved opportunities for public use of the marina, local citizens began expressing increasing opposition to the plan. Their concerns were particularly aimed at the navigable inlet, citing its potential negative environmental impacts as well as the question of funding. At a county-sponsored public forum on development plans in Bolsa Chica, environmentalists and boating interests voiced such opposing positions over the ocean inlet that Supervisor Harriett Wieder, whose district included Bolsa Chica, decided to conduct a mail survey of her constituents. She discovered that 42 percent of those responding to the poll opposed the navigable inlet outright, but another 42 percent

---

9. The deadline was given a 3 year extension to 1990,

were in favor of the inlet provided it didn't cost them anything. With that sense of a significant division among the local residents, Supervisor Wieder spoke out in opposition to the inlet. The inlet was a critical piece Signal's development plans for its principally water-oriented Bolsa Chica project. It seemed the first crack in Signal's marina plans for Bolsa Chica was beginning to open. Recognizing the sea of conflicting views as to how Bolsa Chica should be developed, in 1988 Supervisor Wieder proposed the formation of an alliance of interested parties that was to come up with a compromise plan that would give all sides something to go home with. The group was called the Bolsa Chica Planning Coalition and its final product was to be known as the Bolsa Chica Coalition Concept Plan. It is discussed later in this chapter.

Wetlands as a Four-Letter Word

Toward the end of the 1980s, fallout from Signal's tussle with the Coastal Commission over the extent of wetlands in Bolsa Chica had reached political and civic circles throughout the county. And with the Amigos in the spotlight as the instigator of the battle, it wasn't altogether surprising that when the organization submitted its application to participate in the 1987 Huntington Beach Fourth of July Parade, it was turned down because a banner on their float read, "Bolsa Chica *Wetlands*." The word was just too political.

SB 1517

By 1987 it was probably becoming clear to Signal that the cost of its ambitious marina plan was growing out of sight. Contributing to the concern was the fact there was increasing hesitation on the part of the state to fund the navigable channel, a key feature of the 1973 agreement and the certified Marina Plan. Signal approached State Senator Marian Bergeson, requesting that she sponsor a bill that would establish a special district covering Bolsa Chica. A special district could issue its own bonds, assess landowners, collect taxes, and use the funds to pay for the inlet and the marina's infrastructure. The Senate Bill 1517 attracted a firestorm of opposition from a number of directions, including the County of Orange, the City of Huntington Beach, the Amigos, and individual citizens.

In a February 1988 city council hearing, a standing room only audience heard more than 50 speakers voice opposition to Senator Bergeson's bill. City officials expressed concern that the special district would have such wide-ranging powers that it would overlap and conflict with the jurisdictions of many local agencies. Also, the financial indebtedness of the residents in the district under SB1517 would be substantial. In addition, there was uncertainty as to what effect the special district would have on the funding of the wetland restoration. It appeared that the bill was requested entirely out of "real fear [of failure] or paranoia" (as one internal city memo put it) and was designed strictly for the benefit of Signal. To elicit citizen support for the bill, Signal launched a letter writing campaign, organized by Signal publicist Wayne Clark under the guise of a paper organization called "Citizens for Bolsa Chica Marine Park." But sensing the widespread opposition to the bill, Senator Bergeson eventually pulled the measure from consideration.

Signal did not give up on its hopes of using a special district to fund some of its obligations. In its development agreement with the county, the company included a statement, "Upon the request of [Signal], parties [Signal and county] shall cooperate in exploring the use of financing districts for financing [Signal's] obligation for public improvements, land acquisitions, features and services."

The Coalition

By the mid 1980s, many who were involved with Bolsa Chica were getting pretty weary of it, not the least of which were the people at Signal. They had the Amigo's lawsuit occupying their attention, their LUP had problems getting past the coastal commission, other governmental agencies were showing increasing hostility toward the marina plan, funding of the implementation of the plan was becoming more and more of an uncertainty, and to top it off, Shell Western E & P, the holder of the oil lease in Bolsa Chica from 1984-1986, was planning to spend something around $50 million on upgrading its wells. Concerned that a marina immediately adjacent to its oil operations might lead to flooding of its wells, the oil company was not about to offer its blessings to Signal's marina plan.[10] So Signal found itself desperately looking for a solution for Bolsa Chica that would satisfy the many factions that had interests in the wetland, the various governmental agencies, the community, the oil company, and Signal's 28,000 stockholders. In 1988 a call once again came to those organizations and agencies involved with Bolsa Chica to form a group for the purpose of resolving the question, "what to do with Bolsa Chica?" Forming a group to discuss Bolsa Chica certainly was not a new idea; Bolsa Chica study groups and tasks forces had been meeting off and on since the 1970s. But this one seemed to carry a promise of success. What made this so special?

So on Monday afternoon, November 21, 1988 representatives of the Amigos entered yet one more meeting room to join yet one more group to find answers for the fate of the Bolsa Chica wetland. This time the group was called the Bolsa Chica Planning Coalition.

County Supervisor Harriett Wieder, together with Huntington Beach Mayor John Erskine, was the originator of the idea for the Bolsa Chica Planning Coalition. The coalition principal members were the Amigos, represented by President Shirley Dettloff and Executive Director Adrianne Morrison, Signal, the State Lands Commission, Orange County, and the city of Huntington Beach. Interest in the proceedings of the Coalition rapidly grew and attendance often approached 50, including more than a dozen key support members such as the EPA, the California Coastal Commission, state Department of Fish and Game, the Coastal Conservancy, U. S. Fish and

10. Apparently the oil lease gave the oil company certain rights over what took place in Bolsa Chica if it encroached on the company's ability to produce oil.

Wildlife Service, Army Corps of Engineers, and at least two civic organizations, CARP and the Sunset Beach LCP Citizens Advisory Committee. Representatives from the ports of Los Angeles and Long Beach, Sea and Sage Audubon Society, the Sierra Club, local newspapers, and several individual citizen observers often attended coalition meetings as well.

Signal Landmark Senior VP Jeff Holm recalls that Paul Cook, then Huntington Beach's city administrator, suggested a plan that the coalition eventually adopted. Cook called Holm in early 1987 to offer advice as to how to get the Bolsa Chica project out of its rut. Cook suggested that Signal confine its residential development to behind the Cross Gap Connector and offer the rest of the lowland for restoration. In other words, get the Amigos and the rest of the opposition off Signal's back by eliminating the marina, the commercial development, the navigable inlet, and all the accompanying complications and headaches. Cook's plan was essentially one of the alternative designs in Signal's 1981 LUP. Holm agreed to offer the plan to the coalition as an alternative to the marina plan.

The Facilitator

If history were to repeat itself, the coming together of several factions with as dissimilar goals as those involved with Bolsa Chica was bound to collapse without someone holding the joints together. The group needed a facilitator. Even before the group got to the heart of its work, choosing a facilitator could have been contentious, but a facilitator selection subcommittee agreed to let the Amigos choose the person for that job. The person selected to fill the position was Joe Bodovitz. Bodovitz was well known among coastal protection activists and was an ideal choice. A former San Francisco newspaper writer with an intimate knowledge of environmental law and state politics, he was the first executive director of the San Francisco Bay Conservation and Development Commission (BCDC), the first executive director of the California Coastal Commission, executive director of the California

161

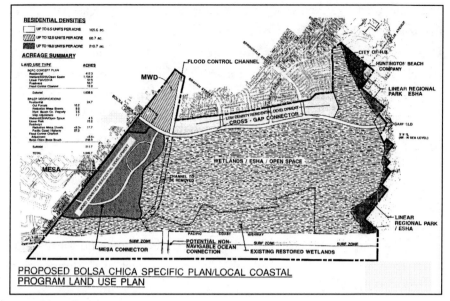

RESIDENTIAL DENSITIES

UP TO 6.5 UNITS PER ACRE   165.6 ac.
UP TO 12.5 UNITS PER ACRE   60.7 ac.
UP TO 18.0 UNITS PER ACRE   210.7 ac.

ACREAGE SUMMARY

PROPOSED BOLSA CHICA SPECIFIC PLAN/LOCAL COASTAL
PROGRAM LAND USE PLAN

9-2. The Coalition Concept Plan. Development would be limited in the lowlands to 185 acres of low density residential units and about 200 acres of mixed residential units on the Bolsa Chica Mesa. The balance of the lowlands would be restored. (Map courtesy County of Orange)

Public Utilities Commission and later, president of the California Environmental Trust. In spite of his environmental background, Bodovitz was lauded for his evenhandedness in dealing with the extreme opposite positions that the coalition principals would initially bring to the table. He would call members between meetings and pick their brains. When the next meeting took place, he pretty much knew what members were thinking and was prepared in advance to deal with conflicts as they came up.

The Coalition Concept Plan

In six short months, after reviewing at least four alternative plans for Bolsa Chica, the coalition produced a compromise for Bolsa Chica in May of 1989 that both sides came to accept (Figure 9-2). In the plan, Signal agreed to a major concession: eliminate its marina plan, including a navigable inlet and the extensive residential and commer-

162

cial development. Although it had pushed for total restoration of the lowlands, the Amigos conceded a strip of low density residential development along the back side of the lowlands, adjacent to previously developed land, amounting to 185 acres on which up to 900 houses were planned. It was recognized at the time that the property contained about 120 acres of designated wetlands, but the Amigos was willing to compromise on that point (and accept the criticism) in exchange for Signal's significant concessions. Besides, Signal still had the Coastal Commission and the Army Corps of Engineers[11] to approve the filling of those wetlands,[12] a gamble that the Amigos was confident would pay off in the end.

The Coalition Concept Plan was never intended to be formally submitted to the Coastal Commission. It was considered a broadbrush, some say vague, concept. But the commission staff, having attended the coalition meetings, was able to brief the commission of the nature of the plan. The staff made it very clear in a public report that the plan was inconsistent with the Coastal Act due primarily to the filling of the 120 acres of wetlands.

With the Coalition Concept Plan as written, the Amigos' long standing mission of preserving all of the Bolsa Chica wetlands seemed to some to have failed. The Amigos had agreed to allow the filling of about 120 acres of wetlands in exchange for the elimination of the marina plan and the preservation of over 1000 acres of wetlands. In the Amigos' eyes, considering what Signal gave up, the coalition plan

---

11. The Army Corps of Engineers has the responsibility of enforcing Title 33, Chapter 26, Subchapter IV, Section 1344 of the U. S. Code that regulates the filling of wetlands. The original legislation appeared in the Clean Water Act as Section 404 when congress passed the Act in 1972 and hence the document needed to allow the filling of wetlands is referred to as a 404 permit.

12. It appears unlikely that Signal would have secured a 404 permit for filling the wetlands in the 185 acre parcel. A possible sign as to the Corp's position on the issue came from a comment from the Bolsa Chica Project Engineer for the Corps, who was quoted in 1993 as saying "houses don't belong in wetlands." However, had Signal been successful in getting a 404 permit, although rarely used, the EPA does have veto power over Corps issuance of such permits.

was still a major victory. And the Coastal Commission and the Corps of Engineers had not yet spoken. With much fanfare, the Coalition Concept Plan was released to the public in the Fall of 1989. Signal paid for a full page ad in several newspapers announcing in two inch letters how a developer and an environmental group had been able to work together for a common goal. The Coalition Plan not only occupied lots of local newsprint, it attracted attention in Washington. In a 1993 study commissioned by the President's Council on Environmental Quality, two projects were singled out as examples of successful private/public partnerships, the Irvine Co. Open Space Reserve Plan and the Bolsa Chica Coalition Plan.

Years of conflict over the future of Bolsa Chica seemed to have been washed away with a single document. Initially both pro-development and environmental interests praised the plan...until the Coalition Plan's details (or lack of them) were more carefully scrutinized.

The Bolsa Chica Conservancy

The Bolsa Chica Conservancy was established in 1990 as part of the Coalition Agreement. To launch the organization, Signal provided $25,000 as startup funds. Its founding executive director was Dr. Victor Leipzig. Included in its functions is the operation of an interpretive center at the corner of Pacific Coast Highway and Warner Avenue. The center is considered a temporary facility until a permanent one is built somewhere in Bolsa Chica. The center contains a number of public educational displays explaining coastal wetlands ecology and history. Other functions of the Conservancy are conducting public tours of the wetland, scientific investigations of various aspects of the wetland ecology, and restoration projects.

The Lawsuit Settlement

In spite of one defeat after another, the Amigos persevered on the legal front for ten years, appealing every loss and re-filing when necessary. With the coastal commission certifying Signal's Bolsa Chica

Marina Plan LUP in 1986, the developer had one more bit of business to iron out in order to clear title to its property and move forward with its project. In 1989, Lucy Dunn, a Signal vice-president and general counsel, contacted Lynda Martyn, the attorney handling the Amigo's lawsuit and asked if a meeting could be arranged in San Francisco, where Martyn's office was located. Martyn agreed and after several discussions during lunches and strolls along San Francisco's bustling streets, the two consented to enter into mediation that would help put together details of a settlement of the Amigos' lawsuit. Martyn was hesitant at first, preferring to see the lawsuit through the courts.[13] If the Amigos' lawsuit had been successful, it would have had immense impact on the many boundary settlements involving wetlands in which the state was involved in the past and the ones contemplated in the future. Up to that point, the core of the Amigos' lawsuit had never been heard in court. But a settlement through mediation, Dunn argued, would leave both sides with something they sought in a relatively short time, whereas once litigation got to the trial phase, court decisions and the inevitable appeals could take another ten years to unfold and ultimately the process would leave behind one winner and one loser. Besides, a much trimmed down development plan, which was very close to the Amigos' goals, was being considered at that moment by the Bolsa Chica Planning Coalition. Martyn eventually agreed to mediation. It took two marathon sessions to forge the details of a settlement, and in May of 1989 Martyn wrote to Signal's attorneys to offer a settlement, to which Signal agreed. The Amigos board of directors debated details of the settlement for several months and the board gave its final approval in September of 1989.

In the ten years that the Amigos pursued its lawsuits, legal costs amounted to well into six figures. Besides its educational program, fund raising to support the lawsuits became the Amigos' major activity. The two chief fund raising events the organization depended on for

---

13. State Deputy Attorney General Greg Taylor, who was representing the various state codefendants, also was opposed to a settlement.

legal funds were the Bolsa Bash and the "Running is for the Birds" 10K run. Typically a Saturday night bash would raise, say, $5000 and Sunday morning the Amigos treasurer would write out a check for $5000 and mail it to the Amigos' attorneys, an amount, by the way, that fell far short of what was actually owed. Fortunately the Amigos attorneys agreed to proceed with the lawsuits in spite of the organization's inability to keep up with its legal costs. As part of the settlement, Signal agreed to cover the Amigos' ten years of legal expenses.

The Coalition Backlash

By signing the Coalition Concept Plan, the Amigos agreed to stay out of the planning process for Bolsa Chica as long as residential densities remained as agreed upon in the plan. The Plan was to stay in force as long as Signal was able to acquire all of the required permits. Signal thus had hoped to neutralize the Amigos as the company turned its attention to developing the 185 acres of lowland and the 200 acres on the Bolsa Chica Mesa.[14] Over the years the Amigos had concentrated its energies on preserving the wetland while regarding the mesa as important but secondary to its primary mission. The Amigos thoroughly understood the mesa's role in the overall health of the Bolsa Chica ecosystem.[15] In spite of the restrictions in the coalition agreement, the Amigos protested features of the mesa development that would have had a negative impact on the wetlands, such as urban drainage into the wetlands, lack of protection of ESHAs on the lower mesa, or inadequate buffers along the mesa edge. Such action got the Amigos into legal hot water, which will be covered in the next chapter.

---

14. Signal briefly began referring to the Bolsa Chica Mesa as "Warner Mesa" in the late 90s, but apparently the name did not stick.

15. The Amigos stated mission, proclaimed in 1976, was: "...to advocate the preservation, restoration, and maintenance of the Bolsa Chica, to encourage the public acquisition of all the wetlands and sufficient surrounding open space to create a viable ecosystem, and to provide education about the importance of wetlands."

That under the Coalition Plan the Amigos agreed to residential development in 185 acres of the lowland did not go down well for some activists in the community, many of whom were long-time Amigos members. And then word leaked to the press that Signal, as part of the lawsuit settlement, had agreed to cover the Amigos' 10 years of legal expenses, not unusual action in similar situations and considered a win for the organization. Long standing friends quickly turned into adversaries. Epithets such as "traitors," "sell-outs," "charlatans," and "pay-off" began to appear in quotes in the local media and in the newsletters of environmental organizations, and more than one prominent newspaper editorial referred to the Amigos as "Amigos de Koll."[16]

Dissension in the environmental community against the Amigos rose to a peak at the January, 1996 Coastal Commission hearing on Signal's Land Use Plan (To be covered in the next chapter). The Amigos had been asked by other activist organizations whether the Amigos was going to oppose Signal's plans for the development of the Bolsa Chica Mesa. The Amigos, still flush with what was generally considered a victory, wanted to express its support for the Coalition Plan that resulted in the preservation of over 90 percent of the lowlands. On the day of the coastal commission hearing for Signal's mesa development, it was standing room only. Seeing over 100 speakers' slips, the chairman announced that to simplify matters, all those wishing to speak in favor of the project were to line up on the right side of the room, all those opposing the plan line up on the left side. The Amigos couldn't oppose a plan they had signed, so they found themselves uneasily standing in the "support" line with Signal lobbyists and pro-development advocates in three-piece suits. That was more than opponents to the plan could bear. At the conclusion of the eight hour hearing, as the Amigos members were passing through the Crowne

---

16. Named after Koll Real Estate Group, who had become manager of Signal's operations in Bolsa Chica.

Plaza hotel lobby, they were pelted with jeers and catcalls in what could only be described as running a gauntlet.

10

EIRs, EISs, LCPs, IPs, Etc

The decade of the 90s was a curious time for Bolsa Chica in that two mutually exclusive but parallel pathways were being followed simultaneously. One trail was Signal's push to see its much scaled-back, coalition-inspired plan through the permit process and the commencement of construction. The other path was the efforts of the Amigos and others to secure the preservation of the entire Bolsa Chica wetlands by urging the ports of Los Angeles and Long Beach to fund the purchase and restoration of the property. Since both Signal's development plans for Bolsa Chica and the state's design for the wetland's restoration would offer significant environmental impacts, both the California Environmental Quality Act and California's Coastal Act would be coming into play regardless of which pathway was followed.

The Environmental Impact Report

In addition to the requirement that development projects within the coastal zone must satisfy requirements of the Coastal Act through the LCP process, all projects regardless of location also must follow the California Environmental Quality Act (CEQA). Among other CEQA requirements, if a project appears to present a potential, significant impact on the environment, that usually requires the preparation of an

Environmental Impact Report (EIR). If the impact appears negligible, a Negative Declaration (ND) is usually sufficient. The preparation of a Mitigated ND may be acceptable if a project's negative impacts are limited and can be easily mitigated to an insignificant level. The decision whether a full EIR or an ND is needed is usually determined within the staff of the lead agency.

EIRs serve a number of purposes. They...

- force a closer examination of a project's impact and alternative plans on its surrounding environment
- reveal serious impacts that may not be evident otherwise
- identify ways of mitigating significant impacts
- provide permitting agencies an important decision-making tool
- provide the public detailed information about a project
- provide the public assurances that the environmental impact of a project will have been minimized

What EIRs don't do is...

- argue for or against a project
- analyze possible legal issues related to the project
- compare economic advantages or disadvantages of a project

For complex projects such as the Bolsa Chica Marina Plan or the Bolsa Chica Wetland Restoration, an EIR can be quite lengthy, amounting to thousands of pages divided into several individual volumes. Besides one or more volumes describing the project, its impact, and proposed mitigation measures, accompanying volumes usually contain background technical information often prepared by consultants hired by the preparer. On information supplied by the applicant, the lead agency initiates the preparation of a draft EIR (DEIR). DEIRs can be written by the lead agency's own staff, by another public agency, by a private contractor, by the applicant, or by a team consisting of two or more of these parties. In all cases, the cost of the preparation of an EIR is paid by the applicant. Since the preparation of a DEIR for a major project can be highly labor intensive, it is common to have it done by a private firm that specializes in that work. It is usually contractually agreed among the key principals in the project, the applicant, the lead agency, and the preparer of the EIR, how much each party will be involved in the preparation of the document. Frequent consultation with other agencies is usually required throughout the EIR preparation process if the project affects their jurisdictions such as, for example, the Department of Fish and Game or the county flood control district. Regardless of who prepares the DEIR, in the end the lead agency is responsible for the report's objectivity, adequacy, and accuracy and the agency must be prepared to defend the document before the appropriate governing bodies.[1]

A typical DEIR must examine every conceivable impact a project might have on the surrounding environment, including natural resources, traffic, air and water quality, and infrastructure to name just a few. Not only is the environmental impact of the completed project under scrutiny, so is the impact of its construction phase. Information needed for the EIR may be gathered from the applicant, previous EIRs, experts in the various areas that potentially would be affected by the project such as geology or wildlife, other public agencies, the public, the scientific literature, and other credible sources.

All information is organized in an EIR in a very predetermined format. In addition to an assessment of the preferred plan for a project, an EIR must examine alternate plans to determine if there might be other feasible approaches to the project that would cause a lesser impact on the environment than the preferred plan. A "no project" alternative is also included. For each aspect of the project that causes a significant

---

1. This aspect of the process often annoys some members of the public, who wonder why a public agency is standing up before a governing body apparently defending a private developer's project.

negative impact on the environment, mitigating measures must be identified that lessen the impact to insignificance. Since some adverse environmental impacts may be considered unavoidable and unmitigatable, the document must show that any such environmental impacts are outweighed by specific economic, legal, social, technological or other benefits. The explanations for claiming such benefits are known as "Statements of Overriding Considerations"

Once a DEIR is completed, it must be circulated for a certain interval of time for review by other agencies and the public. All comments and questions that are submitted must be responded to, usually in an addendum or a separate volume of the final EIR. While the examination of impacts need not be exhaustive, if comments reveal major questions or omissions of issues that were overlooked in the DEIR, or new information is made available that makes a significant change in the EIR, the document must undergo revisions, after which the draft is recirculated for additional review. Only after all these steps are completed can the EIR be considered final. The final EIR is then forwarded to the appropriate body for approval such as a planning commission, city council or county board of supervisors.

Should a project involve the federal government in some way such as being carried out or funded all or in part by Washington, requiring federal permits or being located on federal government property, an Environmental Impact Statement (EIS) also may be required. The intent, format, and content of an EIS are essentially the same as for an EIR and thus the two documents can usually be combined into one document provided the appropriate federal agency approves the merger. When a project involves a federal agency or is funded by a federal agency, such as the Bolsa Chica wetland restoration, the Coastal Commission may require a review of the project to determine if the project is consistent with the Coastal Act. The process may be a "Consistency Determination" in the case of purely federal projects, or a "Consistency Certification" if a federal project is being carried out by a non-federal entity.

The Bolsa Chica EIR(s)

The first Bolsa Chica EIR was prepared in 1980 for the county by the firm Phillips Brandt Reddick, Inc. The DEIR addressed three alternative plans for Bolsa Chica. One plan depicted medium to high density residential development on the Bolsa Chica mesa and on 110 acres along the northeast portion of the lowland. The balance of the lowland, some 1100 acres, would be set aside for wetland restoration. The second plan envisioned maximum residential and commercial development over the mesa and lowland with only 300 acres of restored wetland. The third alternative plan was the general layout for the so-called Marina Plan LUP that was ultimately approved by the Coastal Commission in 1986. It consisted of 5700 mostly water oriented residential units, and 530 acres of public land that would include a navigable ocean inlet and other waterways, a public marina and about 330 acres of restored wetland.

Signal's Marina Plan had encountered difficulties in getting past the Coastal Commission through the 1980s and was replaced in concept by the 1989 Coalition Plan. In 1990, since it looked like Huntington Beach would soon annex Bolsa Chica, Signal agreed to let the city of Huntington Beach be the lead agency in the preparation of a new EIR/EIS[2] following the lines of the Coalition Plan. The resulting DEIR received a barrage of negative reviews from a number of community organizations, individuals, and the county. Most disapproval was directed at the residential densities proposed and their impact on city services, noise, and air pollution. The filling of wetlands to accommodate residential construction in the lowlands and the loss of ESHAs on the mesas caught the eye of many reviewers. In a memo to the city, county Coast Section Planning Chief Ron Tippets submitted 17 pages of comments and corrections covering nearly every section of the DEIR. The city released another draft of the DEIR in 1992, which again failed to satisfy many local activist organizations and apparently,

---

2. An EIS was required because at the time the Army Corps of Engineers was to construct the ocean inlet.

Signal. Signal appeared to have lost patience with Huntington Beach and in 1993 broke its agreement with the city and in a highly controversial move, transferred its development applications to the county.

Opinions abounded regarding Signal's motivation for bailing out of the city as its lead agency. The official reason coming from Signal was that the city had at least one major project on its agenda (Seacliff IV) and did not appear to have the time to devote to a project as complex as Bolsa Chica. In addition, the county had more experience than the city in dealing with wetlands, having been working on restoration plans at Bolsa Chica and Upper Newport Bay, and was involved in planning Wieder Regional Park on the Huntington Mesa bluff top. Members of the city staff had a different view, which Signal Vice President Lucy Dunn denied: the Huntington Beach city council had recently changed from a pro-development majority to a slow growth one[3] and thus the chances that Signal's Bolsa Chica development plan would get past the city council were considered slim. In late December,1992, the year before the switch, Signal Vice President Dunn was quoted as saying, "...we have always planned on working with the city, and we look forward to dealing with the City Council." She was further quoted that her company had the option of going to the county if negotiations with Huntington Beach fell apart, but she said that prospect was unlikely, that all of the council members are fair and open minded on the Bolsa Chica issue. Orange County Chief Planner Tippets opined that the reason the company's plan would not be approved by the city was due to turf wars within the Huntington Beach planning department. Regardless of the reason(s) for the switch, it generated additional animosity toward Signal, for it was stipulated in the Coalition Agreement that Signal would process its development through the city. The city urged Signal and the county to reverse their decision, but neither would yield. The Amigos, who had carefully

---

3. The election of Vic Leipzig and Dave Sullivan to the Huntington Beach city council in the November, 1992, election shifted the council to a slow growth majority that consisted of the two plus Ralph Bauer, Linda Moulton-Patterson, and Grace Winchell.

followed the Coalition Agreement up to that point, began to question whether the agreement was still a valid document.

Now that the Bolsa Chica project was its responsibility, the county turned to prepare yet another EIR. The new DEIR was released for comment in December of 1993. The project proposed in this EIR, like the city's earlier versions, was generally patterned after the Coalition Plan. It was to include a total of 3410 residential units on the 200 acres of the Bolsa Chica mesa and 876 units on the approximately 185 acre lowland parcel adjacent to the existing residential development. Also envisioned in the plan was the establishment of a 1106 acre wetland ecosystem consisting of the restoration of 620 acres of existing wetlands. To mitigate the filling of wetlands in the lowlands, the EIR proposed the creation of 99 acres of new wetlands in Bolsa Chica plus 129 acres of new wetlands to be established off site. In addition, 102 acres of Environmentally Sensitive Habitat Areas (ESHAs), buffers and other forms of open space were included in the plan.

The 1996 LCP

In 1996 Signal submitted an LCP amendment for Bolsa Chica to the Coastal Commission that followed the general design of the preferred plan in the 1993 EIR with some modifications. The 1996 LCP, patterned after the Coalition Plan, had been endorsed by the county board of supervisors and was forwarded to the Coastal Commission. In its report to the commission, the commission staff pointed out that in spite of the fact the new plan was drastically different compared with the previously certified 1986 Marina Plan, it was not much of an improvement and certification of the new plan should be denied. Signal argued that the 1996 LCP was not new, but merely a derivative of the 1986 plan. The 1996 LCP "builds on and reflects the key elements of one of the two land use alternatives defined in the certified 1986 LUP," the company explained.

The 1996 LCP proposed setting aside 1,098 acres of wetlands, ESHAs, and buffers, placing 2400 homes on about 200 acres of the

Bolsa Chica mesa and up to 900 homes on the 185 acres of lowlands, 120 acres of which were designated as wetlands. As in the Marina Plan, the company depended on parts of Sections 30233 and 30411 of the Coastal Act that allows building in wetlands if they are so severely degraded that major restoration is needed. Then no more than 25 percent of the seriously degraded wetland may be developed into a "boating facility" provided the remaining acreage is restored. By building and selling 900 homes on the lowlands, Signal projected it would be able to set aside about $41 million toward the cost of the restoration of the wetlands. Added to that Signal offered about $7 million that would have derived from sales of homes on the mesa. Signal pointed out that there was no other source of funding for a wetland restoration if no boating facility was included; it was the only game in town, the company insisted. But the plan they were proposing did not include a boating facility. But yes, Signal argued, the 1996 LCP "…continues to include a boating facility, but a far more environmentally sensitive and non-disruptive kayaking boating facility."

The Coastal Commission staff had known even before Signal had submitted its LCP amendment that the company intended to build on some wetlands. The staff in its report to the commission emphasized that the Coastal Act did not allow wetlands to be filled just to build houses on them, a kayaking dock notwithstanding. The staff previously had warned Signal for that reason alone it was unlikely the LCP would be approved. And Signal was quite aware of the existence of the wetlands. The EPA had noted in 1989 that about 100 acres of wetlands were scattered in the general area in which Signal planed to build houses, and in 1994 Signal's own consultant delineated nearly 90 acres in the same area.

In addition, the LCP proposed that in order to support the increase in traffic that would be generated by the density of development on the mesa, Warner Avenue would have to be widened, necessitating the filling of Warner Pond, a designated ESHA. The destruction of ESHAs is forbidden by the coastal act. However, in spite of these obvious deficiencies plus others, which prompted the staff to recommend denial, the majority (8 to 3)[4] of the commission rejected the staff advice and certified the document.

The Bolsa Chica Land Trust

The Bolsa Chica Land Trust (BCLT) was formed in 1992 to advocate the preservation of all of Bolsa Chica, lowlands and uplands. Many of the founders of the BCLT were Amigos members who had become dissatisfied over the Amigos de Bolsa Chica being a co-signer of the Coalition Plan and all that implied. This was in spite of the fact the plan had totally eliminated the Marina Plan and preserved over 90 percent of the Bolsa Chica wetlands.

In March of 1996 the BCLT along with Huntington Beach Tomorrow, the Shoshone-Gabrieliño Nation, the Sierra Club, and the Surfrider Foundation filed a lawsuit against the Coastal Commission and every agency and landowner that had anything to do with Bolsa Chica.[5] The lawsuit claimed the commission's actions of certifying Signal's Bolsa Chica 1996 development plan in January were contrary to requirements in the Coastal Act. The major points of the lawsuit were:

1. The commission allowed development in the 185 acre parcel that contained wetlands.

2. The commission allowed the filling of Warner Pond, a designated ESHA.

3. The commission allowed Signal to "relocate" the eucalyptus ESHA, that is, destroy it and replant other trees at another site.

4. The commission allowed inadequate buffers between the residential development and the wetland.

---

4. Voting *no* were commissioners Sara Wan, Francesca Cava, and Fran Pavley. Mrs. Wan had joined the commission during the hearing to fill the position vacated by Madelyn Glickman, who had resigned.

5. The League for Coastal Protection filed a companion lawsuit with the BCLT suit.

5. The commission allowed inadequate protection for archeological sites.

In its findings released in June of 1997, the court agreed with the BCLT on points 1 and 2. The Coastal Act is clear in that the filling of wetlands just to build houses on them is prohibited, just as the staff had advised the commission. As for point 2, the court stated that the Coastal Commission did not offer sufficient justifications for the filling of Warner Pond or offer less damaging alternatives. The other three points, including the relocation of the eucalyptus ESHA, were upheld in favor of the commission. The findings regarding the development in the wetlands and the filling of Warner Pond were enough for the court to order the LCP back to the commission for reconsideration. And the court awarded the BCLT legal costs.

The county returned to the Coastal Commission in October of 1997 and the commission followed the court orders regarding building in the lowland and the filling of Warner Pond, but again the commission gave approval for the relocation of the eucalyptus ESHA, based on the court decision that it was permissible to do so. That action was appealed by the BCLT and in April, 1999, the appeals court found in favor of the BCLT on the question of the relocation of the eucalyptus ESHA, stating that the trial court had erred in allowing the trees' destruction. In addition, the appeals court agreed with the trial court that development in the wetland and the filling of Warner pond were not permitted by the Coastal Act. But by then, the finding concerning building in the wetlands had become moot since Signal had sold most of its lowland holdings to the state in February of 1997. Besides the issues on development in the wetland and the filling of Warner Pond, Signal also lost an appeal regarding the court's order for the payment of the plaintiffs' legal fees. The costs were shared among the defendants.

The court decisions forced three significant changes in Signal's plans for its development project in Bolsa Chica. The removal of the eucalyptus grove ESHA on the bluff would have provided additional

178

space for Signal's development on the lower bench, but with the court blocking the trees' removal, land available on the lower bench for construction was reduced not only by the area of the ESHA, but also by the required buffers around the ESHA. And Warner Pond could not be filled in order to widen Warner Ave. Accordingly, to eliminate the need to widen the street, the anticipated traffic generated by Signal's mesa development had to be reduced. The company's mesa development was cut from 2400 units to 1,235 units. Finally, Signal had to drop all plans for homes in the lowlands. That gave the state the opportunity to purchase 880 acres of Signal-owned lowlands in February of 1997.[6] That purchase resulted in over 90 percent of the lowlands being in public ownership.

The 2000 LUP

Due to the sale of most of the company's lowlands to the state, Signal's development was now limited to the Bolsa Chica mesa. Signal's latest LUP for the development of the mesa was brought before the Coastal Commission in November, 2000. The LUP envisioned up to 1,235 residential units spread over the lower and upper benches. But the commission staff had an astonishing proposal.
Since the lower bench…

- contained two major ESHAs that had been protected by court order, the eucalyptus grove and Warner Pond, plus their buffers,
- was a significant foraging habitat for raptors,
- was immediately adjacent to the wetlands and an important part of their ecosystem,
- contained stands of endangered tar plants,

---

6. The lowlands that remained in private hands were the 43 acre Fieldstone parcel and the 51 acre Edwards Thumb. The Fieldstone property was purchased by the state from Signal in 2005.

...the entire lower bench deserved protection. What was more astonishing was the commission approving the staff's recommendation without deliberation or dissent. Following several hours of public testimony, Commissioner Shirley Dettloff opened commission discussion with a personal narrative of the decades of conflict over the future of Bolsa Chica. Other commissioners briefly expressed their individual thoughts about Bolsa Chica, after which the commission chair fittingly invited Dettloff to offer the motions that incorporated the staff's recommendations. The end effect was that Signal was limited to developing about 65 acres on the upper bench of the Bolsa Chica Mesa with an additional 34 acres set aside for open space.

Signal filed a lawsuit against the Coastal Commission, claiming that the decision of the commission was based on the "wacky logic" of the commission staff, as Signal's attorneys phrased it. Signal claimed that it was the victim of inverse condemnation or a taking. Taking is legalese for a governmental body denying a landowner the use of his property so that it could be converted to public use. In its counterargument, the Coastal Commission interpreted the Coastal Act, backed up by previous court cases, that a taking may be claimed only if the landowner is denied *all* economically viable use of the property. Furthermore, a taking cannot be asserted at the LUP stage. Since Signal was free to develop the upper bench, the commission's action did not appear to be a taking. Eventually Signal dropped the action and turned its attention to the development of its upper mesa project, called Brightwater.

Brightwater

Brightwater is the name Signal gave its residential development on the 65 acres of the Bolsa Chica upper bench. The development is planned for 347 single family homes, some of which enjoy views of the lower bench, the ocean, and the Bolsa Chica wetlands. Occupation of the Brightwater homes began in December, 2007.

As it seems every chapter of the story of Bolsa Chica proves to be controversial, the Brightwater project is no exception. Initially the project as proposed by Signal was to be a private, gated community with very limited public access. Being in the coastal zone, the project must comply with the Coastal Act with regards to public access to coastal resources. The Coastal Commission required Signal to open the development's roads and walks to the public and to provide more public parking facilities. Other changes over Signal's initial plan included wider buffer zones around ESHAs and a filtration system for storm water that empties into the Pocket Wetland.

While the environmental community had hoped to see the entire Bolsa Chica mesa preserved as open space, the building of houses on the upper mesa has provoked intense emotions for another reason. As related in Chapter 1, the Bolsa Chica Mesa was occupied by native Americans at least 8000 years ago. That is more than 3000 years before Stonehenge and the major Pyramids of Egypt. The archeology of Bolsa Chica has been under investigation since the 1920s, and over that time an enormous amount of artifacts have been unearthed, at least a reported 100,000 items by Signal's archeologists alone. In 1978 Signal asserted that archeologists had thoroughly investigated Bolsa Chica and all artifacts had been cleared from the area. But as development of the upper mesa approached, archeological investigations intensified and significantly more discoveries were made.

In 2008 it was revealed that a total of 174 "sets" of human remains had been unearthed from the upper mesa. Half of the remains were uncovered during archeological digs prior to Signal's groundbreaking in June of 2006, and half of the 174 had been removed since. The great number of remains that was discovered prompted an analyst from the California Native American Heritage Commission to comment that the mesa site is one of the densest concentrations of Native American remains in the state, making the site internationally important. Apparently the California Native American Heritage Commission as well as the Coastal Commission was unaware of the magnitude of the number of remains until December, 2007. Due to the site's significance, the California Native American Heritage Commission had repeatedly recommended that building on the site should not be permitted, but state law allows developers to remove Native American remains from building sites provided the remains are reburied at other sites. Reburials must be under the supervision of representatives of appropriate Native American groups, Gabrieliño/Tongva and Juaneños in the case of Bolsa Chica. Internments as well as the reporting of the initial discoveries must be conducted in a timely manner, which in the instance of Signal's mesa development, did not appear to be the case. In a reported agreement between Signal and the Native American groups, the company has promised that all artifacts and human remains were to be buried by July 1, 2009.

Amigos' Legal Tangles Anew

During the November 2000 Coastal Commission hearing, the Amigos spoke in opposition to certain features of Signal's mesa development that would have had negative impacts on the wetlands below. The Amigos supported the staff recommendation of preserving the lower bench due to the bench's ecological connection to the wetland. In addition, the Amigos expressed its opposition to Signal's plan to construct a series of six storm drains that were to direct runoff from its mesa development into the Bolsa Chica wetlands. One drain, to be located just south of the Warner Ave bridge, was to be six feet in diameter and have a headwall[7] 20 feet across. Other drains would flow into outer Bolsa Bay, Warner Pond, and the pocket wetland. Not only would the drains represent an ecological risk to the wetlands, the six foot drain also would mar the lower mesa bluff with a 20 foot wide concrete structure, a clear violation of Section 30251 of the Coastal Act that regulates visual impacts. The six foot drain would have been in full view of travelers on Warner Avenue and on Pacific Coast Highway, which is a county scenic highway. In addition, the Amigos expressed dismay that

---

7. A headwall is a broad concrete frame that goes around the drainpipe.

Warner Pond, a designated ESHA, would be converted into a storm water catch basin. But with the Coastal Commission order preserving the low bench, storm drains that would have emptied into Outer Bolsa Bay and Warner Pond were no longer needed. Still, a single drain was to empty into the Pocket Wetland. That one drain was allowed under the 1997 sales agreement in which Signal was given authorization to allow runoff to flow into the wetland below the project. Runoff into the wetland is to be minimized by strict water use regulations in the Brightwater development through features such as "smart" irrigation systems[8] and the use of low water-requiring plantings. In addition, the drain is required to have filters installed to prevent road residue and other potentially toxic matter from entering the wetlands. Unfortunately such filters are only effective during dry weather; during heavy rains, the capacity of the filters is often exceeded.

Signal interpreted the Amigos' public comments at the November, 2000 Coastal Commission hearing as opposing mesa development, which could be seen as a violation of the 1989 Coalition Plan Agreement. In January of 2001 Signal's attorney notified Amigos that the company intended to compel the Amigos into arbitration to resolve the dispute. Then, in February, Signal filed a court petition to order the Amigos into arbitration over the alleged violation. Signal's position was that when the Amigos signed the 1989 Coalition Plan Agreement, the organization was bound to support "the plan." The Amigos countered that Signal's petition did not precisely state how the organization violated the Coalition Plan Agreement. And besides, there was the overriding question of whether the 1989 Coalition Plan was still a viable document. As one legal consultant labeled it, the Coalition Plan was a mere skeleton the bones of which had collapsed through a series of past actions by Signal. For example, the company unilaterally moved its planning process from the city of Huntington Beach to the county of Orange. Under the coalition agreement, the company was to consult with other signers of the agreement before such action

---

8. Watering systems that respond to weather conditions.

was taken. Furthermore, the development plan presented at the 2000 Coastal Commission meeting which Signal accused the Amigos of criticizing was not the plan proposed in 1989; Signal's development plans had gone through at least one major revision since the Coalition Plan was released. And even if the plan were the same plan, the Amigos was not "bound to support the Plan if it failed to meet substantial permit requirements of local, state and federal laws."[9] Realizing the weakness of its position, Signal eventually agreed to drop its action against the Amigos.

The Bolsa Chica Foundation

While the Amigos' goal from its very beginning was public education concerning the need for preservation and restoration of the Bolsa Chica wetland, a second front involving political advocacy had to be launched. That involved direct contact with regulatory agencies and elected officials at all levels. But more importantly, it meant active participation in the electoral process, that is, providing financial support for travel and other expenses to influence legislation and for the election of state, county, and city office holders. Due to such political activities, the Amigos de Bolsa Chica was prevented from acquiring what is referred to as 501(c)3 status by the Internal Revenue Service. While the Amigos de Bolsa Chica was considered a non-profit organization and exempt from paying income taxes, lacking 501(c)3 status prevented donors from including their donations to the Amigos as deductions for charitable contributions on their income tax forms. Donors recognized this and continued to contribute generously to support the organization's cause with the knowledge what was at stake. However, the Amigos could not appeal to major donors such as charitable foundations for funds and had to depend on fundraisers and independent donors for the bulk of its income.

Once the need for political action was reduced by the sale of most of the Bolsa Chica lowland to the state, the Amigos moved to estab-

---

9. Quote from the Coalition Plan.

lish a formal, separate organization in 1997 known as the Bolsa Chica Foundation,[10] which did acquire 501(c)3 status. Thus while all political activities, though reduced, remained with the Amigos, all educational functions were transferred to the Foundation. This included the development of exhibit and tour materials, the training of docents, the maintenance of a research library, and other associated activities. The foundation was able to obtain some major foundation grants to support its educational programs. In 2005 when it appeared that the Amigos' goals in the wetlands had been substantially met and its role as a strong political force in the community was no longer needed, the Amigos merged with the Foundation. The Amigos de Bolsa Chica was granted 501(c)3 status and the foundation name was retired.

Annexation

As related earlier, Bolsa Chica emerged as an unincorporated county island surrounded on three sides by the City of Huntington Beach. Obviously with Bolsa Chica being within the city's sphere of influence, annexing the property to the city appeared to be a foregone conclusion. Nothing is a foregone conclusion when it comes to Bolsa Chica. Signal first approached the city in 1972 requesting that the city consider accepting jurisdiction over Bolsa Chica. The city rejected the proposal based on the lack of a master plan at that time for the development of the land.

Signal returned to the city in 1976 with an annexation proposal. Initially the city was supportive of the idea, for it had some definite advantages, such as the ability to control development and collect tax revenues. Getting the city to rezone Bolsa Chica to residential/commercial to match its marina aspirations was apparently Signal's major reason for requesting annexation. Citizens and organizations including the recently-formed Amigos de Bolsa Chica, argued that annexing and rezoning Bolsa Chica would cause its assessed value to

10. An informal arm of the Amigos that was referred to as the foundation had been conducting educational activities since 1984.

skyrocket, making it impossible for public acquisition that was anticipated. The county assessor refuted that idea, but other events occurring
at the time strengthened the public's opposition to annexation. The
Coastal Commission had just placed Bolsa Chica on its target list for
purchase, but then a few months later Bolsa Chica was removed from
the list due to the lack of specific restoration plans for the wetland, as
was explained by state officials. In spite of the setback, Assemblyman
Dennis Mangers was able to secure $3.6 million in the 1977 state budget
for the purchase of the Bolsa Chica wetland. The debate over annexation continued for 2 more years, but each time it came before the city
council, annexation of Bolsa Chica was eventually rejected. And at the
same time, Signal turned down offers to purchase the wetlands.

At least four other attempts to annex Bolsa Chica have been made
since 1976 and each one was set aside for various reasons. In 2008
Huntington Beach agreed to annex Signal's 65 acre residential development on the upper Bolsa Chica Mesa, but in an unusual arrangement in which annexation is to occur in 11 phases as development
proceeds.

In 2008, the city council ordered its staff to engage a consultant to
look into the annexation of the entire Bolsa Chica property. According
to regulations governing annexation, the city and landowner(s) must
agree to the process. In the case of Bolsa Chica, over 90 percent is
state owned. A representative of the State Lands Commission felt the
state was essentially neutral on the subject. Assuming the city abides
by the agreement with Signal regarding the phased annexation of the
company's 65 acres, that apparently leaves the city to decide whether to
bring the state-owned Bolsa Chica property into its embrace, resulting
in the entire Bolsa Chica becoming part of the city.

Throughout most of the debates over annexation of that portion
of the Bolsa Chica Mesa that is destined for development, one of
the questions most often raised was, "Annexation before or after
development?" There are distinct advantages to the city for annexation before development. The city can receive permit fees and other

up-front charges. There is greater control over building standards such as setbacks, street widths, park dedications, and a myriad of other details. Signal has insisted on a phased annexation after each segment is developed, denying the city of these benefits; most fees would go to the county and construction would be under the county's building standards.

It is not known how many trees were sacrificed to provide the paper in the name of the California Coastal Act, the California Environmental Quality Act, and a countless other local-, state- and federal-mandated documents that have been generated over the last three decades in connection with Bolsa Chica. Nearly all of these documents for the most part became obsolete by the end of the 1990s. But wait. There is still restoration to deal with.

11

The Road to Restoration

Signal's certified 1996 LCP generally followed the concept of the Coalition Plan. The plan led to litigation and the eventual revocation of that part of the LCP that dealt with building in the Bolsa Chica wetland. With Signal's plans for any development in the lowlands eliminated, the state was able to step in and purchase a major portion of the lowland property. The purchase brought the state's Bolsa Chica ownership up to about 1200 acres or over 90 percent of the lowlands. The next step was restoration.

Restoration

Signal had always used restoration as the fulcrum to make its development plans for the Bolsa Chica wetland possible. The company depended on portions of Sections 30233 and 30411 of the Coastal Act that allow building in wetlands under certain conditions. Signal had claimed that these sections were included in the Coastal Act for the specific purpose of implementing the 1973 Bolsa Chica plan, even though the wetland is not mentioned in the document by name. State officials have denied that assertion. In order to take advantage of the Coastal Act, it was Signal's position that development was the one and only source of funds for the restoration of the wetlands. In a full page newspaper ad in April, 1978 Signal hammered the message that, outside of the ecological reserve, Bolsa Chica was nothing more than an oil field and any restoration would be at great taxpayer's expense if Signal's development plans were not approved. If Signal's plan were to be implemented, a portion of the proceeds from the waterside development was to go toward the cost of restoring much of the Bolsa Chica wetlands. Signal continued its public relations campaign that touted the catchphrase, "Today's Wasteland, Tomorrow's Wetlands." However, in 1997, by selling the vast majority of its wetland holdings, Signal was released from contributing toward any major wetland restoration.

The Need for Restoration

In 1981 the Department of Fish and Game determined that there were 1292 acres of historical wetlands in Bolsa Chica of which 1000 acres were severely degraded as defined in the Coastal Act and in need of restoration. The damage to the wetlands was the result of the insults Bolsa Chica suffered from its time as a hunting reserve followed by several decades as an oil field. And while much of the area retained some characteristics of a viable wetland, restoration was not going to be easy. The dam constructed by the gun club in 1899 was the beginning of the end for Bolsa Chica's millennia of existence as a functioning estuary. Then, starting in 1940 when the first drill bit pierced its soggy soil, the wetland would eventually be crisscrossed with raised maintenance roads and several miles of pipelines, and peppered with over 200 drill pads, all of which essentially destroyed much of the wetland's natural topography. Also, there were likely the inevitable pockets of petroleum residues, discarded drilling mud, rusting, obsolete equipment, all types of industrial waste, and other potentially toxic contaminants, some concentrated in unlined sumps throughout the wetland. Clearly such materials would be hazardous to the wildlife for which the restored wetland was designed to provide a safe haven.

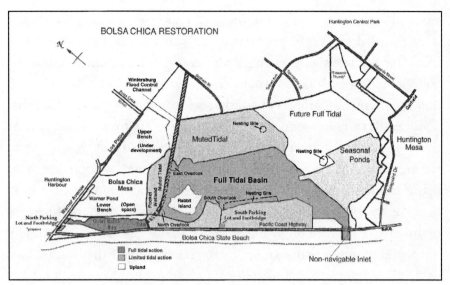

11-1. The restoration plan. The full tidal basin receives unrestricted tidal flow from the non-navigable inlet. The muted tidal wetlands receive limited tidal flow through three culverts that connect it to the full tidal basin. The Pocket Wetland receives water from Outer Bolsa Bay via a culvert through the dike that separates the two bodies. (Map courtesy California State Lands Commission).

A critical point, which will be covered in more detail later, is that the wetland restoration at Bolsa Chica was not being carried out in some remote, uninhabitated space but in close proximity to a highly urbanized area and a fully operating oil field. That factor placed additional constraints on the restoration project.

Restoration Defined

The word restoration is usually defined as bringing something back to its initial state. When one restores an antique desk, for instance, or a Model T Ford, the idea is to return the items back to their original factory condition. That was not the case for the Bolsa Chica wetland. First of all, what was its "original" condition? As was discussed in Chapter 1, Bolsa Chica went through a long series of geological changes from being undersea to a river mouth to a deep lagoon to the shallow wetland of more recent times. Assuming we knew what the wetland was like during any of these various stages, which one should it be restored to? We're pretty sure we know what the wetland was like after the late 1800s when better surveys were conducted, but the page is fairly blank before that period. Earlier survey maps showed nothing more than property boundaries (Frontispiece) but few internal features. But a map produced in 1901 (Figure 7-2), for instance, is relatively detailed in showing the many sloughs and islands that made up the wetland. Should that be the restoration plan? To duplicate those many circuitous channels and sloughs that meandered over its 1400 or more acres would have been the kind of engineering and financial nightmare only taken on by major theme parks. Instead, an essentially unnatural design was drawn up for the restoration of the Bolsa Chica wetland, a design that consisted of a group of overlapping, straight-sided trapezoids that more or less followed the lines of the oil roads (Figure 11-1). But that is not a bad thing.

The goal of the Bolsa Chica restoration was to provide as wide a variety of habitats for as wide a variety of wildlife as was possible, resulting in a functioning ecosystem, and that was essentially accomplished. Perhaps a more appropriate and reassuring definition of wetland restoration comes from the National Research Council: Restoration is, "...*returning an ecosystem to a close approximation of its conditions prior to disturbance. Accomplishing restoration means ensuring that ecosystem structure and function are increased or repaired, and that natural dynamic ecosystem processes are operating effectively again.*" In other words, a restoration must lead to a working ecosystem, and that appears to be the case in Bolsa Chica.

In addition to the problem of how to design one of the largest coastal wetland restorations ever attempted in California, the state was confronted with another question: how to pay for the restoration. Early estimates of the cost had reached $100 million. Since Signal was released from its obligations of funding restoration, another source of funds was necessary. As it turned out, the source of most of the funds to accomplish the restoration of the Bolsa Chica wetland was identified nearly ten years before the funding was even needed.

The Ports Sail into the Picture

Beginning in the 1980s and throughout the 1990s, the Ports of Los Angeles and Long Beach were experiencing unprecedented pressure to handle more shipping capacity, particularly for imports flooding in from the Pacific Rim. Since the ports contribute about $100 billion a year to California's economy, their situation could not be ignored. Ports such as Seattle and even gulf and east coast ports were more than eager to siphon off any highly lucrative shipping business that the local harbors could not handle.[1] There were times cargo ships from the world's ports of call were arriving at Los Angeles/Long Beach harbor at such an increasing rate that many have had to anchor outside the harbor and wait for an open berth. To accommodate the demand, it was clear to the port authorities that they had to enlarge their cargo handling facilities. But in order to do so, they would have to expand out into the open water of San Pedro Bay. That is, to construct wharves, warehouses, truck yards, and administrative buildings, the ports must create more dry land by filling submerged lands and tidelands. But according to the Coastal Act, the filling of such marine habitats is allowed only if it is beneficial to the public, such as for the construction of a harbor, but with an essential condition.

The loss of fish and wildlife habitats by creating landfills in the waters of Los Angeles and Long Beach harbors must be mitigated or compensated for by the restoration or creation of habitats elsewhere.

---

1. In 2008, the Mexican government announced that provided it can find the funding, it is considering construction of a $2 billion freight handling port on the west coast of Baja California to compete with the Los Angeles/Long Beach facilities. The widening of the Panama Canal also will have a critical impact on the local ports' competitiveness, since super size cargo ships from the Pacific Rim will be able to reach gulf and east coast markets directly. That is actually cheaper than unloading cargo on the West Coast and shipping it east by rail or truck. These events may reduce the need for harbor expansion and hence future funding for wetland restoration.

The "elsewhere" could be within the boundaries of the harbor, known as "on-site mitigation," or at some distant site, or "off-site mitigation." Since there was no appropriate open space within the harbors to carry out mitigation, off-site mitigation was the only solution. For instance, the port of Los Angeles paid about $60 million for the restoration of Batiquitos Lagoon in San Diego County to mitigate the loss of habitats from harbor expansion conducted in the1990s. Until Bolsa Chica was restored, the Batiquitos project, completed in 1996, was the largest coastal wetland restoration undertaken in Southern California. The amount of restoration at Batiquitos was considered sufficient to offset the filling of over 600 acres of tideland in the harbor, but more was needed. Other mitigation sites were sought, but they had to conform to certain guidelines. They must be in the general geographical region of the ports, a successful restoration must be technically feasible, and the restoration must replace the filled habitat with similar habitat. In addition, to allow the ports to maintain their construction schedule, the sites must be ready for restoration.

During the 1990s, the most likely candidates for port-funded restoration besides Batiquitos were the Ballona wetland on Santa Monica Bay and Bolsa Chica. Other potential wetlands were not deemed timely candidates because of various reasons such as being under litigation or under private ownership with an unwilling seller. While Ballona was a possible site for restoration, a couple of factors eventually eliminated it from consideration. First, at the time, the portion of Ballona wetland marked for restoration was only about 230 acres, too small to satisfy the extent of fill contemplated by the ports. Also, the settlement of a lawsuit filed by the Friends of Ballona Wetlands had resulted in the owner of the property, Howard Hughes, pledging $10 million toward the restoration of the wetland, which would have further reduced the ports' mitigation credits.

That left Bolsa Chica, which had sufficient area and apparently was ripe for purchase. The timing could not have been better. By court order the Coastal Commission was forced to reverse its approval of Signal's development of 185 acres of lowland. The court decision eliminated the possibility of any development in the lowlands and left the landowner with few choices for what to do with the property. For all practical purposes, the Bolsa Chica lowland was, from the owner's perspective, a white elephant. For the ports and all those who supported the preservation of the Bolsa Chica wetland, the situation presented a fortuitous, once-in-a-lifetime opportunity. The ports' representatives had been attending the Coalition meetings and were fully aware of the potential for capturing significant mitigation credits should Bolsa Chica be in line for purchase and restoration. And the Amigos had been lobbying the ports since the Coalition was meeting to make sure the ports' interest in Bolsa Chica remained high.

As the story of Bolsa Chica unfolded over the decades since the 1973 agreement, more and more wetlands underwent restoration. Initially about 210 acres were restored in 1978. Then, more of the wetlands would be restored based on the 1979 Marina Plan. And then according to the 1989 Coalition Concept Plan, 1100 acres[2] were earmarked for restoration. But by the 1990s, there was doubt among the various agencies that Signal would ever secure final permits to build in the wetland, apparently eliminating Signal as a source of restoration funding. In 1995 the U. S. Department of Interior officially invited the ports to participate in funding the purchase and restoration of the Bolsa Chica wetland in exchange for mitigation credits. Representatives of eight state and federal agencies gathered together and hammered out the details of the ports' mitigation plan for the Bolsa Chica wetland two years before the sale of a major portion of the wetlands to the state was completed in 1997. A memorandum of understanding was eventually signed in 1996 by all eight agencies and the ports, an historical event in itself. Gray Davis, Lt. Governor and chair of the State Lands Commission at the time, commented that he could not remember another instance when so many governmental agencies had met and agreed on such a major issue.

---

2. Less the part of the 300 acres of the State Ecological Reserve already restored in 1978.

What made the Bolsa Chica restoration plan unique was that, unlike the restoration at Batiquitos Lagoon where the ports played an integral management role in the planning and construction of the project, Bolsa Chica was going to be a "pay and walk away" arrangement. The restoration was to be managed by a team from the original eight governmental agencies that brokered the restoration plan with the ports. From that time on, the team was referred to as the "Bolsa Chica Steering Committee" (Table 11-1).[3] The agreement that was put together involved the ports depositing funds into an account known as the Kapiloff Land Bank Fund and in exchange the ports would receive mitigation credits against the acreage of submerged lands and tidelands they planned to fill.

Jack Fancher, a wildlife biologist with the U. S. Fish and Wildlife Service and a member of the Steering Committee, served as the Coastal Program Chief for the Service and Project Manager for the record-setting Bolsa Chica restoration.

Matching Mitigation

Mitigation to offset the loss of fish and wildlife habitat must be true mitigation, that is, the loss must be balanced equally or better both qualitatively and quantitatively by a gain of similar habitats. While a variety of habitats were to be filled in the harbor, much of the ports' expansion involved the loss of deep water habitat. Therefore at least half of the Bolsa Chica restoration had to be deep water that would accommodate significant fish populations. That would be accomplished by excavating the central portion of the full tidal basin to a depth of at least 3 feet below mean lower low water (MLLW).[4] As for

---

3. It was originally intended that the U. S. Fish and Wildlife Service was to hold ownership and management responsibilities of the newly restored wetland, but the agency opted out and the state Department of Fish and Game was given the management role with the State Lands Commission as the landowner.

4. Mean lower low water is the average depths of the lowest of the two low tides for each day calculated over a 19 year period, which is known as the National Tidal Datum Epoch.

196

Table 11-1. Members of the Bolsa Chica Steering Committee.

Agency	Member
U. S. Fish and Wildlife Service	Jack Fancher
National Marine Fisheries Service	Bob Hoffman
U. S. Environmental Protection Agency	Tom Yocom
U. S. Army Corps of Engineers	Larry Smith
California State Lands Commission	Jim Trout
California Department of Fish and Game	Terri Stewart
California Coastal Conservancy	Peter Brand
California Resources Agency	Chris Potter

other habitat types, thirty five percent of the basin must be between minus 3 feet and plus 2.5 feet from MLLW, providing for intertidal mudflats, and the balance must be between plus 2.5 feet and plus 5.5 feet above MLLW, creating emergent salt marsh.

The calculation of how much mitigation credit the ports received for providing restoration at Bolsa Chica depended on the biological worth of the waters to be filled and the relative value of the wetland to be restored. For example, deep, outer harbor habitats have greater biological value than the relatively more shallow areas around wharves and are thus given higher priority. Thus it was determined that restoring one acre of highly diverse Bolsa Chica wetland habitat would offset the loss of 2.64 acres of shallow water habitat while the same acre of restored Bolsa Chica wetland would mitigate only 1.32 acres of deep water habitat.

The Restoration Plan

Figure 11-1 shows the general plan of the wetlands restoration. The project area was divided into two major habitats, the Full Tidal Basin of 367 acres, which would include the deep water habitat and the intertidal mudflats. A 181 acre portion, referred to as the muted tidal area, would create an emergent salt marsh. The 42 acre "pocket wetland"[5] at the foot of the Bolsa Chica mesa and adjacent to the Wintersburg Channel also was established as a muted tidal wetland. The pocket wetland was connected to Outer Bolsa Bay by a culvert and thus was not hydrologically linked to the main restored area. Not included in the restoration project at this time were the Future Full Tidal area and the Seasonal Ponds, two areas to be discussed later.

Cleanup Questions

Once the agencies signed the agreement that detailed how the restoration was to be funded, attention was focused on technical elements of the restoration. Several questions were raised: First, how badly contaminated was the wetland from remnants of the oil field operations? Obviously a 60 year old oil field would not be expected to be free of the myriads of soil contaminants, some highly toxic, that are commonly associated with the exploration, production, and processing of oil and gas. So while a purchase and restoration plan was in place, by law the state could not acquire the land until it was cleaned up or that a guarantee of it being cleaned up was in hand.

The Ecological Risk Assessment

To arrive at a definitive answer to the question of contamination, in 1996 one of the member agencies that oversaw the mitigation plan, the U. S. Fish and Wildlife Service, launched an Ecological Risk Assessment, a program that identified the types and concentrations of chem-

---

5. The narrow strip of wetland between the Bolsa Chica mesa bluff and the Wintersburg flood control channel, known as the Pocket Wetland, had once been proposed in the 1960s as a utility easement to serve a 1800 megawatt nuclear power plant and 50 million gallon per day desalination plant to be built on a man-made island off the Huntington Beach coast. The plan was eventually dropped, but the Metropolitan Water District ("MWD") retained the property until it was temporarily held by the Bolsa Chica Land Trust and then deeded to the state in 1997 to be part of the restoration. MWD's switch yard was to be located on a 50 acre parcel off Graham Street that is presently owned by Shea Homes.

ical contaminants in the Bolsa Chica lowland and determined what contaminants may pose a risk to wildlife.

The Service carried out extensive sampling and testing in Bolsa Chica involving some 1700 core soil samples, over 100 water samples, and more than 250 tissue samples taken from a wide variety of animals. Each sample was tested for the presence of any of 237 known toxic chemicals. In addition, sediment and water samples were tested to determine if they presented any signs of toxicity toward test invertebrates or fish. Out of the 237 possible contaminants, about 50 were identified to be present in Bolsa Chica at concentrations that were deemed high enough to cause a risk of adverse impacts on plants and animals in the wetland. None of the contaminants were at concentrations deemed hazardous to humans. And to everyone's relief, the overall results indicated that the oil field was not as badly contaminated as was first anticipated. As stated by several Steering Committee members, "There were no surprises."

How Clean Is Clean? The Cleanup Plan

The second question was: to what degree would cleanup have to reach? It was clear that funds available for the purchase and restoration of Bolsa Chica would not be sufficient to conduct the almost impossible task of 100 percent removal of all contamination. That question was answered through the part of the Ecological Risk Assessment in which the results of the sampling were compared with tolerance levels of specific contaminants for wildlife. As each probable contaminant was studied, its impact on future wildlife was assessed and that led to the Cleanup Plan. The decisions that went into the Cleanup Plan had to be based for the most part on the scientific evidence, but some approaches had to be made for practical reasons. For example, there were some areas that were only moderately contaminated, but their high habitat values would be destroyed in order to carry out decontamination of the area. It was decided that preserving the habitat outweighed the risk presented by the contamination. Soils that contained high levels of contamination were hauled to a hazardous waste dump. It was decided that soil that contained levels of contamination not deemed sufficiently harmful to justify disposal in a hazardous waste dump was to be sequestered deep within earthen structures such as levees and elevated overlooks.

Who Does the Dirty Work?

Finally, who was going to conduct the cleanup and who was to pay for it? Since the Regional Water Quality Control Board had been the overseer of several cases of oil contamination cleanups, it was the agency of choice for monitoring the cleanup, and it agreed to fill the role. As far as who pays, normally both the landowner and the oil lessee are jointly responsible for any oil cleanup. In the case of Bolsa Chica there was initially considerable reluctance on the part of the responsible parties to fund the whole cleanup operation. There had been several prior oil lessees in Bolsa Chica and the present lease was in the name of a consortium known as CalResources, a combined company consisting of Shell and Mobil oil companies. Phillips Petroleum, the immediate prior oil lessee, also was tapped to contribute to the cleaning up of the oil field. From the beginning the oil companies could not agree among themselves how to manage the cost of the cleanup, raising the possibility that the deal could collapse. To avoid that possibility, the Steering Committee contributed $4 million toward the cost of cleanup.

Clinching the Deal

The State Lands Commission scheduled a news conference for the morning of February 11, 1997 to announce the completion of the details for the funding of the purchase and restoration of the Bolsa Chica wetland. The event was held in the parking lot of the state ecological reserve, across from Bolsa Chica State Beach. But the anticipation of the large turnout was dulled by the announcement that while Signal had approved the sale of 880 acres of its lowland property to the state, and the ports had agreed to providing the funding, the oil companies that were operating in the wetland had yet to agree on the particulars of the cleanup. State and federal officials had been working on the deal for several months and were ready to announce its closure at the news conference. But as late as the night before of the news conference, wording of press releases had to be changed from certainty to uncertainty. It was said that negotiations were still going on in the parking lot via cell phone as the news conference speakers tried to make something out of the non-event.

The next opportunity for the golden announcement was to come on the following day, when the State Lands Commission was to hold a meeting at Huntington Beach City Hall. The scenario had all the trappings of a suspense film. The commission, chaired by Lt. Governor Gray Davis, had convened for the purpose of approving the state's purchase of 880 acres of Bolsa Chica lowland from Signal and accepting the dedication of another 25 acres of the Pocket Wetland that had been owned by the Metropolitan Water District. Even as the meeting opened, the commission's action could not go forward because the oil companies still had not come to a mutual agreement concerning the cleanup and the state could not act until the question was settled. While waiting to hear from the oil companies, the commission patiently listened to about a dozen public speakers, all of whom supported the commission's action to acquire the 880 wetland acres.

Following the public testimony, a five minute break was called, which extended to over 30 minutes. More suspense. When the session was reconvened, CalResources Governmental Affairs Manager William Harper quietly announced that his company and Phillips Petroleum had arrived at an agreement, albeit verbal. As soon as the applause faded the commission voted on Chair Davis' motion to approve the acquisition of the 880 acres of Bolsa Chica lowland, provided the oil companies delivered a written agreement to the commission by noon

11-2. Members of the Amigos de Bolsa Chica celebrate the state's purchase of 880 acres of Bolsa Chica wetlands with a dawn breakfast at the Ecological Reserve south parking lot. (Photo courtesy Amigos de Bolsa Chica)

on the following Friday. More applause accompanied by cheers. The resolution was signed in green ink.

On Saturday the 15th, in celebration of the acquisition, which was consummated on Friday as promised, the Amigos held a dawn *al fresco* breakfast at the Bolsa Chica parking lot (Figure 11-2). The dawn event was symbolic, as Amigos Treasurer Terry Dolton put it, for it represented a new dawn for the Bolsa Chica wetland.

In an inter-office memo to Signal employees, the sale of the 880 acres of Bolsa Chica lowlands to the state was referred to as a "company triumph." The sale eliminated the company from any restoration obligations, estimated at $50 million, or cleanup responsibilities, provided some good PR, resolved several litigation actions over wetland development, and brought in some cash during an apparent dry season for the company. Signal also planned to get a tax write-off from the sale. In the sales agreement, the company noted that it would claim the difference between the assessed value of the property, $31 million, and the sales price, $25 million, as a charitable contribution to the state.

How Does One Design a New Wetland?

As explained earlier, the decision was made not to duplicate what the Bolsa Chica wetland was like at any particular time in its history, but to construct a place that would have the maximum diversity of coastal wetland habitats. As outlined in Chapter 6, coastal habitats are generally categorized into several zones. The Subtidal Zone refers to that part of a wetland that is under water all the time, regardless of the tide. In the Bolsa Chica restoration plan, the Subtidal Zone would be in the Full Tidal Basin, which may reach as much as 6 or 8 feet in depth at maximum high tides. These depths provide feeding grounds for diving birds such as mergansers, pelicans, grebes, scoters, and cormorants as well as habitat for innumerable wetland and marine fish species and plants such as eel grass.

The Intertidal Zone is submerged at high tides and exposed during low tides. In Bolsa Chica, large portions of the Intertidal Zone consist of gently sloping mud flats, the water's edges of which are enjoyed by birds that normally feed by wading in shallow water, like egrets, herons, avocets, stilts, and many types of ducks. The mud flats are enormously rich in algae and invertebrates such as crabs, clams, worms, and other food for probing birds such as curlews, godwits, and willets. Birds that feed on insects and other invertebrates on the surface, such as plovers and sandpipers, are also observed at the water's edge. These birds often can be seen congregating on the mud by the thousands during low tide.

The Low Wetland is submerged during most high tides, supporting the growth of those plants especially adapted to that habitat, such as cord grass. Cord grass has been planted along the upper edges of the mudflat to attract the endangered California Light Footed Clapper Rail, which prefers to nest among that aquatic plant. The High Wetland gets wet only during the very high tides. Pickleweed, which is necessary for the endangered Belding's Savannah Sparrow for both food and nesting, is particularly suited for high wetland habitats.

Restoration Plan Introduced to the Public.

Knowing the enormous interest in Bolsa Chica in the community, the Steering Committee went out of its way to assure that the restoration plans received maximum public exposure. Between May of 1997 and October of 1999, at least seven well attended open forums were presented to the local community on various aspects of the restoration plan.

Early Paperwork

In November, 2001 the Coastal Commission approved the Consistency Determination for the restoration project that was submitted by the lead agency, the U. S. Fish and Wildlife Service. The Army Corps of Engineers and the Regional Water Quality Control Board issued their permits for the restoration in the Spring of 2002.

Variations on the Restoration Theme

A number of alternative plans for the restoration of Bolsa Chica was studied as part of the preparation of the Environmental Impact Report that was issued in 2001. Most of the alternatives involved various locations of the inlet (south end, opposite Rabbit Island, or near Warner Ave.), whether there should be an inlet at all, and whether or not some or all of the Wintersburg Channel should flow into the newly restored wetland. These alternatives are discussed below.

The Tidal Opening

A key feature of the restored wetland was the inclusion of an opening to the ocean, an absolute necessity for a fully functioning coastal wetland. An inlet allows the incoming tide to deliver cool, oxygenated, life-giving seawater into the full tidal basin. A direct ocean inlet also assures relatively constant salinity and temperature in the waters of the wetland. An inlet would restore the natural tidal conditions that existed prior to 1899 when the gun club constructed the dam across the wetland's main channel. It was decided that the new inlet be located about 2 miles south of where the inlet's historical site was prior to 1899. Alternatively, openings at the historical site at Warner Avenue or one opposite Rabbit Island were considered but rejected for a number of reasons. Either of these plans would have required extensive and costly re-engineering of the bays. The mud flat in the outer bay would have to be removed to allow sufficient water flow into the wetland. The mud flat has become an enormously rich feeding habitat for thousands of migratory birds. Also, inlets at these locations would have resulted in the loss of considerably more parking spaces and other facilities at the state beach than the preferred plan. Finally, the alteration of inner or outer bays, which had become relatively well functioning habitats since their restoration in 1978, was not deemed ecologically justified.

Types of Inlets

Inlets that allow seawater to enter an enclosed bay can be either natural, that is, without jetties, or protected with jetties. A natural opening has the tendency to meander up and down the beach as littoral (near shore) currents scour one side and drop sand on the other. These currents tend to switch direction depending on the season, resulting in a back and forth movement of the inlet. A natural opening at Bolsa Chica would have required setting aside about 1000 feet of beach for the inlet to wander. Not only would such an itinerant inlet have played havoc on the operation of the state beach, the cost of a 1000 foot causeway for Pacific Coast Highway to span the inlet's ambling would have been prohibitive. As proposed in the preferred plan, the placement of short rock jetties would anchor the opening to a set location. To minimize their effect on sand movement, the jetties would be short, just reaching the low tide line.

Work on the Bolsa Chica inlet jetties began in February of 2006 and when work was completed about 72,000 tons of rock had been barged from Santa Catalina Island for the jetty construction.

Alternatives to an Inlet

Inclusion of the new opening in the restoration plan was not without controversy. Opposition to an inlet from several quarters raised a number of concerns, including the loss of beach (about 5 acres), the inlet's possible effect on sand transport along the beach, and the prospect that outflow from the wetland would be a source of pollutants for a beach that has been one of the cleanest in the region.

The inclusion of a direct ocean inlet as part of the Bolsa Chica restoration was opposed by a number entities, including the California Department of Parks and Recreation, due to the loss of beach, and curiously, at least two environmental organizations, The Bolsa Chica Land Trust and the Surfrider Foundation. The Amigos strongly supported it. Two alternatives to an inlet were offered, namely underground culverts to deliver sea water to the wetland, and the existing channel from Huntington Harbour to serve the newly restored wetland.

One proposal was to use culverts up to 20 feet wide that would pass from the wetland under Pacific Coast Highway and extend out to sea. Tidal action would then be the moving force to transport seawater in and out of the wetland. A number of problems became evident when the culvert plan was reviewed. The seaward openings of the culverts would have to be complex structures that would prevent sand and other objects from being swept into the culverts. Periodic inspections would have to be carried out by divers and regular maintenance would be needed to rid the walls of the culverts of fouling marine growth such as algae and invertebrates, which would eventually block flow if allowed to accumulate. Chemical antifouling would have to be conducted frequently with the use of chlorine or other toxic agents. Since one of the functions of the newly restored wetland was to improve the local fishery, many important fish such as California halibut, which depend on wetlands for foraging and raising their young, would probably avoid using the culverts to enter the wetland. In the final analysis the culvert plan, which had never been attempted before at that scale, and would have cost between about 2 to 10 times that of the preferred inlet and bridge configuration, was discarded.

Another proposal was offered that would eliminate any type of inlet and instead depend on water coming from Anaheim Bay via Huntington Harbour to supply tidal flow into the newly restored wetland. It was calculated that the volume of water required from Anaheim Bay would not provide sufficient tidal flow to fully support the wetland's biological diversity, even with additional dredging of the water's path or the widening of the channel under the Warner Avenue bridge. In addition, it was calculated that the velocity of the tidal flow through Huntington Harbour would be increased from 3 to 4 times its present level. It was uncertain what the increased flow velocity would do to structures in its path such as bulkheads and slips. There was also the concern over the quality of the water. The water's route would flow through a busy marina and residential area, a route that is also the terminus of two major flood control channels (The Bolsa Chica[6] and the Wintersburg channels). Concluding that the restored wetland would simply end up as a backwater of Huntington Harbour, the steering committee dismissed this alternative plan early in the planning process.

There was another concern raised that the new inlet as proposed would cause bacterial contamination to the nearby Bolsa Chica State Beach in the same manner that the inlet to the Talbert Marsh was suspected to have caused a contamination situation at Huntington State Beach. One group, which represents the surfing community, in public statements and in publications opposing the inlet referred to the inlet as a "storm drain" in spite of the fact no significant source of urban runoff was to flow into the newly restored wetland. Another potential source of contamination were the large numbers of birds that were expected to inhabit the newly restored wetland. To answer this

---

6. This is a misleading label, the channel having nothing to do with Bolsa Chica. It is named after Bolsa Chica Street, along which it runs from Rancho Road south to Edinger Avenue, then west until it empties into Huntington Harbour.

11-3. A dredge was brought in on dry land and assembled. The full tidal basin was then flooded to sufficient depth to float the dredge, which then did the final contouring of the basin bottom. (Photo courtesy Moffatt and Nichol Engineers)

concern, before the inlet was constructed the prime contractor for the restoration, Moffatt and Nichol, carried out a series of computer simulation models that measured the bacteriological impact various populations of birds would have on the nearby state beach. The company found that even under the worst case scenario involving maximum probable bird densities in the restored wetland, bacteriological counts on the beach would be about one tenth the level that would trigger a beach closure.

The Bolsa Chica Conservancy began testing the water in the inlet for bacterial contamination starting from the very day the inlet opened and continued for over two years. In addition, the Orange County Sanitation District and the Orange County Health Care Agency had been conducting water testing in the surf during that same period of time at points near the inlet. Results showed that the water flowing out of the full tidal basin had no appreciable impact on the bacteriological quality of the surf at Bolsa Chica. Bolsa Chica State Beach remains one of the cleanest beaches in the state.

The Full Tidal Basin

An area of 367 acres was contoured to become a full tidal basin. That meant the water body was to experience the full effects of the tides as seawater flowed in and out of the inlet. During typical high tides, the water in the full tidal wetland could reach depths of 6 to 8 feet, and during low tides, one could wade across the basin. The basin was initially excavated dry by the use of heavy earth moving equipment. When rough contouring of the full tidal basin was completed in September of 2005, a floating dredge was moved onto the dry basin floor piece by piece and assembled. Enough water was then pumped into the full tidal basin from Inner Bolsa Bay to float the dredge (Figure 11-3). A pipe was led out the still dry inlet to the ocean where the output of the dredge, some 1.2 million cubic yards of sand, was pumped to create the ebb shoal.[7] When dredging was completed, the dredge was lifted out of the basin with cranes, disassembled and trucked to its next job.

To Connect or Not Connect

One of the most frequently asked questions regarding the restoration of Bolsa Chica was why the newly restored area was not connected to the original ecological reserve and make it one large ecological system. With it being restored in 1978, over the years the Ecological Reserve had developed into a relatively well functioning ecosystem. Much of the reserve's qualities would have been heavily altered or even destroyed in order to be connected to the new wetland. It was thus decided to keep the two ecosystems separate.

---

7. In December 2005 whale sightings near the shore of Huntington Beach were reported. It was later discovered that the whales were actually pieces of the black dredge pipe that had broken away during a heavy surf.

The Muted Tidal Wetland.

About 180 acres at the far northeastern corner of the Bolsa Chica restoration site was designated as a muted tidal wetland to provide an emergent salt marsh. The area still contains active oil wells that are elevated above water levels. The wetland is actually three hydrologically separate units that are supplied with seawater from the Full Tidal Basin through three large box culverts. Flow is adjusted by automatic control gates so that the tides in the muted marsh never rise more than one to two feet, in contrast to those in the Full Tidal Basin which may rise and fall as much as 6 to 8 feet. If there was ever an oil spill in the muted tidal wetland, the gates could be closed to prevent contamination of the full tidal basin.

For a variety of reasons, flow into the three wetland units was delayed long after the full tidal basin was flooded. Even with the control gates closed, water was observed entering into the muted tidal wetland. The box culverts had been laid on a bed of gravel which allowed water to seep under the culverts and enter the muted tidal wetland. A contractor was called in to grout (seal) the gravel, but even then, the oil operator refused to allow the opening of the culvert gates until the oil company's oil spill safety measures were totally in place. As of this writing, only one of the units has been opened to muted tidal flow.

The Overlooks

Two elevated overlooks were originally designed for the restored area, one tucked in the north-east corner of the full tidal basin, and one in the north-west corner. Each of these earthen structures gives visitors 360 degree views of the wetland and the land- and seascapes beyond. When the inlet channel was being excavated, a pocket of oil-saturated soil was discovered. On chemical analysis, the soil was not considered sufficiently toxic to require hauling it off to a toxic waste dump. Instead, it was decided to build a third overlook near the walk bridge and safely embed the contaminated soil deep within the overlook structure. This third overlook, shown on the map (Figure 11-1) as the South Overlook,

11-4. Effect of long jetties on the littoral flow of sand. A river mouth protected by jetties where littoral sand transport moves from left to right. Sand builds up against one jetty while the shore on the right is severely depleted of sand. (Photo courtesy United States Department of Transportation, Federal Highway Administration.)

offers visitors an excellent view of the nearby nesting site, the full tidal basin, and Rabbit Island.

Beach Sand Movement and the Flood Shoal

The sand at ocean beaches below the high tide line is in constant motion. The sand moves principally in a path parallel to the beach along a course depending on the direction of the waves and littoral currents. During the winter at Bolsa Chica State Beach, the littoral

211

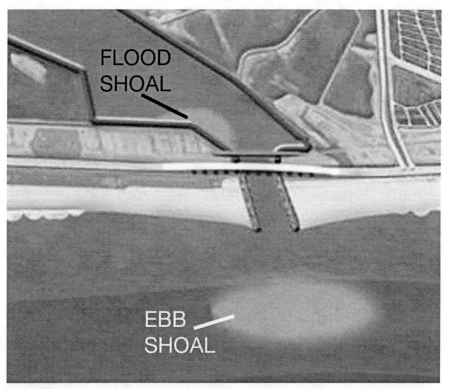

FLOOD
SHOAL

EBB
SHOAL

11-5. Drawing of the location of the Bolsa Chica ebb shoal in relation to the tidal inlet. The shoal was "pre-filled" to reduce sand depletion on nearby beaches. The flood shoal is also shown, which is expected to require removal about every 2 years. (Figure courtesy Moffatt and Nichol Engineers).

current moves from north to south, carrying a considerable amount of sand in that direction. In the summer, the opposite occurs, but the volume of sand is considerably less. Experience has shown that if jetties are too long, sand cannot move around them and piles up on the side of one of the jetties, while the beach sand on the side of the other jetty is washed away and not replaced (Figure 11-4).

Invariably flood tides will carry some sand that is moving along the beach into the Bolsa Chica inlet to accumulate where the inlet widens at the mouth of the full tidal basin, forming what is known as a flood shoal (Figure 11-5). If there is sufficient volume and velocity of the ebb (outward) flow when the tide turns, most of that sand should

212

be carried back out of the inlet and swept away by the littoral current. But eventually enough sand will build up in the flood shoal to the point there is the danger that the inlet will become blocked. If that occurs, the wetland will be deprived of the benefits of the tides and the wetland's biological values will be seriously diminished. Thus maintenance dredging of the flood shoal is imperative and expected to be needed every one to two years.[8]

The inlet's design size (that is, the area of its cross section between high and low tide levels) depends on the volume of water that fills the wetland. That volume is known as the "tidal prism." The calculation of the inlet size is critical, for it must be sufficiently large to allow optimum tidal flushing of the wetland, but if it is too large, the lowered current velocity through it will not be sufficient to keep the inlet clear of sand for an acceptable period of time. And if it is too small, the higher current velocity will cause scouring of the bottom of the channel. The size of the present inlet was calculated based on the tidal prism of the new full tidal basin plus the tidal prism expected of the wetland that would occupy the Future Full Tidal area.[9]

The Ebb Shoal

One of the critical features of the restoration is not even visible nor within the boundaries of the restored wetland. It is the ebb shoal, a sand bar that was constructed off the beach immediately opposite the inlet opening. As described above, a certain amount of sand is expected to enter the inlet during flood tide and then flow off shore during an ebb tide. Some of the sand that is diverted offshore by the ebb tide will accumulate into a so-called ebb shoal that is opposite the inlet

---

8. A portion of the funds for restoration have been set aside for maintenance dredging. As expected, dredging was needed by the end of 2008 and carried out during the spring of 2009.

9. For the mathematically curious, the formula for calculating the size of the inlet is $A_c = 0.000469\ P^{0.85}$ where A_c is the cross section of the inlet in square feet below mean sea level, and P is the wetland's tidal prism in cubic feet between the mean of the lowest low tides and the mean of the highest high tides.

11-6. Thirty foot interlocking sheet piles were installed along the eastern edge of wetland to prevent seawater from entering the adjacent groundwater. (Photo courtesy Moffatt and Nichol Engineers)

(Figure 11-5). The diverted sand is prevented from following its normal course along the shore and nearby beaches are therefore deprived of that sand. After several years, a natural ebb bar will reach an equilibrium state and its effect on littoral sand drift will be minimized. By constructing ("prefilling") a 50 acre ebb shoal off the Bolsa Chica inlet during restoration, the equilibrium state was attained at once, thereby avoiding significant sand loss on adjacent beaches. As required by the Coastal Commission, the sand that was used to fill the ebb shoal was very carefully selected for grain size to assure it would perform like a natural ebb shoal and be appropriate for deposition on beaches.

The Wintersburg Flood Control Channel.

One of the early alternate designs of the Bolsa Chica restoration was to allow the Wintersburg Channel to empty into the newly restored full tidal basin. In another alternative design, a weir was to be constructed on the channel levee facing the wetland. Should heavy rains raise the water level in the channel to near overflow, the water would overflow and deliver water into the wetland rather than backing up into adjacent neighborhoods. It has long been recognized by wetland biologists that occasional doses of fresh water invigorate the growth of plants and animals in a salt marsh, but it was decided during the planning process that even dry weather flow might deliver too much fresh water into the wetland, which would be detrimental to marine wetland plants. In addition, the channel's levels of urban pollution would not be compatible with a healthy wetland. Based on the comments expressed during public meetings and in writing by several stakeholders including environmental organizations and the city of Huntington Beach, it eventually was decided that the channel's outflow would remain in its original configuration, emptying into Outer Bolsa Bay. The doses of fresh water in the newly restored wetland will have to come entirely from rainfall.

The Groundwater Barrier

Residential development abuts the eastern boundary of the Muted Tidal Wetland. The wetland is flooded with seawater on the high tides, and while only to relatively small depths, there is the possibility that the seawater could migrate underground into the adjacent neighborhood and contaminate the subsoil. To prevent that, a groundwater barrier consisting of 30 foot interlocking sheet piles (Figure 11-6) was installed along the property line adjacent to the houses, which would prevent seawater from seeping into the nearby community. However, the barrier also prevents high groundwater levels from draining from the residences into the wetland during times of heavy rain, which could cause flooding. Consequently the groundwater barrier contains a sump that was designed to capture any water that accumulates on the residential side. The water is then pumped into the wetland.

A Place to Nest

Prior to Bolsa Chica State Beach becoming the enormously popular beach that it is today,[10] the beach was the site of tens of thousands of nesting birds during the spring and summer months, as were most other sandy beaches in Southern California. Certain species of birds prefer to nest on plain sand with little or no foliage present. That is, a nest to them is simply a shallow depression in the sand, sometimes decorated with a few pebbles or fragments of seaweed and driftwood. Among these species is the endangered California Least Tern, as well as other species of terns, skimmers and the threatened Snowy Plover.

Once the beaches were purchased by the state and had undergone improvements for public use, hoards of beachgoers began to arrive and the birds fled to find appropriate but scarce nesting sites elsewhere. For instance, many birds found the unpaved oil field maintenance roads in Bolsa Chica to their liking. Whenever that occurs, federal laws that protect migratory birds force parts of the oil field to be off limits to traffic during the nesting season. Other level surfaces such as abandoned airfields and the flat decks of unused ocean-going barges have also been taken over by breeding pairs. In the new restoration, three nesting sites totaling about 20 acres were created to accommodate beach nesting birds.[11]

The Seasonal Ponds

An area of about 140 acres, located in the southwest corner of the Bolsa Chica lowlands, consists of a number of pools that are filled

---

10. Before the state purchased the beach in 1961 that is now known as Bolsa Chica State Beach, it was the site of an eclectic collection of tents and cardboard shacks housing homeless squatters and summer campers. It was principally famous for its mile high pile of trash, reportedly amounting to over 300 tons, giving the beach the name "Tin Can Beach." Bolsa Chica State Beach is now the second most popular beach in Southern California with 2.7 million visitors a year. (Huntington State Beach is first with 2.9 million visitors a year (2006 figures)).

11. Two highly successful nesting islands were constructed in inner Bolsa Bay as part of the 1978 restoration.

with water much of the year, but especially following the rainy season. The area is somewhat isolated from most of the oil activities in the wetland, providing a unique, undisturbed plot that provides resting, feeding, and nesting sites for a great number of birds. Because it is already a functioning, heavily used habitat, it was decided to leave it as is, with perhaps only some minor rehabilitation.

The Fieldstone Property

In the northeast corner of the Bolsa Chica lowland was a 42.5 acre trapezoidal parcel long known as the Fieldstone property. Over the years it has had a number of owners, including the Fieldstone Company, hence its name. Signal was the last private owner, having purchased the property in October of 1997. When the state purchased the 880 acres of lowlands in February of 1997, it was anticipated that the Fieldstone parcel eventually would be included in the restoration. But initially the sale was delayed by the landowners and then later put on hold because of a contamination problem. The undeveloped property, which is at the dead end of Graham St., was immediately adjacent to a 1970s housing development, making it a convenient dumping ground for excavated soil and building and industrial waste. The true nature of the wastes was not fully known until early 1999 when the land was examined for possible sale to the state. Major concern was focused on PCBs that were detected in a few sites on the property. PCBs are a large class of industrial chemicals that were used for decades in a great variety of applications but recently they have been suspected of being carcinogens and their use was banned.

Also of critical concern was the discovery of traces of the PCBs in the soil around the homes immediately adjacent to the site. Possibly the PCBs were dumped on the home sites before they were developed and much of the contaminated soil was then moved to the Fieldstone parcel where it was as much as 6 feet deep in some places. No one would claim responsibility for the PCBs and eventually the cleanup was turned over to the state Department of Toxic Substances. The state agency first replaced all the contaminated soil around the affected homes, then attacked the contaminated sites on the Fieldstone property itself, hauling out over 6700 cubic yards of soil. The state eventually purchased the property in July of 2005 even though the cleanup wasn't officially completed until September of that year. The property underwent some contouring to allow it to become part of the adjacent muted tidal wetland. Feeder channels and culverts were constructed to allow limited tidal flow into the wetland. A 10,000 square foot pad and access road from Graham St. was also included in the work to provide a site for the office of the Ecological Reserve manager.

The Future Full Tidal Area

A parcel consisting of 248 acres in the south-east corner of Bolsa Chica lowlands, which was part of the 880 acre state purchase, has been designated as a Future Full Tidal Basin. Like the Muted Tidal Wetland, this area still has active oil extraction activity that would have made it prohibitive for the state to buy out the wells. Thus this area has been set aside until that unpredictable day when the oil is depleted and the oil company removes its wells and cleans up remnants of its operations. Once restored, the Future Full Tidal area is expected to afford Los Angeles and Long Beach mitigation credit for an additional 80 acres of harbor expansion. Since this area is already mostly below sea level due to subsidence, little excavation will be necessary to convert it to an extension of the full tidal basin.

Edwards Thumb

This curiously named[12] 42 acres in the south-east corner of the Bolsa Chica lowlands is still owned by Signal and as of this writing it continues to be in active oil production. In spite of its relatively small size, the parcel is a critical part of the overall plan for Bolsa Chica, for it is a potential green belt connection between the wetland and

---

12. Like a thumb, it is a narrow parcel pointing in a north-easterly direction. It is named after Edwards Street that is immediately east of it.

Huntington Beach's Central Park. Like the Future Full Tidal area, it will have to remain an oil field until its resources are deemed depleted and purchase by the state occurs.

Tying It All Together

The full tidal basin, the muted tidal wetland, the future full tidal wetland, and the already existing seasonal ponds made up the four major sectors within the Bolsa Chica restoration project. While these areas represent separate habitats, for a variety of reasons they must interconnect. It already has been pointed out that the muted tidal wetland is to receive its water from the heart of the wetland, the full tidal basin, through three water control structures. Neither the future tidal wetland nor the seasonal ponds need to receive water from the full tidal basin unless extreme dry conditions occur. In that case, control structures can allow water to enter these areas. And in extreme wet weather, provisions have been installed to allow excess runoff to drain from these areas into the full tidal basin. All of these provisions to transfer water from one sector to another is necessary not only for ecological reasons, but also to protect from flooding the many oil wells that are still operating in some of these areas.

Restoration Commences

Cleaning Up

With Bolsa Chica having been an oil field for over 60 years, the project was faced with a major task: the elimination of remnants of the oil operation in the full tidal area. Restoration was complicated by the fact the state had to buy out the wells that were in the full tidal portion. Oil leases usually afford the oil companies protection against loss due to action by the oil field owner. While an owner normally has the right to order an oil company to abandon its wells, the owner must reimburse the oil company for the cost of removing the wells and more importantly, for lost future revenue. That is, the landowner has to pay what the oil company estimates it would have earned for the life of the wells had they been allowed to continue pumping. That is what occurred in Bolsa Chica. Part of the restoration expenses was the cost of compensating the oil company for the deactivation of 64 oil wells.[13]

Removing Oil Wells

The deactivation of an oil well is a complex process that must be carried out in steps, each of which is carefully monitored. First, all of the machinery and pipes that appear above ground must be removed. The heavy concrete foundation on which the pump was placed is then demolished and removed. Wells can have several thousand feet of an iron rod, which transmits the familiar up and down movement to the pump at the bottom of the well. This must be removed. Then the inner pipe (known as the tubing) that also could amount to several thousand feet and which conducts the oil to the surface is taken out in sections. Explosive devices are lowered into the outer casing of the well and detonated. This punches holes in the casing so when concrete is poured into the casing, it oozes out of the casing and fills any spaces between the casing and the soil, effectively sealing the well hole. The casing is cut off well below the excavation level and welded shut. Thus no oil or gas can rise to the surface and contaminate the wetland.

By the time cleanup operations were completed, nearly 37 miles of steel pipe, 2700 tons of concrete rubble and about 600 truckloads of contaminated soil were hauled out of Bolsa Chica. Some of the low level contaminated soil was used as the core for the construction of the levees, nesting sites, and elevated overlooks.

Restoration work had already begun in October of 2003, one year before the official groundbreaking, with the removal of about 500 power poles and 64 oil wells and accompanying structures in the area that was to become the full tidal basin.

---

13. Not all were in production, however.

11-7. Bolsa Chica restoration groundbreaking ceremony on October 6, 2004. Top photo: from left to right, Cathy Green, Huntington Beach Mayor; Rodney McInnis, SW Regional Administrator, NOAA; Eugene Voiland, President and CEO, Aera Energy; Lt. Governor Cruz Bustamonte; Lynn Scarlett, U. S. Department of Interior; Steve Westley, State Controller; Mike Chrisman, Secretary, Department of Resources; Col. Leonardo Flor, Dep. Commander, Army Corps of Engineers.

Bottom photo: Amigos past presidents Chuck Nelson, Jim Robins, Mary Ellen Houseal, Vic Leipzig, Terry Dolton, Linda Moon, Herb Chatterton, and Dave Carlberg. (Photos courtesy Amigos de Bolsa Chica)

Groundbreaking

With much fanfare, groundbreaking for the restoration occurred on October 8, 2004. Representatives from the eight agencies who oversaw the restoration plan plus other governmental officials grasped Home Depot's best- selling shovels and posed for the media, followed by several past presidents of the Amigos de Bolsa Chica (Figure 11-7). It was said that Governor Arnold Schwarzenegger was to attend the groundbreaking, but Chapman University was dedicating their new

11-8. Steering Committee Representatives celebrating the Bolsa Chica restoration groundbreaking: Peter Brand, State Coastal Conservancy; Chris Potter, Resources Agency; Jack Fancher, Fish and Wildlife Service; Tom Yocom, Environmental Protection Agency; Terri Stewart, Department of Fish and Game; Jim Trout, State Lands Commission; Larry Smith, Corps of Engineers, and Bob Hoffman, National Marine Fisheries Service. (Photo courtesy Jim Milbury, NOAA)

film school on the same day and the Governor obviously had a closer affinity to film than wetlands. Lieutenant Governor Cruz Bustamonte attended in his place.

Heavy rains in February, 2005 made the Bolsa Chica wetland too wet to allow construction and restoration had to cease. Before construction could continue, 140 groundwater wells had to be installed to dewater the wetland. Work was resumed several weeks later.

In April of 2005 PCH traffic was detoured around the construction site to clear the way for construction of the highway bridge that would span the new inlet (Figure 11-9). During bridge construction, remnants of the coast highway of the 1920s was unearthed complete

Table 11-2. Sources of restoration funding.

Source	$ (millions)
Ports of Los Angeles and Long Beach	102
Propositions 40 and 50 bond issues	20
Interest	20
Msc. sources	5.7
TOTAL	147.7

with curbs and lane markings. Bridge construction was completed in 2006 and the very first vehicle traffic crossed the new PCH bridge on January 9. Workers then turned to the construction of a second bridge that would serve a 25 acre plot adjacent to PCH. This area contained numerous oil wells that had been slant drilled under the highway and into the state's off shore oil field.

The Final Accounting

Initially the combined sum of $76 million, equally divided between the two ports, was transferred to the restoration fund in 1997, providing mitigation credit for 454 acres of filled submerged and tideland habitat. Out of the $76 million came $26.7 million for the purchase of 880 acres of Bolsa Chica lowland. But once restoration work was underway, it was evident that additional funds would be necessary. The Steering Committee was prepared to trim the project to save money, but the ports eventually increased their final contribution to a combined sum of $102 million, giving them a total of 534 acres of mitigation credits.[14] Two state bond issues (Propositions 40 and 50[15]) contributed $20 million, and since the bulk of the funds was not spent until 2004 when the major restoration construction phase was begun, the funds

---

14. The source of the ports' resources comes in part from fees charged for everything that passes through the port facilities as well as from docking fees, terminal leases and other services. For instance, the ports typically charge shippers about $150 per 20 ft. container and $25 per car. A typical docking fee for a 900 foot container ship is about $5000 per day (2000 figures).

15. Signal reportedly gave $350,000 to the Yes on Proposition 50 campaign.

Table 11-3. Restoration Expenses

Expenses	$(millions)
Purchase	26.7
Cleanup	5.5
Planning	7.0
Oil buyout and removal	11.2
Construction	71.2
Agency oversight	4.1
Operations and management set aside*	15.0
Future restoration	2.5
Total	147.7

*Funds for management personnel and maintenance costs such as dredging the inlet.

11-9. To avoid any traffic interruptions on State Highway 1, Pacific Coast Highway, a four lane detour had to be provided around the inlet bridge construction site. (Photo courtesy Moffatt and Nichol Engineers).

were invested in the interim and they earned another $20 million in interest (Table 11-2). The final cost of the restoration, which included the purchase of the 880 acres, planning, cleanup, construction and

11-10. On the morning of August 24, 2006, about 100 spectators watched as equipment removed the last sand berm to allow tidal flow into the newly restored Bolsa Chica wetland. (Photo courtesy Craig Frampton)

administration was $147.7 million (Table 11-3), with about 10 percent of that set aside for future operations and management costs.

Time for Celebration

In the predawn hours of August 24, 2006, a group of about 100 lined the railing of the Pacific Coast Highway bridge that spanned the new Bolsa Chica ocean inlet and watched as earth moving equipment demolished the last sand berm that had prevented seawater from entering the inlet (Figure 11-10). That task was completed just before 6 am as the tide turned and seawater began entering the inner reaches of the wetland for the first time in 107 years (Figure 11-11). The sound of popping Champaign corks blended with the roar of nearby PCH traffic and the hiss of the incoming seawater as it passed under the bridge. Amigos and others celebrated the culmination of 30 years of fighting for the preservation and restoration of the Bolsa Chica wetland. On the day of the inlet opening, several past presidents of Amigos rushed to the Bolsa Chica wetland to witness the filling of the full tidal basin (Figure 11-12). Figures 11-13 and 11-14 are views of the full tidal basin. Figure 11-15 is a splendid aerial view of the entire Bolsa Chica wetland.

For an event that officials from the State Lands Commission wanted to be low key, along with the 100 onlookers, the opening attracted a flock radio, television, and print media reporters and photographers. In addition to local coverage, reporters from the Associated Press news service were present and their account appeared in a number of papers across the nation, including the San Francisco Chronicle and the New York Times.

Has restoration been accomplished?

The restoration plan included a requirement for periodic biological monitoring of the newly restored area. Surveys were conducted in 2007 and again in 2008. Bird counts were carried out every two months during the course of the two years. During 2007, 99 species were sighted, and in 2008, the count was 136, most of which were shorebirds. Using a variety of nets, biologists surveyed the waters of the full tidal basin for fish present. Fish species increased from 19 in 2007 to 41 in 2008. All of the fish seen in 2008 were represented by both adult and juvenile forms, indicating the wetland was performing one of the major functions of a coastal wetland, a fish nursery. In addition, bottom samples revealed rich populations of crabs, oysters, clams, mussels, worms, and other invertebrates of all kinds. Other surveys have revealed healthy areas of eel grass throughout the floor of the full tidal basin, and cord grass that had been planted on the mud flat along the eastern edge of the full tidal basin is beginning to spread.

As we opened this chapter we defined restoration of a wetland as, "...returning an ecosystem to a close approximation of its conditions prior to disturbance." In the short two years that the Bolsa Chica tidal inlet has been delivering sea water to the new-old wetland, the

11-11. Tidal water flows under the two bridges that span the new tidal inlet. The narrower bridge serves the 25 acre slant oil drilling site, the second bridge carries Pacific Coast Highway traffic. (Photo courtesy Moffatt and Nichol Engineers).

11-12. Amigos past presidents Peter Green, Chuck Nelson, Shirley Dettloff, Linda Moon, Tom Livengood, Mary Ellen Houseal, Dave Carlberg, and Jim Robins visited the Bolsa Chica wetland immediately following the opening of the inlet to witness the filling of the full tidal basin. (Christopher Wagner, 2006, Huntington Beach Independent. Reprinted with Permission.)

227

11-13. View looking east over the recently restored full tidal basin from the south overlook. During low tide, exposed sand bars have become popular loafing sites for thousands of shorebirds. In the distance, operating oil wells are visible in the muted tidal wetland. (Photo the author)

11-14. View looking north over the full tidal basin from the south overlook. Rabbit Island is in the background with the Bolsa Chica Mesa beyond. (Photo the author)

228

11-15. Aerial view of the completed restored wetland. (Photo courtesy Moffatt and Nichol Engineers)

restoration seems to have been a success, as reflected in the significant increase in the wetland's biodiversity since the inlet was opened to the sea in 2006. It is perhaps too soon to claim a perfect victory for the Bolsa Chica wetland. It is understandable why the restoration project requires an additional eight years of biological monitoring before a final assessment is made. But from all indications so far, for those few folks who began meeting in kitchens and living rooms during the 1970s and for all those who followed, their hopes and dreams may be very close to fulfillment.

Selected Bibliography

Chapter 1. Prehistory of Bolsa Chica

Altschul, J. H. and D. R. Grenda. Islanders and Mainlanders. Tucson, Arizona: SRI Press, 2002.

Boulé, Mary. California Native American Tribes Gabrielino Tribe (California's Native American Tribes). Vashon, WA: Merryant Publishers. 1992.

Eberhart, H. "The Cogged Stones of Southern California." American Antiquity 26. 3 (1961): 361-370.

Johnston, Bernice Eastman. California's Gabrieliño Indians. Los Angeles: Southwest Museum, 1962.

Kroeber, A. L. Handbook of Indians of California. New York: Dover Publications, 1976.

McCawley, William. The First Angelinos: the Gabrielino Indians of Los Angeles. Novato, California: Ballena Press, 1996.

Miller, Bruce W. The Gabrieliño. Los Osos, California: Sand River Press, 1991.

Chapter 2. The Spanish and the Missions

Aviña, Rose Hollenbaugh. Spanish and Mexican Land Grants in California (M.A. thesis). Berkeley: University of California Press, 1934.

Beebe, Rose Marie and Robert M. Senkewicz. Lands of Promise and Despair: Chronicles of Early California, 1535-1846. Santa Clara and Berkeley California: Santa Clara University and Heyday Books, 2001.

Chapman, Charles E. A. History Of California: The Spanish Period. New York: The Macmillan Company, 1926.

McPherson, William. A Hundred Years of Yesterdays-Land Grant Policies and the Ranchos. Santa Ana: Orange County Centennial, Inc., 1988.

Meadows, Don. Orange County Under Spain, Mexico and the United States. Whittier: California Historical Publishers, 1963.

Weaver, John D. El Pueblo Grande-A Non-Fiction Book About Los Angeles. Los Angeles from the Brush Huts of Yangna to the Skyscrapers of the Modern Megalopolis. Los Angeles: Ward Ritchie Press, 1973.

Chapter 3. The Rancho Period
En el Rancho Grande

Carpenter, Virginia. Ranchos Of Orange County: Chronologies Of Early California. Orange, California: The Paragon Agency Publishers, 2003.

Cleland, Robert Glass. The Cattle On A Thousand Hills: Southern California: 1850-1880. San Marino, California: The Huntington Library, 1951.

Dana, Richard Henry. <u>Two Years Before the Mast</u>. New York: Modern Library, 2001.

Friis, Leo J. <u>Orange County Through Four Centuries.</u> Santa Ana, California: Friis-Pioneer Press, 1982.

Hanna, Phil Townsend. <u>California Through Four Centuries: A Handbook of Memorable Historical Dates.</u> New York: Farrar & Rinehart, Inc, 1935.

Smith, Sarah Bixby. <u>Adobe Days</u>. Lincoln: University Of Nebraska Press, 1987.

Wilson, Florence Slocum. <u>Windows On Early California</u>. Pasadena: The National Society of the Colonial Dames of America, 1971.

Chapter 4. Abel Stearns: A Yankee *Ranchero*

O'Flaherty, Joseph S. <u>An End and a Beginning: The South Coast and Los Angeles, 1850-1887.</u> New York: Exposition Press, 1972.

Wright, Doris Marion. <u>A Yankee In Mexican California – Abel Stearns, 1798-1848.</u> Santa Barbara, California: Wallace Hebberd, 1977.

Chapter 5. Guns and Oil

Crump, Spencer. <u>Ride the Big Red Cars: The Pacific Electric Story</u>. Glendale, California: Trans-Anglo Books, 1988.

Milkovich, Barbara. <u>A Study of the Impact of the Oil Industry on the Development of Huntington Beach, California, Prior to 1930</u> (MS Thesis). Long Beach: California State University, Long Beach, 1994.

Talbert, T. B. <u>My Sixty Years In California</u>. Huntington Beach. California: Ben Franklin Press, 1982.

Tompkins, Walker A. <u>Little Giant of Signal Hill: An Adventure in American Enterprise</u>. Englewood Cliffs, N. J.: Prentice-Hall, 1964.

Chapter 6. Wetlands, Tidelands and Submerged Lands

Bakker, Elna S. An Island Called California-An Ecological Introduction to its Natural Communities. Berkeley: University of California Press, 1971.

Greenfield, Roseanne. The Bolsa Chica Wetlands of Huntington Beach: The Changing Environment, Land Use Patterns, and Cultural Values of Its Inhabitants From 500 A.D. To The Present (MA Thesis). Fullerton, California: California State University, Fullerton, 1990.

Kennedy, Victor S. (Ed.) Estuarine Perspectives. New York: Academic Press, 1980.

Miller, David C. Dark Eden: The Swamp in Nineteenth Century American Culture. Cambridge, Eng: Cambridge University Press, 1989.

Mitsch, Wilham J and James G. Gosselink. Wetlands. Hoboken, N.J.: John Wiley & Sons, 2007.

U.S. Environmental Protection Agency. Economic Benefits of Wetlands.

(http//www/epa.gov/owow/wetlands/facts/fact4.html)

Chapter 7. The Bolsa Chica Wetland in Jeopardy

California Coastal Commission. The California Coastal Commission: Why It Exists and What It Does. San Francisco: California Coastal Commission, 2002.

Dillingham Environmental Company. An Environmental Evaluation of the Bolsa Chica Area. La Jolla, California: Dillingham Environmental Company, 1971. In 3 vols.

Slade, David C. [et al.]. Putting The Public Trust Doctrine to Work: The Application of the Public Trust Doctrine to the Management of Lands, Waters and Living Resources of the Coastal States. Washington, D.C.: Coastal States Organization, 1990.

Chapter 8. The Amigos Emerge.
Grass Continues to Grow

Aldridge, James A. Saving the Bolsa Chica Wetlands. Fullerton, California: Amigos de Bolsa Chica/California State University, Fullerton Oral History Program, 1998

EDAW, Inc. Report to the Bolsa Chica Study Group: Background, Issues and Considerations in Planning for the Long Range Uses of the Bolsa Chica Area. Newport Beach, California: EDAW Inc., 1979.

Chapter 9. The 1980s (continued)

Fulton, William and Paul Shigley, Guide to California Planning. Point Arena, California: Solano Press Books, 2005.

Chapter 10. More Paper: EIRs, EISs, LCPs, IPs, Etc

Kreske, Diori L. Environmental Impact Statements: A Practical Guide for Agencies, Citizens, and Consultants. New York: Wiley, 1996.

Chapter 11. The Road to Restoration...
Is Paved with More Paper

California State Lands Commission, United States Fish and Wildlife Service, and the United States Army Corps of Engineers. Final EIR/EIS for the Bolsa Chica Lowlands Restoration Project. 2001. In 6 vols.

Zedler, Joy B. (ed.). Handbook for Restoring Tidal Wetlands. Boca Raton, Florida: CRC Press, 2001.

Epilogue

"A Dream Became A Reality"

When the Amigos de Bolsa Chica was first formed over 30 years ago, no one ever thought that many of its members would still be a part of the organization, still "fighting the good fight" whenever and wherever they were needed. The organization began its life in 1976 with one mission, to "save the Bolsa Chica Wetlands" and it soon became an educational group, a lobbying organization, and a political force, always changing as the times demanded.

The story of the Bolsa Chica is as much a story of saving wetlands as it is a story of the people who dedicated a good part of their adult lives to the cause. I don't think that those who were sitting around a coffee table in a home near the wetlands ever thought that 33 years later they would have achieved their goal of seeing the Bolsa Chica Wetlands saved and restored. Many of these same people stood on the bridge over the tidal inlet channel at 4 a. m. on August 24, 2006, toasting the achievement with champagne as they watched ocean waters flow into the wetlands. They had been through the battles and on that clear morning they witnessed their years of hard work and dedication become what many thought could never happen, a reality. This success could not have been possible if it were not for this band of citizens and the thousands who contributed to this victory. It was the housewife

237

who never thought she would be involved in the political process; the professors who lent invaluable expertise and scientific information to the fight; the thousands who contributed money to pay for scientific reports, lawsuits, and educational materials; and government officials who gave support to the cause – the list is endless.

The great success of the Amigos was due to their ability to understand the governmental and political process and the important role these various bodies would have in saving this invaluable resource. Hundreds of meetings were held at city, county and state levels. Amigos had to learn how to deal with and how to present themselves to those governmental bodies, the members of which would be the people who would, with a push of a button, the raising of a hand, a spoken aye or nay, determine the future of Bolsa Chica. Amigos learned how to become lobbyists and how to hold their own in high level meetings, thus earning the respect of many elected and appointed officials regardless of their own position on the future of Bolsa Chica. The Amigos pressed the Ports of Los Angeles and Long Beach to use Bolsa Chica for mitigation to offset the ports' expansion, eventually allowing all of the wetlands to be saved. The Amigos learned a very important lesson, and that was to persuade the "powers that be" with scientific evidence and not sentiment. Decisions were made based on proven science and not emotion. Also patience played a very important role. Obviously members of the Amigos have patience. They knew that every step they took was a step forward in saving the wetlands. Even when criticized they took the criticism and kept moving forward. Many people were critical of the role Amigos played in the Coalition which allowed a limited number of homes to be built in the lowlands, but critics did not know what was happening behind the scenes. The Amigos knew that federal and state law could prevent such building in the wetlands. Of course this was a risk! Would the federal and state agencies follow their own regulations? But unless you are willing to take a risk, you may not be able to move forward. Much had been achieved during the Coalition process. The connector to Huntington Harbour had been eliminated, commercial development stopped, an ocean entrance allowing boating removed from the plan, an increase in the number of wetlands acreage, all achieved during the Coalition process.

Achieving these goals took the work of hundreds, but some members of the organization went well beyond mere membership. Out of the Amigos membership were 14 Huntington Beach mayors, of which three were Amigos presidents. Also among Amigos members were two State Coastal Commissioners, a County Supervisor, two State Legislators, and several appointees to various state and local boards and commissions. Over the years, members testified hundreds of times before local and state entities, including the State Lands Commission and the Coastal Commission. Average people who had never been involved in politics found themselves in Sacramento and Washington D.C. seeking support by relating the story of Bolsa Chica. They walked the halls of the State Legislature, successfully lobbying for the defeat of five special interest bills that supported development at Bolsa Chica. They met with Coastal Commissioners, City Council Members, County Supervisors and Planning Commissioners, State Legislators and members of Congress. They earned the reputation of being honest, fair and above all they were trusted because the information they presented always had a scientific basis that was backed by professional scientists. It must be remembered that all of these individuals also had full time jobs, so the time they gave to the cause was invaluable. During this time, ballot box politics was also a part of the Amigos' focus – helping to get people elected to positions where they could be influential. There were times when no one ran for any office without having a picture being taken at Bolsa Chica and making the commitment to support its preservation.

Other organizations also were a part of this success. The Bolsa Chica Land Trust was dedicated to saving the Bolsa Chica mesa and played a significant role in preventing development on portions of the uplands and lowlands through a precedent-setting lawsuit. The Bolsa

Chica Conservancy was formed out of the Coalition and remains a vital force today by operating the Bolsa Chica Interpretive Center and conducting numerous educational and scientific programs.

The word Amigos, meaning friends, also had a personal meaning for the members of the Amigos. Friendships which span 30 years were developed, as members worked together toward a common goal. The Bolsa Chica story demonstrates how ordinary people became extraordinary when called upon to accomplish a goal so that future generations would always have a priceless natural resource as part of their environment.

– Shirley Dettloff

Presidents of Amigos de Bolsa Chica

1976, Herb Chatterton

1977-78, Ken and Rhoda Martyn

1979, Herb Chatterton/Dave Carlberg

1980-81, Peter Green

1982-84, Lorraine Faber

1985-86, Mary Ellen Houseal

1987-88, Vic Leipzig

1989-90, Shirley Dettloff

1991-93, Terry Dolton

1994-95, Chuck Nelson

1996-97, Tom Livengood

1998-99, Dave Carlberg

2000-02, Linda Moon

2003-04, Jim Robins

2005-06, Tom Anderson

2006-07, Tom Anderson/Dave Carlberg

2008-09, Dave Carlberg

Index

("t" indicates the item is in a table, "f" in a figure)

About the Author

David Carlberg is a 100 percent Southern Californian. He was born in Los Angeles, schooled (K-PhD.) in Los Angeles and Avalon, Santa Catalina Island, and now living in Huntington Beach ("Surf City"). Now a retired microbiologist, David has held positions in both the private sector and academia. He has worked as a chemist and an executive for a major pharmaceutical company, as a research scientist in the aerospace industry working in astrobiology and biological warfare detection, as a consultant in the medical device, pharmaceutical and motion picture industries, and as a professor of microbiology at California State University, Long Beach. He is married to wife Margaret and has two sons, Howard and Marvin.

David is the author of four books on microbial genetics and environmental and industrial microbiology. His first brush with the environmental movement came in the early 1970s when he joined a group opposing a nuclear power and desalination plant that was proposed for an artificial island off the Huntington Beach coast. Then, a new issue appeared, the transformation of the Bolsa Chica Wetland into a clone of Marina del Rey. He joined the Amigos de Bolsa Chica in 1977, holding a number of positions on its board of directors, including president in 1979, 1999, and 2008-9.

"To the Amigos de Bolsa Chica—the best friend a wetlands ever had."

11-16. In commemoration of the Amigos' 16th anniversary, local artist Neill Ketchum designed a 35 foot wide outdoor mural depicting the Bolsa Chica Wetland and the plants and animals that reside there. The mural was inspired by Ketchum's illustrations in a children's book on the Bolsa Chica adventures of a Clapper Rail. The mural was painted by a crew of 15 amateur and professional artists between October and December of 1991 and was dedicated on January 11, 1992. Those who worked on the mural were Tom Anderson, Manuel Brito, Dave Carlberg, Angela Dutra, Arnie Ehlers, Sara Faber, Jose Garcia, Giana, Pat Keppler, Jack Ketchum, Neill Ketchum, Perry Mart, Adrianne Morrison, Karen Peoples, and Robert Richert. Known as the "Railing Wall," the mural is located behind the building at 5811 McFadden Avenue in Huntington Beach. (Photo courtesy Amigos de Bolsa Chica)